The Teaching for Social Justice Series

William Ayers—Series Editor
Therese Quinn—Associate Series Editor

See You When We Get There:
Teaching for Change in Urban Schools
GREGORY MICHIE

Echoes of Brown:
Youth Documenting and Performing the
Legacy of *Brown v. Board of Education*
MICHELLE FINE

Writing in the Asylum:
Student Poets in City Schools
JENNIFER MCCORMICK

Teaching the Personal and the Political:
Essays on Hope and Justice
WILLIAM AYERS

Teaching Science for Social Justice
ANGELA CALABRESE BARTON, with
JASON L. ERMER, TANAHIA A. BURKETT,
and MARGERY D. OSBORNE

Putting the Children First: The Changing
Face of Newark's Public Schools
JONATHAN G. SILIN and
CAROL LIPPMAN, Editors

Refusing Racism:
White Allies and the Struggle
for Civil Rights
CYNTHIA STOKES BROWN

A School of Our Own:
Parents, Power, and Community at the
East Harlem Block Schools
TOM RODERICK

The White Architects of Black Education:
Ideology and Power in America,
1865–1954
WILLIAM WATKINS

The Public Assault on America's Children:
Poverty, Violence, and Juvenile Injustice
VALERIE POLAKOW, Editor

Construction Sites: Excavating Race,
Class, and Gender Among Urban Youths
LOIS WEIS and MICHELLE FINE, Editors

Walking the Color Line: The Art and
Practice of Anti-Racist Teaching
MARK PERRY

A Simple Justice:
The Challenge of Small Schools
WILLIAM AYERS, MICHAEL KLONSKY, and
GABRIELLE H. LYON, Editors

Holler If You Hear Me: The Education of
a Teacher and His Students
GREGORY MICHIE

see you when we get there

TEACHING FOR CHANGE IN URBAN SCHOOLS

gregory michie

foreword by
GLORIA LADSON-BILLINGS

 Teachers College
Columbia University
New York and London

To young teachers everywhere,
to my parents, whose love and support never waver,
and to Lisa, who woke me up.

Published by Teachers College Press, 1234 Amsterdam Avenue, New York, NY 10027

Library of Congress Cataloging-in-Publication Data

Michie, Gregory.
   See you when we get there : teaching for change in urban schools / Gregory
Michie ; foreword by Gloria Ladson-Billings.
      p. cm. – (The teaching for social justice series)
   Originally presented as the author's thesis.
   Includes bibliographical references.
   ISBN 0-8077-4520-0 (cloth : alk. paper) – ISBN 0-8077-4519-7 (pbk. : alk. paper)
   1. Minority women teachers–Illinois–Chicago–Case studies. 2. Education,
Urban–Illiniois–Chicago–Case studies. 3. Critical pedagogy–Illinois–Chicago–Case
studies. I. Title. II. Series.

LB2837.M45 2004
370.11'5'091732–dc22

                                                                        2004051762

ISBN 0-8077-4519-7 (paper)
ISBN 0-8077-4520-0 (cloth)

Printed on acid-free paper

Manufactured in the United States of America

12 11 10 09 08 07 06 05   8 7 6 5 4 3 2 1

contents

series foreword

Teaching for social justice is the living heart of good teaching. Rather than a fad or a trend, an add-on or a gimmick, teaching for social justice can be thought of as the nucleus of the entire educational enterprise. What is our work fundamentally about? What are we teaching for? If we are concerned with human fulfillment, enlightenment, and freedom, if our teaching aspirations include a better world for all, then we are within the realm of teaching for social justice.

We as educators underline at the outset that schooling is never neutral—teaching is always *for* something and *against* something else. Teaching can be geared, for example, toward obedience or expression, toward conformity or creativity, toward the status quo or change. The important thing for educators at all levels is to know that authentic choices are available, and to become conscious of what might be at stake. At the deepest, most profound level, education is in search of truth and freedom, it is *for* enlightenment and human liberation, or else it becomes entangled in mystification, prejudice, command, and control.

We teachers might, at the start, choose to embrace as principle the idea that our teaching will stand for truth and knowledge, liberation and freedom, and always against oppression. Truth may elude us, of course, may only partially be found, but our eyes can remain open, our minds stretched. Our pursuit of freedom may fall short, or it may be achieved only contingently, but our path can still be clear. Our fundamental stance and our most basic goals can guide us—it is to our deepest human values that we must aspire in our teaching lives.

The philosopher Hannah Arendt (1958) argues that

> education is the point at which we decide whether we love the world enough to assume responsibility for it and by the same token save it from that ruin which, except for renewal, except for the coming of the new and the young, would be inevitable. And education, too, is where we decide whether we love our children enough not to expel them from our world and leave them to their own devices, nor to strike from their hands their chance of undertaking something new, something unforeseen by us, but to prepare them in advance for the task of renewing a common world.

Arendt provides a useful frame for considering teaching's moral and political landscape. We can see that school is a natural site of hope and struggle—hope hovering around notions of a future, struggle busting out over the direction that future should take, the shape it could assume, the meanings it might encompass. Who can participate? What do we want for the children? And for ourselves? What worlds might we dream into being? What tools, skills, and accumulated wisdom should we offer the young, the coming generation? What might they create for themselves? Each of these questions invites us to reflect, debate, consider, and make judgments from conflicting claims; in doing so we raise questions, doubts, challenges about the aims and the content of education, and the practice of teaching.

Teaching for social justice is always more possibility than accomplishment, more a project of people in action than a finished condition. It requires a continuing identification of the obstacles to human fulfillment, the gaps and the inadequacies, and the ongoing challenge of figuring out what is to be done. The process of education—of discovery, illumination, and liberation—is rarely neat, logical, smooth, and obvious in its advance; it is more often messy, rough, unpredictable, and inconsistent. It can be halting and it can be slow, but it can also surprise us with its suddenness, with a power to rearrange everything around us.

Teaching for social justice is teaching *of, by,* and *for* the people. Its themes include:

- *Democracy*: Not as some waving flag or an inert monument, but as an ongoing project requiring participation, engagement, and creative input from all.

- *Activism*: Moving toward action, away from complacency, passivity, cynicism, despair; reaching beyond the superficial barriers that wall us off from one another.
- *History*: Reminding us of the powerful commitment, persistence, bravery, and triumphs of our justice-seeking forbears, of women and men who sought to build a world that worked for us all, of abolitionists, suffragists, labor organizers, civil rights activists, liberationists, and gender transgressors.
- *Public space*: Seeking those places where the meaning of equality and freedom are worked out on the ground.
- *Self-awareness*: Knowing what we owe one another, what is fair and not, who we are in the world.
- *Social literacy*: Resisting the devastating effects of consumerism and the destructive power of familiar social evils—racism, sexism, and homophobia.
- *Imagination*: Releasing the imagination to act on behalf of what the present demands and what a more just society might look like.

This kind of teaching can be thought of as creating and building upon a new 3 R's: relevant, rigorous, and revolutionary. It involves the positive transformation of people's lives, their environments, communities, and entire societies. It is based on dialogue not monologue, problem-posing rather than pat, fill-in-the-blanks answering, reflection and action rather than passivity. Teaching for social justice is the practice of democracy toward a more humane social order.

William C. Ayers
University of Illinois at Chicago

Therese Quinn
Art Institute of Chicago

REFERENCE

Arendt, H. (1958). *The human condition*. Chicago: University of Chicago Press.

foreword

I probably have the details wrong, but my recollection of meeting Greg Michie is at a professional conference several years ago. As is typical of these huge gatherings, most of the people one meets begin to blur. However, I do remember Greg approaching and asking me to write a book jacket review for his first book, *Holler If You Hear Me* (1999). I presumed that he was a young assistant professor and agreed to give the manuscript a quick read and send him the review. I believe I was quite slow in responding to his request, and, after an additional prompting from him, I took the time to read the manuscript.

What captured my attention was his incredible story-telling ability. Too often, graduate school wrings out every last bit of creativity from students. Their writing becomes dense and alienating and, in an attempt to impress a perceived intelligentsia, they create 200-word sentences that no one really understands. Greg's work did not have those typical markers. I do not mean to imply that Greg's work was simplistic and without intellectual heft. On the contrary, he wrote in a way that melded important ideas with engaging language. *Holler If You Hear Me* (1999) is an incredible book that has become a staple in my classes. However, it was not until after I had written the review for the book that I learned that Greg was just beginning his graduate school career. That is perhaps a lesson for those of us who advise graduate students. We should probably allow them to develop their own intellectual signatures and stop trying to force them to trace ours.

My relationship with this book, *See You When We Get There: Teaching for Change in Urban Schools*, is different. As Greg was completing his dissertation research, he asked if I would be willing to serve as an external member of his committee. Knowing both his commitments and his writing skill made this an easy decision for me. When I read the dissertation, I knew immediately that it was a book. This is a rare experience. Although many students believe their dissertations are books, few actually are. Books, at least those that are good, require a strong narrative voice that tells a compelling story. *See You When We Get There* does just that.

This is the story of young teachers of color who believe in the promise and possibility of their students. The power of this book is in Michie's ability to bring each teacher's story to life. Instead of being preoccupied with generalizations and themes, Michie illuminates the uniqueness of each teacher. Rather than paint a picture of miracle workers, he exposes the gritty, frustrating, and ultimately rewarding work of teaching in urban classrooms. This book presents no prescriptions or panaceas. It underscores the mundane and the mindlessness that surround working in entrenched bureaucracy. However, it leaves readers with hope because it introduces them to people who know what it means to teach for larger social purposes. Michie helps us know about both teaching and the teachers. Nancy, Freda, Toni, Cynthia, and Liz are real teachers whom we have an opportunity to learn from, but Michie is careful not to construct them solely as teachers. We come to know them as people. We learn of their relationship with the author, their students, their school communities, and their own identity and sense of self.

Reading this book reminds me of my early (and not nearly so successful) teaching years. But I clearly identify with the idealism, energy, and enthusiasm of the teachers Michie profiles. My first year of teaching early adolescents taught me a lot about teaching and a lot about myself. I learned that what I want for students is not always what they or their parents want. Most of my students were struggling to be successful in the classroom. However, one student was a clear standout. She was smart, inquisitive, and creative. Whenever other students ran into difficulty, they found their way to Rachel for help. I had big plans for Rachel. Rather than seeing Rachel go to the neighborhood high school, I was positioning her for one of the slots in the city's highly selective, all girls' school. There she would have access to excellent teachers, challenging peers, and a first-rate curriculum. I presented this idea to Rachel's mother who was a school crossing guard. Very quickly the mother set me straight.

"I know you want Rachel to go to that school across town and I know it's an excellent school. Rachel will be smart wherever she goes. But, at that school Rachel will be a little fish in a very big pond. If she goes to the neighborhood school, she'll be a big fish in a small pond. And, by being the top student she will have a better chance at getting a scholarship. We're poor people and the only way Rachel is going to get to college is with a scholarship. She'll get lost in that fancy school. She'll stand out here in the neighborhood." This parent's savvy understanding of the way schools work and the family's own economic reality made me realize that Myles Horton was right—"the people with the problems are the same people with the solutions." The teachers in *See You When We Get There* understand how important it is to study both their subject area and their students. They understand the incredible reciprocal nature of the teaching–learning experience, and they understand what it means to assume the responsibility of teaching. It is a job that requires twice as much listening as speaking, and all of Michie's teachers are good listeners.

The reason I can attest to the teachers' listening ability is that Michie so clearly and powerfully includes the students' voices. If the students were not permitted to come to voice, the volume would reveal some monumental silences. While I typically am mesmerized by excellent teaching, I found myself drawn to the students' voices throughout. Like a mirror, the students so accurately reflect what is happening in the classroom and in their interactions with these marvelous teachers.

See You When We Get There speaks to new teachers, prospective teachers, and veteran teachers. To new teachers, this book is a reminder that it is not their job to try to be saviors who "rescue" the students from their families and communities. Rather, teaching is about a complex set of interactions, intellectual development, and social responsibilities. To prospective teachers the book cuts through the romance of many stories of teaching and learning and omits the shock value. Unlike many tales of teaching Michie's does not attempt to tell stories through rose-colored glasses or rely on our fears, prejudices, and biases. Finally, for veteran teachers this is a book that reminds us why we started on this journey in the first place. It reminds us that we can learn from our neophyte colleagues and that we have a responsibility to nurture their hope and enthusiasm.

Greg Michie is a new generation teacher educator. Not content to understand teaching from a distance, Michie brings us up-close and personal insights on the lives of young teachers of color. These are stories that have been begging to be told. However, their authors are too busy with the all-consuming work of teaching in schools and classrooms where students are struggling to achieve. In many ways Michie serves as an interlocutor, a cultural translator who works hard to faithfully relay their stories. His careful documentation brings them and their students alive for readers. This is the kind of book that serves as an antidote to the mindless tactics of punish, test, and punish again that hold our schools hostage. In these pages is a vision of the possibilities that teaching should and could hold for us all.

Gloria Ladson-Billings

acknowledgments

I never have words adequate to the task when it comes to thanking those who have supported and stood by me, so to all of you, know that my appreciation is far greater than my ability to convey it.

My heartfelt thanks to the five teachers portrayed in these pages—Liz, Cynthia, Freda, Toni, and Nancy—for being so generous with your time, and for always reaching toward something better for your students. Each of you placed an uncommon amount of trust in me by allowing me to tell part of your story as I saw and heard it. I hope I haven't let you down.

This book began as my doctoral thesis, and a number of fellow graduate students at the University of Illinois at Chicago provided encouragement and insight at various points along the way. Thanks to James O'Brien, Horace Hall, Therese Quinn, Kalani Beyer, Gini Sorrentini, Raphael Guajardo, Young Joo Kim, Patrick Roberts, Andrea Brown, Rick Russo, Terry Jones, Elizabeth Alvarez, Laurence Hadjas, Peter Hilton, Dave Walsh, and Heather Duncan. Special thanks to Pauline Clardy and Cynthia Robinson, whose support and friendship throughout the dissertation process and beyond have been steadfast.

Bill Ayers has been friend, counselor, confidante, and one of the best teachers I've ever known. He shepherded me through this project—from beginning to end—with patience, keen observations, and his customary good humor. My dissertation committee, too, provided wisdom and counsel, while also challenging me to rethink my work in important ways. My appreciation to Annette Henry, Bill Schubert, Bill Watkins, and Pamela Quiroz—and an extra thank you to Gloria Ladson-Billings for fitting my project into her busy schedule.

My work for the past 3 years has been as codirector of the GATE@UIC Alternative Teacher-Certification Program, and I feel as if I've learned almost as much about teaching in that time as I did during my years in the classroom. If that's true, it's thanks in large part to the interns in GATE cohorts I through III, whose dedication and hard work as first-year teachers never failed to amaze me. If anyone worked harder than them, though, it was Amy Rome, who as codirector of GATE@UIC has been the heart and soul of the program, as well as a tireless advocate for Chicago schoolchildren, and a good friend. Thanks also to the staff at Golden Apple: Dom Belmonte, Gloria Harper, Nellie Quintana, Jim Pudlewski, Norm Crandus, Brigid Gerace, and Renee Dolezal.

Although I no longer teach full-time in Chicago's Back of the Yards neighborhood, I still spend a lot of time there, and I continue to be inspired by the many people who are dedicated to opening doors of opportunity for the youth in that community. Among others are Father Bruce Wellems, Oscar Contreras, Diana Rubio, Angelo Chavez, Father Ed Shea, Miguel Cambray, David Lozano, Salvador Chavez, Claudia Alvidrez, Claudio Rivera, Magda Banda, Irasema Salinas-González, Patty Brekke, Brigitte Swenson, Steve Hermann, Alfredo Nambo, Mayra Almaraz, Gonzalo Flores, Marcey Reyes, Rhonda Hoskins, Valerie Brown, and Sandy Traback. I'd also like to express my gratitude to the young men and women who have participated in the Reflections groups, both at Holy Cross and at Hamline School, over the past several years. Your presence is a sign of hope for us all.

A big thank you to the folks at TC Press who helped guide me through the twists and turns of the publication process: Carole Saltz, Catherine Chandler, Aureliano Vázquez, Dave Strauss, and Leyli Sheyegan. Thanks, too, to Steven Slaughter, who donated his time, energy, and creativity to designing the cover.

Other friends and colleagues have lent helping hands and listening ears, or have called or emailed to say hello at just the right time: John Dahl, Mike Baer, Sarah Cohen, Dave Coronado, Bob Fabian, David Mac-Williams, Penny Lundquist, Christina Hernandez, Julie Cajune, Sarah Howard. And to my former students at Seward

School and the Golden Apple Scholars Summer Institute—too numerous to name—I miss you and think of you often.

Lisa Espinosa is the most amazing person I know. She inspires me every day, and reminds me of what is beautiful in life by the way she lives hers. She probably knows this book better than I do, having spent many late nights listening as I read long passages over the phone, always providing patient advice, helpful questions, and, when needed, tough criticism.

Finally, my family somehow manages to make me feel loved and supported from 800 miles away, and has been a constant source of strength during tough times. Mom and Dad; Kirk, Kelley, and Jack; Lynn, David, Sadie, and Simon—thanks for all the goodness you bring to my life. I love you all.

1

other people's stories

It's only a few minutes into the first day of school, and the seventh graders sitting around six tables, arranged in a large rectangle so that everyone can see each other, are still getting their bearings. Some are coolly surveying the scene; others sit with bodies curled more tightly. Either way, outwardly most are doing a pretty good job of following the unwritten rules of seventh grade: acting only mildly interested, as if this first day is no big deal.

The teacher—a young Latina less than a year out of college—passes out a spiral notebook to each student. She tells the group that these will be their daily journals, and assures them that they'll be doing a lot of writing in her class. Suddenly, a look of panic crosses her face, then vanishes so quickly that I wonder if anyone else even noticed. "Wait–" the teacher says, "I forgot to say my name, didn't I?" She laughs to herself and touches a hand to her head. All eyes are turned her way. "My name is Nancy Serrano," the woman says. "And I will be your teacher."

A teacher introducing herself to her first class is always a moment filled with drama, but this one had some added poignancy for both Nancy and me. We'd met in this very building—Quincy Elementary School, a huge, factorylike structure that serves close to 1,000 students on Chicago's south side—nearly 10 years earlier. At the time, Nancy was an eighth grader dreaming of becoming the first in her family to go to college, the sixth of nine children born to a Mexican immigrant mother she described as "really strong and really stubborn." I was a 28-year-old, white, middle-class transplant from North Carolina stumbling through my second year as a public school teacher, an outsider to the kids I was teaching in many ways.

Nancy and I got to know each other pretty well that year. Along with four classmates, she volunteered to help me put together a homemade "book on tape" of Sandra Cisneros's *The House on Mango Street*. We'd meet one or two mornings a week before school to read and discuss the stories, and over time we developed a closeness that's difficult to achieve in a class of 30 students. When the girls graduated at the end of the year, we all promised to keep in touch.

During high school, Nancy took a part-time job waiting tables at a Mexican restaurant only a block from Quincy, and whenever I stopped by, we'd spend time catching up. In the spring of her senior year she told me she'd been awarded a scholarship and would be heading to DePaul University to study education. "One day I plan to teach at Quincy," she told me the next fall when I visited her on campus. "I think the kids will look at me different. They can say, 'My teacher lives in my neighborhood. She's lived here all her life. She's just like me.'"

Five years later, she's standing in front of her own classroom in the same school where she spent 9 years as a student. Thinking about her pathway to this point, I'm overwhelmed once again by her determination and strength. "I went to this school," Nancy tells her students later. "I was in these classes. I sat in your seat."

In a school district where only 13% of the teachers are Latino—even though Latino children comprise 36% of the system's student population—the power of Nancy's presence would be difficult to overestimate. But her return wasn't only of statistical significance. More important than Nancy's coming back to Quincy was what she'd come back to do. While in college, she'd been pushed to question the inequities she saw around her, and she now had words to wrap around some of the ideas she'd long felt but couldn't quite express. She knew the children in her community were struggling in many ways—against poverty, racism, lack of opportunity, feelings of inferiority—and she felt an intense passion, maybe even a calling, to help them better understand these obstacles, and to strategize ways to overcome them. Nancy saw teaching as a way to make a real difference in the lives of kids who were growing up much as she had. She wanted to change the world, and she wanted to begin in her own back yard.

I knew from personal experience that Nancy—whose story you'll read more about in Chapter 6—wasn't alone in her conviction. As an instructor in the Golden Apple Scholars program, I'd worked with a diverse group of undergraduate pre-service teachers from across Illinois who were committed to teaching in what the program terms "schools of high need." One thing I observed over several summers in the program was that many of the participants of color, especially those who'd grown up in urban areas, had come into teaching with the understanding that issues of equity and justice should be central to a teacher's work. They'd seen firsthand that public schools were failing many of the kids in their neighborhoods, but they held on to the belief that things could be made different, that with the collective efforts of young people such as themselves, schools could become engines of positive social change. Many hoped to teach in communities like the ones in which they'd been raised, and felt committed to working with students with whom they shared racial or cultural backgrounds.

This is not a new phenomenon, of course. In the African American community, particularly, there is a long tradition of conceptualizing teaching in this way. Cultural critic bell hooks (1994), in describing her schooling experience as a young girl growing up in the apartheid South, writes that at that time, in that place,

> teaching was about service, giving back to one's community. For black folks teaching—educating—was fundamentally political because it was rooted in antiracist struggle. . . . Almost all of our teachers at Booker T. Washington were black women. . . . We learned early that our devotion to learning, to a life of the mind, was a counter-hegemonic act, a fundamental way to resist every strategy of white racist colonization. Though they did not articulate these practices in theoretical terms, my teachers were enacting a revolutionary pedagogy of resistance. . . . Teachers worked with and for us to ensure that we would fulfill our intellectual destiny and by doing so uplift the race. My teachers were on a mission. (p. 2)

Nancy and many other young teachers of color see themselves as being on a similar mission, but this would be hard to tell from reading educational research. In part, that's because the bulk of such work continues to be quantitative and prescriptive, its "conclusions" often seeming far removed from what actually goes on in real classrooms. Teachers, in these studies, are viewed not as interpreters of their own experience or potential agents of change but as implementers of programs, deliverers of curriculum. In the current climate of hyperaccountability in schools, such research has become resurgent, while the voices of teachers have slipped further into the shadows. We are, as Mike Rose (1995) has noted, in dire need of more up-close looks at committed teachers and the spaces of hope they struggle to create in their classrooms—what Rose calls "rich, detailed images of possibility" (p. 4).

But even in accounts of teaching that do zoom in close on classroom life, stories such as Nancy's are still hard to come by. Historically, narratives about attempts to teach against the grain of a broken educational system have usually come from the perspective of white teachers. My own memoir of my teaching experiences in Chicago, *Holler If You Hear Me* (1999), followed in a long line of such work stretching back to classic books by Herbert Kohl and Jonathan Kozol in the 1960s. In recent years, black women scholars such as Gloria Ladson-Billings, Michele Foster, Jacqueline Jordan Irvine, and Annette Henry have countered this tendency by chronicling the "culturally relevant" pedagogy of a number of African American and African Canadian teachers. But despite these important contributions, the recorded story of attempts at teaching for change in America's schools has, in large measure, retained a distinctly vanilla flavor.

This book represents my effort to portray the classroom lives of Nancy and four other young teachers of color, and to explore what "teaching for change" means to them. In observing and interviewing these teachers, I wanted to learn more about how they understand their experiences: their pathways to teaching, their day-to-day challenges in the classroom, the factors that motivate and constrain their work with urban kids. I wanted to know what they believe about the purposes and possibilities of public education, and to find out how (or whether) they manage to renew themselves in the current climate of high-stakes testing and teacher deprofessionalization. In short, I wanted to hear their voices and document their teaching stories, while also taking a measure of my own.

••••••••••••

One thing that's important to keep in mind as you read this book is that no story tells itself. In shaping the teacher narratives that follow, I had to make countless choices—locating patterns and drawing connections, emphasizing certain themes or events while downplaying others, figuring out what to include and what to leave on the cutting-room floor. Such decisions necessarily reflect my own history, values, and preoccupations as much as they do the teachers'. To begin to understand these stories, then, you first need to know something about mine.

I was born in 1963 in a tiny town in the North Carolina mountains, just off a winding stretch of the Blue Ridge Parkway. At the time, my parents both worked at a boarding school for teenagers who'd had trouble in previous schools—my mother as a teacher and "house parent," my father as recreation director and, eventually, principal. My mom had been born and raised in the South, the daughter of a red-dirt Georgia farmer and a college-educated teacher, the granddaughter of a Presbyterian minister. My dad's parents emigrated from Aberdeen, Scotland, a few years before his birth in 1928, and raised their three children in Hamburg, New York, a suburb of Buffalo.

Most of my childhood was spent in Charlotte, North Carolina, and in many ways, it was idyllic. I remember lots of good times: building a clubhouse out of wood scraps in our back yard, picking honeysuckle at a nearby creek, lip-synching with neighborhood friends to "The Age of Aquarius," wearing a homemade Evil Knievel costume on Halloween, playing endless games of Kick-the-Can on summer evenings. Our family was textbook middle-class: no lavish vacations or outings to what we called "fancy" restaurants, but my brother and sister and I always had what we needed. I felt safe and loved and, most days, quite happy.

Of course, the early 1970s were something of a tumultuous time, so I also have vivid memories of the social and political issues that swirled around me. Court-ordered busing to desegregate schools began in Charlotte in 1970—the year I started second grade—and I recall hearing news stories about black students being harassed at local high schools. African American families had started moving into the neighborhood where we lived, and "For Sale" signs popped up in the yards of white residents faster than you could count them. One morning on my way to school, I walked past the house a black family had just bought to see the word "NIGGER" spray-painted on the front in huge, jagged letters.

My parents were both Democrats, and my mother was an unassuming but committed activist on issues of racial and economic justice. My own first foray into political activism came when I was nine: My best friend, William Goodrum, and I spent several afternoons riding our bikes around the neighborhood putting "George McGovern for President" flyers in mailboxes. I'm sure I only minimally understood McGovern's platform at the time, but I do remember having a strong sense that I was doing something important. Naturally, I was crushed that November when Richard Nixon was reelected to the presidency in a landslide decision. Growing up, as I did, in Jesse Helms country, I would unfortunately become accustomed to such election-night disappointment.

Throughout my young life, I spent almost every Sunday in the pews of Seigle Avenue Presbyterian Church. With the exception of my parents' influence, the experiences I had there probably had more to do with shaping the person I am today than anything or anyone else. It's said that Sunday morning from 11 to 12 o'clock is the most segregated hour in America, but Seigle Avenue was different. There, across the street from Charlotte's largest public housing development, blacks and whites from various economic backgrounds worshipped side by side, singing from the Presbyterian hymnal one minute and clapping along with the gospel choir the next. The relationships I formed at Seigle and the time I spent there not only enriched me as a person but helped give me perspective on my privilege, and broadened my worldview in ways schoolbooks never could.

Still, I did like school as a kid. I had lots of creative energy and I was lucky to have numerous teachers who gave me the freedom to explore that side of myself in their classrooms. I remember putting on all sorts of plays and skits, doing a student radio show, performing impersonations over the intercom. In ninth grade, some friends and I wrote and performed songs about labor leaders Samuel Gompers and Eugene Debs for a social studies project, and to this day, I can still sing some of the lyrics. In high school, we made an 8-millimeter home-movie version of *Lord of the Flies*, which at the time seemed like a cool idea and I remember having a lot of fun doing it. In retrospect, it seems kind of creepy.

In college I majored in television and film, but after spending a few unfulfilling years in low-level TV jobs, I moved to Chicago and got a position codirecting an after-school program. From there I became a substitute teacher, and within 2 months—despite the fact that I had no formal preparation or credentials—I had a class-room of my own. I felt woefully underprepared, but I also felt, for the first time, that the work I was doing had a higher purpose. It challenged me, often confounded me, and left me at the end of each day exhausted but determined to do better.

Since I had no formal background in education, my teaching approach grew mostly out of what made sense to me—much of which I'd absorbed either from my parents or from the many good teachers I'd had in public schools. I thought classrooms should be active spaces where kids had regular opportunities to do and make things. I thought students should be encouraged to express themselves, that their voices should be not only heard but valued. I believed kids should feel a connection between what they studied in school and their lives outside it, and should be pushed to think about the world around them. Most of all, I recognized that a meaningful, quality education was crucial for the young people I was teaching, whose communities had been largely neglected by those in power.

Needing certification, I signed up for a master's program, and there I was able to focus, refine, and question my personal theories and beliefs about teaching and learning. I remember being both inspired and challenged by the work of Paulo Freire (1970), whose conception of a problem-posing, humanizing education kept me awake to the larger social forces I was struggling against as a teacher, and that my students and their families had to fight on a daily basis. I was also impacted early on by the writings of several black educators who wrote specifically about teaching African American students: Janice Hale-Benson, Jawanza Kunjufu, and Lisa Delpit all helped me see things in ways I hadn't before.

Most provocative for me was Delpit's (1986) critique of whole-language approaches to literacy and, just as important, of some white teachers' assumptions that they know best how to educate children of color. In "The Silenced Dialogue" (1988), Delpit suggests that "progressive" white teachers must reexamine their own roles in perpetuating the culture of power, and reconsider whose voices get heard—and whose don't—in educational discussions and debates. "Appropriate education for poor children and children of color can only be devised in consultation with adults who share their culture," Delpit writes. "Good liberal intentions," she adds later, "are not enough" (p. 296).

I tried to keep those words in mind throughout my 9 years in Chicago classrooms, and I've attempted to do so in my more recent work as a teacher–educator as well. I've learned a lot over the years by working alongside and talking with black and Latino teachers who have unique understandings of the communities in which they teach, who see their students not as "other people's children" but as their own. The stories in this book are, in part, an effort to continue those conversations, and to give others the opportunity to pull up a chair and listen in.

•••••••••••

I understood going in to this project that I would be an outsider, in many respects, to the people and communities I planned to write about, and that my efforts to convey the meanings of these teachers' experiences would be in certain ways limited and complicated by that reality. I'd learned—the hard way, you might say—that issues of representation are important to keep in mind, especially for a person of relative privilege, like me, writing about people of color.

In my first book, *Holler If You Hear Me: The Education of a Teacher and His Students* (1999), I attempted to portray the complexities both of my work as a teacher and of my students' lives. I'd read plenty of "teacher hero" narratives, and I tried to write against that tradition. Through the stories I told, I hoped to counter stereotypical notions both of what it means to teach in an urban school and—through extensive use of my students' own words—what city kids are like. I wanted to portray the struggles of trying to teach with one eye on all the hope and possibility I saw in my students, and the other on a school system and larger society that seemed intent on shutting them up, shutting them down, and shutting them out.

Initially, response to the book was positive, especially from teachers and teachers in training. In the neighborhood where I'd taught, the reaction of students and community members was overwhelmingly favorable. A Mexican American activist wrote to express her appreciation "for giving these great students a voice and a context for the world to hear and understand. Your treatment of the kids' lifestyles and milieu," she wrote, "was not patronizing or condescending." Former students who'd read the book called or e-mailed to tell me I'd done a good job of portraying their neighborhood and their school experience—that I'd "gotten it right," so to speak. But not everyone thought so.

I began to hear criticism from a few Latinos at the university I attended (and, later, from other academics as well) who said my book was little more than another chapter in the "master narrative"—that of a white do-gooder coming in to "save" their children. "Do you think Michie calculated the sale of his book, going around glorifying his teaching in the barrio?" read one e-mail, which referred to me as "Vinney Vanilly." My intentions, these people said, didn't matter. What mattered was that I was white, and that I was writing about people of color. Those details alone were enough to make the resulting narrative a reminder of the continued colonization of black and brown people by those of European origin. For Latinos who had not sold out to white norms, I was told, my book was painful to read and, in the final analysis, it did more harm than good.

The criticism hurt. It cut deep. It came from people I respect, people I hoped would consider me an ally, and at first I was defensive. I'd worked hard to craft the stories I'd told about my students and their families in a respectful way, I thought, but now it seemed they were being misinterpreted. "I know Latinos get misrepresented," I said to myself, "but not by me. I'm trying to do the opposite. I'm one of the good guys." As time went by and I was able to give it more thought, I recognized that the whining—even if it had been done inside my head—was counterproductive. I knew I had no right to request or expect special consideration. I also knew that if I really intended to try to write the book you're now reading (which began, once upon a time, as my doctoral thesis), I would be wading into even more troubled waters. What I needed to do was listen to the criticisms, take everything in, and read and think more about the issues involved.

So that's what I did. I read Renato Rosaldo's (1993) potent critique of classic anthropological studies, which he explains have been used not simply to examine "them" and how they differ from "us" but to justify imperialism, and to reinforce the notion that certain societies are meant to be dominant while others are meant to be subjugated. I looked to Ruth Behar (1996), who writes of the misrepresentation of Latino people by clueless—and, moreover, humorless—Anglo anthropologists. I reread authors such as bell hooks (1990), who asserts that while white people may be able to comprehend the realities embedded in black literature and history, they "know them differently" than do blacks; and Cornel West (1993), who argues that the root of the problem of representation for black people is their lack of control over the means to represent themselves. I stumbled upon Sherman Alexie's appraisal of Edward Curtis's famous black-and-white portraits of Native Americans, which Alexie, a member of the Coeur d'Alene tribe, calls "moldy old photographs of pathologically stoic Indians" that hold too much power "in a culture where Indians rarely, if ever, get to self-define" (in Cates, 2001). I read Gloria Anzaldúa and Stuart Hall, Patricia Hill Collins and Peter McLaren, Adolph Reed, Jr. and Wanda Pillow, and much more.

I also had dozens of conversations—with professors, fellow graduate students, friends, family, and the teachers with whom I planned to work—about the potential complications of my writing about women of color. (Actually, the plan was never to work only with women teachers, but that's how things worked out. See the appendix for more details about how I selected the teachers.) Liz Kirby, an African American teacher whose classroom you'll visit in Chapter 2, told me she was somewhat reluctant to participate when I first approached her. "I had a fear of being a *There Are No Children Here* subject or a *Hope in the Unseen* subject," she told me. "And I really liked both of those books. But in reading them, I do feel, 'That's another white person telling a black story.' And for me, that makes me think—what's happening? Why don't more people of color tell their own stories? Is it because they can't, is it because they try and it doesn't happen, is it because they're just too busy dealing with their lives to stop and do it?"

Part of the answer to those questions, I think, is that books about people of color written by whites are often unfairly seen by publishers and critics—most of whom, of course, are also white— as being more "objective" than those written from an insider's perspective, and thus are more likely to get published and, once on the shelves, to be more widely read. In that sense, white authors writing about urban issues or communities of color often receive the same sort of "cultural affirmative action" that William Jelani Cobb (2003) says young white music listeners award to Eminem. Though getting my writing published has always seemed difficult at every turn, I'm sure I have a wide range of advantages. One of the unearned privileges that goes along with being a white male, after all, is that whether you're selling insurance, applying for a loan, walking down the street, or pitching a book idea, people tend to give you the benefit of the doubt.

When I told my sister and her husband about the dilemma I was facing around the issue of representation, the difference in their reactions was telling. My sister said nothing for awhile as her husband suggested possible "escape routes" for me. Couldn't you say this, he asked, or this? Wouldn't this solve the problem? He sensed my frustration, and—as a fellow white guy—was trying to help, to find a way out of the predicament. My sister remained quiet as we volleyed ideas back and forth. Then she said, matter-of-factly: "I think what they're really saying is that it's time for white men to just shut up and listen for awhile."

In so many words, that is what a lot of people are saying. And in certain respects, I agree with them. I believe the concerns over power and representation are legitimate and important for researchers in the social sciences to continually keep in mind. Being a member of a privileged group does indeed make it problematic for someone such as myself to write about those who are members of oppressed groups. But at the same time, I agree with Micaela di Leonardo (1997), who laments that, taken too far, identity politics "assumes a Tower of Babel in which groups can never communicate or act beyond their 'primary identities.' . . . This is not how human beings live or ever have lived" (p. 67).

Ultimately, that's where I come down on the issue. Liz, for example, certainly looked at me and saw a white man, and I looked at her and saw a black woman, but I don't think we viewed each other *only* through those lenses—at least not always. We were able to connect as teachers, as advocates for children, as city dwellers, as avid readers, as human beings. We were able to communicate across and through and around and in spite of our differences. Still, it would be a mistake to assume, as many white people seem eager to do, that race and other social distinctions can be quickly and once-and-for-all transcended in personal relationships. Relevant here are the opening lines of Pat Parker's (1990) poem, "For the white person who wants to know how to be my friend": "The first thing you do is to forget that i'm Black/Second, you must never forget that i'm Black" (p. 297).

My interpretation of all five of these women's experiences was limited, without a doubt, by who I am, where I'm from, what I've known and not known. Those factors affected not only what questions I asked them but also what they chose to tell me, and how I heard what they said; what I noticed or paid attention to in their classrooms, as well as how I made sense of what I saw. If I've understood their stories, it's certainly been in a different way than the women themselves do. But I have to believe that the attempt at understanding is still important, and that there is value in the resulting narratives. Partial and imperfect though they may be, they nonetheless reveal glimpses of the meaning these teachers give to their work. While my outsider status unquestionably complicated and colored that effort, it didn't make it impossible.

There are no easy answers. Gloria Anzaldúa (1990), for one, doesn't pretend to provide any. She does, however, make a distinction between white authors who "appropriate" another group's culture in their writing and those who "proliferate information": "The difference between appropriation and proliferation," she writes, "is that the first steals and harms; the second helps heal breaches of knowledge" (p. xxi).

My purpose in cointerpreting these teachers' stories has been to help heal such a breach. Along the way, I've tried to keep my eyes and ears wide open, and to be honest with myself and the teachers with whom I worked. Though I can't escape my privilege, I can try to live my life and do my work in ways that interrupt and challenge it. I can keep listening and learning, bearing in mind that whatever I write, it's sure to be only a modest contribution to a much larger conversation—one in which the final word is never written, and the dust never settles.

....

My experiences as a teacher and teacher–educator tell me that one of the best ways to learn about teaching is to watch dedicated practitioners at work, and to talk with them about why they do what they do, and what factors limit and sustain them. The portraits in this book will give you an opportunity, through my admittedly limited lenses, to do just that with five dedicated young teachers. But as I've mentioned already, none of these stories should be seen as a complete accounting. The narrative is always selective, always a partial telling, only a representation of what it sets out to portray.

When I taught media studies to seventh and eighth graders, I'd introduce them to the idea of representation by holding up a photograph of something—a ladder, for example—and ask them what it was they were looking at. "A ladder," the first few students would always say, staring at me as if the answer couldn't be more obvious, and they'd appear increasingly puzzled each time I said that wasn't the response I was after. Eventually, a lightbulb would click on in someone's head: "Oh! It's a *picture* of a ladder!" It was a simple inroad to a complex idea, but the point was made nonetheless, and the students usually agreed it was an important distinction.

What you'll find here are pictures of five young teachers at work, extended snapshots as seen through my eyes and written by my hand. During the time I visited their classrooms for this project, they all worked in Chicago public schools. I've used their real names, but I've changed descriptive information and identifying markers of most other people and places. The specific context of each teacher's work varied: Liz taught history and African American studies at a magnet high school; Cynthia Nambo worked at an all-girls school, where she was a sixth-grade science teacher; Freda Lin was a high school U.S. history and Asian studies teacher; Toni Billingsley worked at a small charter school where she taught Spanish and reading to middle schoolers; and Nancy taught language arts and reading to seventh and eighth graders at a neighborhood grammar school.

Yet despite any differences, these five teachers share two seemingly contradictory beliefs: that public schools have too often failed poor children and children of color, and that public schools—with considerable effort—can become places of hope and possibility for all kids. They don't always see what they are doing as "radical," and they wouldn't necessarily cite "critical pedagogy" as the bedrock of their work in schools. Indeed, some of their attempts to enact classrooms where concerns of social justice are central may seem modest compared to the more elaborate proposals of critical theorists. But I would argue that the work they are doing is critical in more ways than one, and that reading about the small victories they do achieve can give others needed sustenance to keep resisting systemic restraints, rethinking their practice, and working toward a day when hope and justice are in more abundant supply for all children. See you when we get there.

Photo: Antonio Pérez

2

liz kirby

"In a week or so," Liz Kirby was telling the juniors and seniors in one of her African American Studies classes, "we're going to start reading *The Autobiography of Malcolm X*. So you need to either buy it in the next week or give me 5 dollars to buy it for you."

Several kids' eyebrows raised. "You talking about the one by Alex Haley?"

"Yes."

"That book is about 15 dollars."

"No, it's not," Liz said reassuringly. "It should cost you about 5 dollars."

Around me, students grumbled. "Do we get extra credit for buying it?"

"No, you get regular credit. I really think it's a book you'll want to have in your personal library."

"I don't have a personal li-bury," said a kid with spotless, shiny white gym shoes. "And I'm not gonna read it, so why should I buy it?"

"Excuse me," Liz said, furrowing her brow and turning her body toward him. "Let's be strong. And focused. Can we have a little less resistance and trust me a little bit?"

The kid's face softened. "How long is it?"

"It's . . . " I could tell Liz was searching for a way to answer that wouldn't alienate the skeptics any further. "It goes really fast. It's a quick read."

"That book's about 500 pages," a young man with a radio announcer's voice called out. "It's this thick." He held up a thumb and forefinger about 3 inches apart to show the group. "And like I told my English teacher—if it don't fit in my back pocket, I ain't gonna take it home."

"Can't we just watch the movie instead?" a girl with braces and barely sprouting dreadlocks asked.

"Yeah, let's just watch the movie," several others agreed. I wondered if Spike Lee, who fought so hard to direct the film version of Malcolm X's life in hopes of bringing the story to more young people, had anticipated the possibility of this sort of backfire.

"Look," Liz told them. "I really want you to own this book. I personally believe it's a book that every person who lives in America—black, white, Latino, Asian—should read. I didn't read it myself until pretty recently, but when I did, my first reaction was, All my students have to read this book. It's that powerful."

"But I don't got time to read a thick book like that, Ms. Kirby," whined the radio announcer.

"How do you get to school?" Liz asked him.

"I take the bus."

"There you go," she said. "Read it on the bus every day." He looked thoroughly unconvinced; Liz turned to the class. "I really don't want you guys to be intimidated by the book because of its length. It's an important, important book, and I really think you're going to like it. And I promise you this: You will be a better person for having read *Malcolm X*."

"A'ight, Ms. Kirby," the kid with the sparkling shoes said. "Long as you don't ask us no questions about what was the deeper meaning."

The undercurrent of his comment, it seemed to me, was clear: Liz always asked her students about the deeper meaning of things, and he knew that it would be no different with *Malcolm X*. Liz had told me that one of the goals of her teaching was for her students to become intellectually curious. "I want them to really want to know things, I want them to question," she'd said. "I want them to be able to think independently and decide thoughtfully, so that they can build strong families and strong communities and strong selves. In general, I think America is an anti-intellectual society, and that's so frustrating for me, because how can you make good political decisions when there's no intellectual activity?"

As Liz began to outline the class's four main projects for the upcoming marking period, it was evident that there would be no intellectual vacuum here. "It's going to be an intense quarter," she told the group, "so please prepare yourself for that intensity." In addition to a continued study of slavery and slave rebellions, they would be adding chapters to their own autobiographies, reading and discussing *Malcolm X*, writing a research paper that tied into African American history, and doing a small-group performance to creatively express something they'd learned in the class.

At the mention of the performance piece, a loud groan came from the direction of the radio announcer, whose name, Liz told me after class, was Sherman. "OK, look, Oscar the Grouch," Liz said, laughing. "You have a lot of choice in this. You can do dance, rap, poetry, dramatizations, you can do scenes from—"

"*The Jeffersons?*" Sherman asked.

Liz gave him a look that said she'd had about enough of his silliness. "You could bring in an India.Arie song and do something with that," she suggested. "Or you could do a dialogue between Tupac and Dr. King." The two references to black popular music weren't accidental nor, I would learn, were they uncommon. Liz was a lover of hip-hop, and she frequently wove rap lyrics or song references into her lessons. Posters of Common's CD *Like Water for Chocolate* and The Roots' *Things Fall Apart* decorated one of her bulletin boards. On several occasions in the coming days, I would witness kids come up to her after class to talk about a new video they'd seen or a song they'd heard. Music, for Liz, was an avenue for making connections, one of the many ways she built bridges of common understanding with her students.

"Ms. Kirby, Philip say is it OK if he do his research paper on growing marijuana," asked Quinzell from the back row.

Liz stared him down. "You want to do your paper on black ventriloquists? Let Philip ask the question if he's got a question."

While Liz had cautioned me beforehand that this class was in many ways her most difficult, the static from her students seemed to be more of a show than a genuine display of resistance. Despite the surface negativity, I didn't get the feeling that these kids—most of them anyway—were actually thinking of not reading the book or doing their projects. They seemed to feel the need to play the role of disaffected teens, putting up a front of indifference and alienation, but underneath it all there was trust and respect. When I asked a kid next to me what he thought of the class, he said, "Everybody wanna be with Ms. Kirby."

After the project assignments had been discussed, Liz turned to the main activity she had planned for the day: Several students would be reading aloud their "appeals"—poems or essays inspired by David Walker's *Appeal*, an impassioned antislavery plea published in 1829 by Walker, a free black man who urged slaves to rise up, to fight violence with violence, and to claim their dignity and freedom. Liz had asked her students to compose their own appeals that touched on current or historical issues that affected them, and they had responded, she'd told me, with provocative and insightful pieces.

Racquel Fields, the first to read, waited for the class to settle down before she began.

Today I am writing to bring to your attention
Whether you be white, Black, or somewhere in between
I too have decided to break the patriotic convention
I've found that America is corrupted by politics, and has
    been washed unclean

By the time she'd reached the end of that stanza, the only sound in the room was Racquel's voice.

From the beginning, it has been contradictions, lies, and
    obscenities
Though poorly blanketed with a profound disguise
Do you even dare call this cold ground the land of liberty
Well, I'll tell you what I have read, seen, and interpreted
    through my eyes

As she read on, spotlighting historical injustices from World War II–era Japanese internment camps and U.S. involvement in Vietnam to George W. Bush's questionable election in 2000, the audience listened even more intently, responding aloud to lines that struck them as if they were at a tent-meeting revival: "Mmm-hmmm!" "That's right!" "Say it!" When Racquel was finished—

concluding with the lines, "Race-related, black-on-black, drug-related crimes/America, built on our backs, will fall in due time/Change . . . "—a guy behind me leaned over and said to a friend, "She deep. She need to go ahead and pop a album off. She got more lyrics than Mos Def."

"So what's she appealing?" Liz asked the class.

"How America has been hypocritical since back in the day," Jazmine answered.

"She's finding a lot of inconsistencies with the whole founding of the country," added Rodney. "And with what's going on today, too."

"My point was not to bash America," Racquel said. "I just wanted to show how we have to change and better these things if we don't want to repeat the same mistakes."

Saying that we have to make things better, of course, assumes that it is possible to do so, that bringing about social change is something that is within our collective grasp. Racquel clearly believed that it was, and that notion, Liz told me, was one of the most important messages she tried to get across to her students. "I really hope that in my teaching I can encourage kids to look at their lives and their roles differently," she said. "I want kids to feel—empowered is not the best word, but—connected to their lives and connected to their communities. I don't want them to feel like things just kind of happen around them and there's nothing they can do about it. I want them to understand that each decision they make, like it or not, is a decision, and it has an impact. And I want them to take responsibility for that."

•••••••••••

Making good choices and taking responsibility for one's self and others were themes that echoed throughout Liz's teaching, both in the content of her lessons and in the ways she framed her expectations of her students. The next morning in her world studies class—she also taught a period of U.S. history in addition to her four African American studies sections—she was moving from desk to desk checking homework while her students responded in writing to a journal prompt on the board: "What responsibility, if any, do people have to help those in need?"

Liz stopped next to a kid who'd come in late. "Anthony Valentine, where were you yesterday?"

"Home."

Liz made a mark in her grade book and looked Anthony in the eye before moving on. "You are choosing summer school," she told him. "Don't choose summer school."

"What can I do to raise my grade?" Anthony called after Liz as she moved on to the next student.

"Call me tonight if you're really serious about that," she told him. "We'll figure something out."

Liz zig-zagged her way through the rest of the aisles, then sat down behind a podium, closed the grade book, and addressed the class. "I'm very frustrated with the people who have chosen not to do their homework," she said. "Very frustrated." From what I could tell only a few students didn't have it, but Liz wasn't letting them off the hook. "Just understand that there are consequences to making that decision. You can spend your summer working, spending time with friends and family, or you can spend the summer taking world studies again at a site to be determined—which may not be here at Matheson. It's your choice."

Liz had come to Matheson, long considered one of Chicago's premier public high schools, after spending 2 years at a small charter school on the city's southwest side. For many years, Matheson had parlayed its reputation for excellence into attracting top-notch students—both black and white—from the surrounding community. But during the 1990s, the school's white population had started to dwindle, mirroring a system-wide trend. Some neighborhood residents murmured that Matheson was beginning to slip academically. Others believed the notion of Matheson's demise was more perception than reality, and had been perpetuated mostly by parents who were concerned that the school was losing its racial and economic diversity: By 2001, white student enrollment had shrunk to less than 5%.

From Liz's point of view, such worries were largely unwarranted. "People say we're losing our appeal," she said, "but kids are knocking down the doors trying to go here." The black students at the school, she pointed out, came from diverse backgrounds and brought with them a broad range of experiences, hopes, and dreams. Some were children of professors or attorneys and lived in single-family homes with two-car garages; others lived with relatives in walk-up apartment buildings or in what remained of public housing. A handful had emigrated from places such as Ghana or Jamaica; others were transplants from Mississippi or Tennessee; still others had never traveled more than a few hours' drive from the south side of Chicago. While some struggled academically, many were college bound. As juniors, a number spent their spring breaks visiting historically black colleges and universities, and each year a few seniors won scholarships to prestigious institutions such as Julliard, Columbia University, and Howard. Indeed, visitors to Matheson who subscribed to the "deficit model" of urban schools and city kids didn't have to look far or listen long before the stereotypes began to crumble.

Yet whether her students were fielding offers from esteemed universities or dragging themselves into class late without a notebook or pen, Liz believed her purpose in teaching them was essentially the same. "Education for African Americans has always been about liberation and liberating," she told me, echoing the recent scholarship of Theresa Perry (2003) and calling to mind black educators and freedom fighters from Frederick Douglass and Carter G. Woodson to Mary McLeod Bethune and Fannie Lou Hamer. "But somehow that message has gotten lost. People don't see it, they don't understand it, they don't appreciate it." Liz wanted to rekindle that tradition, and she felt strongly committed to teaching in the black community. "I do feel like I'm 'giving back' in a way," she said, "but I hesitate to say that sometimes because I'm not teaching out of charity. I'm teaching because I really want to teach here. There's a connection."

Liz believed it was extremely important for African American kids to have teachers with whom they could connect culturally and historically. "When you're a black teacher teaching black kids," she said, "I think you have a greater sense of urgency about what they need to know and why they need to know it because you can draw from your own experience. Also, I think a lot of times there's an added degree of trust there, a comfort zone that kids have with you that allows them to open up. I can talk about things like hair and skin color with my students, and it'll be really real, and we'll know exactly what we're talking about. Or when we talk about things that are painful, it's easier for me to understand in a way that a white teacher wouldn't be able to."

But Liz thought some people took that notion too far: first, in thinking that an African American teacher would be effective with black students simply by virtue of her blackness; and second, in thinking that white teachers could never be successful teachers of African American children because they couldn't relate to them in genuine ways. Personal experience, she said, had shown her that neither of those propositions held true in all cases.

"I mean, would I want Ward Connerly as my teacher?" she asked, laughing. "No. Oppression comes in all shapes, sizes, and colors. I've heard some black teachers say some really crazy things to kids, and sometimes people just accept it because they figure, 'Well, they're black. They know what's up.' But even though they're black, they may be bringing very unhealthy practices and philosophies into the classroom."

While Liz had certainly worked alongside white teachers who were insensitive to African American students and didn't demand much of them, she also had white colleagues who she thought did amazing work with black kids. Part of what made them successful, she believed, was their willingness to be honest with themselves about power relationships and their own gaps of knowledge. "Some white teachers aren't really aware of their own privilege," she said. "They haven't begun their own critical self-examination. To teach black kids well, a white teacher has to be able to say, 'I know I'm white and this can get really complicated, so let's talk about why that could be.' Or, 'I know I'm really ignorant about your experience, but I want to know, and I'm open to learning, even though some of what I learn may be hard for me to understand or painful for me to hear.' And kids can read you. They can tell if you're really trying to understand or if you're just going through the motions."

Liz had gotten her own initial taste of cross-cultural teaching when she came to Matheson and, for the first time, had white students in some of her classes. Up until then, she'd worked in schools that were virtually all-black. "A lot of the white parents were on the Local School Council," she explained, "and I had some of their kids in my classes, so I was really conscious of that. I would get kind of nervous in my teaching, thinking my white parents would monitor me closer as a teacher than my black parents. And then after a while I thought, 'You racist! How could you think like that?' You know, giving extra attention to the white kids' parents, and kind of taking the black kids for granted. I never, ever thought I would think that way. But to me, that just shows how deep white supremacy is—in the black community in particular. And I consider myself somewhat educated, you know? Yet I still see myself falling into that kind of thinking."

Liz passed out photocopies of an article from *Time* magazine, "Death Stalks a Continent," which examined the HIV/AIDS epidemic in southern Africa. Her world studies class was wrapping up a unit on Africa in which they'd examined, among other things, imperialism's impact on the continent, political corruption in Nigeria and Zimbabwe, African art forms, the role of the griot, and the history of apartheid. With the AIDS article, Liz was striving— as was her practice in all her history classes—to make connections: between the lesson and her students' lives, the past and the present, the textbook and the front page. "I want you to think about the journal question as we read this," she told the group. I looked back at the board and read it again: "What responsibility, if any, do we have to help those in need?"

Several students took turns reading the first two pages of the article aloud, breezing through a succession of what I thought might be unfamiliar words: *cataclysm, depredation, virulence, promiscuity*. Two main points emerged from the reading: that the spread of AIDS in Africa had been due largely to a lack of education and awareness, and that the United States and other Western nations had been slow to provide needed aid or assistance in the wake of the crisis. At several points, students raised their hands and asked questions—How did the first people catch AIDS? Can you die from diarrhea? Are AIDS cases increasing in the United States?— and Liz did her best to address them, even telling the class about a good friend's battle with HIV. But she kept bringing them back to the question on the board: Do we have a responsibility? Should we help? Is there anything we can do?

"It's horrible and everything," Reena said. "But it's not our responsibility to help."

"If we was in the same situation," added Marcus, "they wouldn't help us. So why should we help them?"

Jermaine, in the back corner, raised his hand. "On a wide scale, I think we do have a responsibility. We have a lot of resources in the United States. We're a first-world country, and we have a responsibility to help poorer countries."

"Stop saying it's our responsibility," Marcus retorted. "Most of those people got theyselves into that situation by doing drugs or something, so if they got theyselves into it, they can get theyselves out of it. If you wanna help, that's on you. But it ain't our responsibility."

After a little more verbal sparring, Liz broke in. "I'm not hearing much of a moral message in our conversation, and that concerns me," she said. "But maybe that's where you guys are right now. Can anybody argue that it's just the right thing to do—that countries should help other countries in need because it is the moral thing to do?"

For a few seconds, no one responded. "I heard this quote," a girl named Treasure finally said. "I can't remember it exactly, but it's basically saying that a person who says they're not doing evil is still actually doing evil by not doing anything good." A bit jumbled, but she had the gist of it.

"So you contribute to the injustice by not responding to it," Liz offered.

Treasure thought about it for a second. "Yeah, I think you do."

When she first came to Matheson, Liz had expected—naively, she now realized—that most of her black students would be on the same page politically, down with the same program. But she quickly found that not to be the case. "You would think that African American kids, because they come from a history of struggle, would be a little more empathetic to things," she told me. "And some of them are. But there's a very strong conservative strain in the black community. It's almost a backlash to what they perceive to be the welfare mythology stuff."

Students in Liz's classes sometimes espoused what she considered to be reactionary stances on a range of issues—from modern-day U.S. imperialism to affirmative action to immigration policy—and she wasn't always sure how to respond. While she believed in being explicit about her own political commitments, she also wanted her classroom to provide a space for genuine dialogue. "Sometimes kids will say things and I'll think to myself, 'They're just not getting it,'" she told me. "But then I think, 'Is it that, or is it that they're not thinking what I want them to think?' And how do I address that? What's my responsibility as a teacher, and what's my responsibility as an African American woman who is very passionate about her culture and who strives very hard to be politically aware?"

Part of her responsibility, Liz had decided, was to bring out the moral implications of historical and contemporary issues. "I try to connect things to a larger theme of goodness and whose world is the world," she said. In most cases, she did so with great subtlety; other times, less so. The next day in world studies, she brought in a cassette of USA for Africa's "We Are the World," which had raised money for famine relief in Ethiopia in the mid-1980s, and made the class listen to the entire song—twice.

....

Liz grew up in a mostly black, middle-class suburb of Cleveland, Ohio, the middle child of two public school teachers: her mother a high school French instructor, her father a teacher of fifth and sixth graders with hearing disabilities. Perhaps not surprisingly, Liz caught the teaching bug early. "I was the kid with the chalkboard who would sit with the dolls and practice penmanship," she told me. "I kept all my phonics books from school, and when my sister was three I remember just sitting with her and going through the words and—I taught her how to read! When I was eight! By the time she was in kindergarten, she was reading at a second-grade level." That year, Liz's little sister was chosen to be the narrator of their school's annual Christmas program. "It was a really big deal," Liz remembered, "because she could read so well and she was only 4 years old. So I knew then that I wanted to teach."

Despite their commitment to public education, Liz's parents—like many public school teachers in northern cities—sent their own children to private schools. "They really struggled financially," she said, "but they just poured all of their money into our educations. They didn't even question it—they just did it." Liz started off in a nursery program that's been heralded as a national model of excellence, then spent her elementary and middle-school years at St. Barnabus, a black Catholic school in Cleveland that features an

Afrocentric curricular focus. From there, she went on to Chalmers Academy, which she described as "a very white, prestigious, elite private school." She chose it because she wanted to attend an academically challenging, competitive high school that would prepare her for a top-notch college. "I definitely bought into the idea that if I went to these really elite schools, that would be the best education for me," she said. "Because I've always been a super-duper overachiever maniac. So in eighth grade, I'm the student who's calculating my GPA—I mean, who calculates their GPA in eighth grade?—just to make sure that I'm going to be the valedictorian, and not Jackie Dillard, who was my arch-enemy second grade through eighth grade." She laughed hard at the memory— the sort of easy, unguarded laughter that frequently punctuated her conversation.

Coming from St. Barnabus, where virtually all of her classmates and many of her teachers were black, and where African American history and values were part of the fabric of the school, Liz found that adjusting to life at Chalmers was a struggle. "It was definitely a culture shock," she recalled. "There were about 80 people in my class, and there were two black girls—myself and another girl—and maybe four black guys. There were a few Asians and one or two Latino students, but that was it. It was almost all white." All of a sudden, Liz began to question who she was, and to examine herself in newly critical ways. "My freshman year, I went through changes," she said. "I went through a little anorexic episode, and at one point I remember thinking, 'My voice sounds so different. Is there something wrong with my voice?' I was dealing with serious identity stuff, and there really wasn't anybody I could talk to about it. I think that really speaks to what happens to a lot of kids of color—especially black kids—who go to those kinds of elite schools, because there's really no support. At Chalmers, they didn't really deal with race. They dealt with diversity, but they didn't deal with race. I resented that experience for a long time."

Despite the lingering bad feelings, Liz acknowledged that attending Chalmers had its benefits. "The work load was very, very rigorous," she said, "and that really prepared me for college. From the beginning, the culture of the school was, 'You work hard.' So I would literally have like 5 hours of homework every night. Not even a question. And it was really important to me that I did well." So intense was her drive to excel in school, Liz told me, that her parents actually resorted to taking books from her as a means of disciplinary action. "This is sick," she said, shaking her head and laughing, "but I remember a huge argument I had with my mother. It was like two in the morning, and I was still studying because I had midterms the next day. And she came in and took my book! That was my punishment!"

In hindsight, Liz recognized that her motivation at Chalmers was misplaced—or at least too narrowly focused. She was overly concerned with test scores and grades, and not conscious enough of the purpose of her learning, of its value or relevance to her life. She questioned little and memorized a lot—an approach that served her well in the traditionally structured classrooms that were commonplace at the school. "I had great grades," she said, "but I didn't really retain the information. I wasn't really turned on to it. My teachers just presented lecture notes, so it became an exercise in learning how to take lecture notes." Again, she laughed. "I'm sitting there, you know, with a tape recorder, desperately trying to write down everything the teacher says."

The good grades at Chalmers earned Liz entry to an Ivy League school, where she spent her first 2 years trying to resist the urge to become a teacher. "I went to college with the intention of seeing if I could entertain something else," she remembered, "thinking that the teaching thing would maybe go away. I was trying to convince myself that I wanted to be a lawyer and make a lot of money, so I started out as a government major. But I hated the classes so much. I didn't like the whole culture of it. It was so against my nature." By the end of her sophomore year, Liz had decided that she could no longer fight the calling she'd first heard as an 8-year-old: She applied and was accepted to her school's undergraduate teacher education program, and signed on for a special concentration in urban studies.

"My friends gave me a lot of heat for switching from government to education," Liz told me. "They were like, 'Why? You're paying loans—a teacher? Teach later.' I mean, I heard everything. But I just felt that if I became a lawyer or an investment banker, I'd just be part of this larger system, I'd just be a cog in the machine, and I wouldn't like it and I wouldn't be passionate about what I was doing." But even when she began taking education classes, Liz found herself falling into a familiar routine: studying hard, doing the work, getting the grades—but for what purpose? "I didn't really like learning until after college," she said. "And I don't want my students to have to wait until they're 22 to really want to know stuff. I went through all those years being a really good student, getting really good basic skills, but—I think it's a shame that I wasted so much time in high school and college without understanding what it means to really learn."

••••••••••••

One important component of real learning, Liz believed—and one that was often given too little attention in schools—was knowledge of self. To make space for self-reflection and self-definition in her "Afro" classes, as she called them, she'd initiated an ongoing autobiography assignment: a yearlong project in which students wrote personal essays that pushed them to examine who they were, what they believed, and what paths they were choosing. "I want them to see that their lives and histories are as important as other histories," she told me.

Liz usually came up with the writing themes, but she'd decided the students should have more input in deciding on new topics. To kick-start their thinking, she'd listed on the board all the autobiographical assignments they'd already completed, followed by a list of six future possibilities:

1. My Greatest Fear and How to Overcome It
2. In 5 Years
3. My Contribution: How I Will Change or Impact the World
4. Who My Friends Are and How They Are a Reflection of Me
5. What Lesson Would I Teach the World If I Could
6. What I Value Most in Life

"So what do you think about these suggestions?" Liz asked the class. It was a simple question, but a brave one. Based on my experience, opening one's ideas to student critique could be a humbling exercise.

"Number 1—that one's too personal for me. I think you need to get rid of that one."

"And number 3–that's a kindergarten one. That's little kid crap." I felt the sting of that comment, and it wasn't even my idea being roasted.

"I understand what you're trying to do, Ms. Kirby," said Ebony, caramel-skinned with long beaded braids. "You're trying to give us some kinda direction and help us find our purpose in life, but—"

"Don't nobody know they purpose in life," Charles interrupted. "Do you know your purpose, Ms. Kirby?"

Liz leaned against a table. "I think I do. I think part of my purpose is to educate."

"But Ms. Kirby, I don't just learn from you," Kevin said. "I learn from Ebony over here, I learn from Kentrell, I learn from Shanice. We all educate each other. So in a way, we're all educators."

"I agree," Liz said. "We're all teachers and we're all learners." She walked over to the desk of a kid who wasn't participating and casually took away the *XXL* magazine he'd been reading. "How about number 5? What lesson would you teach the world?"

"Or how about, 'What Lesson Is the World Teaching Me?'" asked Warren.

"Oooh, yeah!" Charles said. "I'm feelin' that one!"

Liz wrote it on the board. "I like that, too. What else? Other ideas?" The suggestions came faster than she could write them:

"Do the music you listen to reflect your life?"

"Is your father really a role model for you?"

"How can I change society's outlook on my generation?"

"Why are some people's lives so unfair?"

"Hey, Fred," Charles shouted across the room, "you need to write about 'Why do I get jumped every day?'"

"And Charles Jackson," Liz countered, "maybe you need to write, 'How can I be appropriate in the classroom?'"

Behind me, Sierra Sanders muttered: "I couldn't be no teacher. I'd fuck a kid up. You gotta have lots of self-control to be a teacher, and I have no patience for kids."

Sierra, I'd figured out already, was a complicated young woman. On my first day at Matheson, she'd made an immediate impression: "My mind is more advanced than these children," she'd told me then. "I'm on a different level. I'm not being challenged at this school." Instead, she seemed to spend most of her time doing the challenging—criticizing and questioning everyone and everything around her. She sat behind me in the back corner, providing a continuous and often hilarious running commentary under her breath. When a fellow student came in one day wearing a camouflage shirt, bright green shorts, and a bandana around her head, Sierra whispered: "What the fuck she supposed to be—a Ninja Turtle?" Another time, when the girl next to her asked to borrow a sheet of paper, Sierra replied, "What do I look like to you—Office Max?"

Liz saw all kinds of potential in Sierra—she had, after all, been the valedictorian of her eighth-grade class—but getting her to work up to her capabilities had proved difficult. In the last few months, Liz told me, Sierra had seemed to be on even more of a downward spiral: She'd been suspended from school once for fighting, she was cutting class more frequently, and she'd shown up late one recent morning smelling like freshly smoked weed. As bright as Sierra was, she seemed to be headed down a self-destructive path. "She's a really smart girl," Liz said, "but she's making a lot of not-so-smart decisions."

Liz thanked the class for their suggestions and told them they'd be able to select some of the remaining topics for their autobiographies from the list they'd generated. She then asked them to get out their notes on the four slave rebellions they'd been studying: those organized by Gabriel Prosser, Nat Turner, and Denmark Vessey in the southern United States, and the uprising led by Toussaint L'Overture in Haiti. Most of the students obliged by flipping through spiral notebooks or folders, but one kid sat slumped with his head resting on his left arm.

Liz walked over to him. "If I was you, LeJohn, I'd be a little more aggressive about getting out my notes."

"I can't find 'em, Ms. Kirby," LeJohn said as he wiped his eyes and made a halfhearted effort to straighten up in his chair.

"That's unfortunate," said Liz. "But it's not an excuse." She went back to the podium and made a mark in her grade book. "You have to be more responsible." LeJohn, Liz had told me in an earlier conversation, had his share of struggles outside school and was forever behind in his work, but she continued to push him. "I was telling my sister about him one day," Liz said, "about all the stuff he'd been getting into, and she was like, 'His name is LeJohn?' And I said, 'Yeah, and his father's name is LeJeffrey.' And she was like, 'And *that* is Le Problem!'"

Liz had first taught the unit on slave rebellions the year before in response to comments students made during their study of slavery and its legacy in the United States. "Some kids would say things like, 'Slaves never fought back' or 'They didn't do nothing' or 'Slavery was their own fault,'" she told me. "I don't want them to leave my class at the end of the year still thinking that way. If they ever in their lives have another discussion about slavery, I don't want them to say, 'Slaves never fought back.'"

Occasionally, Liz said, students in her Afro classes accused her of being too pro-black in her teaching, but she didn't see it that way. In fact, she rarely used the textbook she was given for the class—written by a black author—because she felt it was biased, simplistic, and academically dishonest. Still, her stances on hot-button issues and the content she chose to present in class had led some of her African American students to conclude that she was too race-conscious. "I really don't see my teaching as being as Afrocentric as my students think it is," she said. "They think I'm a militant. But I guess it's all relative, because I know some people who are much more militant than I am who would probably say I'm a sellout."

Liz spent a few minutes reviewing the dates and locations of the four slave rebellions with the class, then asked if the students had noted similarities among any of the rebel leaders. "They used the Bible and religion to justify their actions," said Kevin, who always sat in the second row with his best friend, Raymond.

"Just like white people used parts of the Bible to justify slavery," Raymond added.

"So what do you think about that?" Liz asked. "We've seen religion used as an oppressive force and also as inspiration to fight oppression. Is using the Bible to promote killing slave owners any better than using the Bible to promote slavery?"

"Religion is hypocrisy," Sierra grumbled behind me.

Liz continued. "Nat Turner basically used Christianity as his anchor for all his beliefs and actions. He said that God was telling him to do what he was doing when he killed all those people. So was Nat Turner a hero or a hypocrite?"

"I say he's a hero because historically God has led people to kill others for his glory," said Celine. "Nat Turner knew what he was getting into and what could happen, but he was so passionate and so led by God that he went ahead and did it."

"I don't agree with that," argued Ebony. "Killing is wrong. Period. He planned the killing of a lot of people and he got a lot of other people killed in the process. That's not a hero. People take Christianity and skew it for their own purposes, but killing is not part of God's plan."

"But what's more wrong—keepin' all those people in slavery or tryin' to do something about it?" asked Warren. "I say he's a hero."

"I think we need to remember that we're all black students in this class," said Kevin. "If this was a class full of white students, we might be looking at this a different way. Like Mexicans look at the Alamo differently than people in the U.S."

I wasn't sure if Kevin had said that for my benefit or not, but Liz used it as an opportunity to draw me into the conversation. "Greg, what do you think?" she asked. "Hero or hypocrite?" I don't think she meant to put me on the spot, but I suddenly felt the intensity of all eyes on me.

"Well, first of all, about what Kevin said—I don't think most white kids are even learning about Nat Turner," I said. "If they've heard of him, it was probably just in passing—maybe in one paragraph of their history book. So that's a problem right there. And what do I think about it?" I paused, still not sure of how to phrase my answer. "I can understand why people who are oppressed and think they don't have any other options turn to violence if it seems like that's the only way things are going to change. So in that sense, I can see why he did what he did. But I still have a hard time saying what he did was right, because I think that, ultimately, violence usually creates more violence. I don't think it's really a solution."

"What I don't understand," said Raymond, taking the heat off of me, "is why they became Christians in the first place. Why would you gravitate to the religion of the people who are persecuting you? I know they were getting threatened and stuff, but how can you just worship somebody else's God?"

"Yeah," Charles said. "How could those slaves look at their situation, at what was happening to them, and still believe in Christianity?"

Liz held her notes to her chest. "I think about that a lot," she said. "That's part of my spiritual struggle right now."

"I think the reason slaves were attracted to Christianity was because it was so promising to them," reasoned Celine. "They had to believe in something."

"Well, I believe in God," Charles said, "but I don't believe in a lot of what churches do. My momma—she give, like, half of her check to the church. And then the pastor got a Rolex, drivin' a Benz—" The students were getting off track a bit, but the comments were flowing so freely now that Liz just hung back and listened.

"God is real," said LeJohn in a bit of a non sequitur, seemingly roused from his sluggishness by the lively conversation. "I feel like God is watching over me."

Then, as if the discussion hadn't expanded enough from its original focus, Marquis broadened things out further. "Do you ever think about what's the point of life if you're just gonna die anyway?" he asked the class. "I mean, even if I survive this, and do that, I'm still gonna die. So what's the purpose of living?"

We all meditated on his words for a moment. "This about to break into religion class," Charles exclaimed. "We in religion class now!"

•••••••••••

It was not uncommon, in Liz's classroom, for discussions about historical and political rights and wrongs to veer into the realm of spirituality and religion. Part of the reason for that, I figured, was the prominent role of the church in the African American community: Many of the kids in Liz's classes, from what I gathered listening to their comments and conversations, had been raised in homes where church-going was a weekly (or twice weekly) ritual, and they often wove biblical references or Christian teachings into class discussions. But beyond that, I discovered, the frequent connections to religion and God were a by-product of Liz's own continuing spiritual journey. "Whatever my central struggle or issue is," she told me, "it always comes up in class."

Like many of her students, Liz had spent most of the Sunday mornings of her childhood in church. But she doesn't remember feeling the spirit move her. In fact, she doesn't remember any-body—spirit or otherwise—moving much at all. "We went to a Presbyterian church," she told me. "You know—very traditional, very boring. It was a black church, but there was no hand-clapping, no gospel music." Yet boring, she soon learned, was preferable to rigid, which was the prevailing atmosphere in her Catholic-school religion classes. "That's where I got that heavy, heavy 'You're gonna go to hell' stuff," she said. "In eighth grade, my religion textbook broke down what sin is—what the specific sins are—and that tortured me for a long time. I think it still tor-tures me."

Neither of Liz's parents were preachy types, but they always made a big deal of the after-church Sunday dinner—which ritual-ly began with a prayer from her father. "He would just pick some verses from the Ten Commandments and say them," she told me with a laugh. "My sister and I would just kick each other under the table. His famous one was, 'Thou shall not kill, thou shall not steal, thou shall not bear false witness against thy neighbor.'" She cracked up at the thought of it. "Over dinner!"

But more than the uninspired Sunday services, the guilt-producing Catholic-school textbooks, and her father's awkward premeal prayers, the religious memories that etched themselves into Liz's mind most indelibly were the images of Jesus she saw as a young child. "In our dining room," she recalled, "we had the ceramic white Jesus figure with the pointy nose and the long, flow-ing hair. And a picture of him, too. Even in our Catholic school—which was a really Afrocentric school—it was still the white Jesus in blackface. And I can't shake that image. A lot of people can't shake that."

That didn't mean she wasn't trying. For months, Liz had been wrestling with a variation of the same question her students had attempted to tackle in class: Was Christianity ultimately a liberat-ing or an oppressive force for people of African descent? If not for slavery, she pointed out, it's a religion that never would have been handed down to her in the first place. "I'm trying to find a space in Christianity for me which I feel is legitimate and authentic and real," she told me. "That's the process I'm in right now. I have to kind of break down everything I've been taught and go back and look at it and see if it's something I really believe."

One problem Liz had with Christian teachings was that, spun a certain way, they could encourage people to be passive in their own lives. "Jesus can become a crutch for people," she said. "You know, they think their glory will come after they die, so they just have to suffer and endure until they get to heaven. But really, Jesus as a historical figure was an activist. He challenged things. So, when people say, 'What would Jesus do?'—well, Jesus wouldn't wait 'til he was dead! Jesus would question and be active and shake it all the way up and risk his life! That's what Jesus would do."

In an effort to sort through some of her questions, Liz had, somewhat hesitantly, joined a weekly Bible study group. "I don't really consider myself a Bible study type of person," she told me. "But I was hoping that exchanging ideas and talking about stuff would help me settle some of my spiritual issues." Instead, additional uncertainties had cropped up. "There are some things I wonder about," she explained. "Like, I question how God can watch everybody. How can he be watching everybody when there are some people who seem like their lives aren't being watched at all—they suffer all this hardship, right? So what is that about?" Yet despite the persistent doubts, she believed the study group was good for her. "In a way," she said, "I think the process of questioning Christianity is actually leading me back to it. It's helped me see a clearer relationship between God's purpose and my own."

A big part of that purpose, Liz believed, was to educate black youth, and for her, that meant tending to both the mind and the spirit. She wasn't out to influence students to adopt or disavow any particular religion, but she wanted to do what she could to help them along in their spiritual journeys. "You can teach kids skills for days and days and days," she told me. "But eventually I think you arrive at a point where there are questions that link back to some concept of God and spirituality—like goodness, and looking out for other people, and building strong communities, and being kind and empathetic. Otherwise, you're just kind of teaching in a vacuum."

There is a passage from Philippians, Liz told me, that she comes back to again and again when thinking about her teaching. She couldn't remember the exact phrasing, but the essence of it is, "Whatever work you do, you do it for God." Keeping those words in mind, Liz said, helped keep her focused on the road ahead. "You're not just working for your own benefit," she explained. "You're really doing the work of God. So that's what kind of pushes me to keep trying to be the best teacher I can be, and pushes me to keep working hard. Beyond the general care and concern that I have for kids or even the community, that's also what keeps me going."

....

It was a Friday morning just before Liz's first-period U.S. history class, and she didn't yet look fully awake. The week had been a hectic one, and Liz had been up late the night before grading tests and responding to student essays. Added to that was the fact that she'd been "off coffee" for the past 10 days, a sacrifice which had left her struggling with her energy level most mornings. "I really notice the difference," she told me. "And you know, I didn't even start drinking coffee until I came to the public schools."

As students filled the room and took their seats, a voice came over the intercom to remind teachers of that day's doughnut sale fund-raiser. "I want to shoot the intercom," Liz said to me. "I hate it. It makes me feel like I'm in a George Orwell novel." Clearly, her day had not gotten off to a good start. But then, as if on cue, a girl in overalls came bounding into the room and gave Liz a huge bear hug. "Good morning, Ms. Kirby," she said excitedly, then turned to me and smiled broadly. "Ms. Kirby's like a mother to me," the girl said, hugging Liz one more time before bouncing off to her seat. It was a better pick-me-up, I felt sure, than any cup of coffee could've been.

For the past 2 days, Liz's U.S. history class had been looking at the causes of the 1929 stock market crash and its effects on both big business and working families. Today, feeling the pressure to keep pace with board-mandated curriculum guidelines, Liz had planned to move on to the Great Depression. Her students had other ideas.

"Ms. Kirby, can we talk about the economy?" Afina asked.

"We are," Liz said.

"No, but I mean like what's going on now. 'Cause isn't our economy getting messed up—like with Montgomery Wards closing and everything?"

"Yeah," a girl added between applications of Carmex. "Gas costs a dollar ninety-six on 79th Street."

"It seems to me like there's a lot of similarities now to how it was before the market crashed back then," said Karen, who was wearing a T-shirt that depicted a bird's eye view of a slave ship's hold with the words BLACK HOLOCAUST underneath. "People are spending money they don't have. They're buying things on credit that they don't really need and can't afford."

Liz raised a finger in the air. "I'm going to tell you a lesson I don't want you to ever forget: Your credit is more important than your money."

"Why?"

"Because if you have bad credit, you're not going to be able to buy anything. If you have good credit, you can take advantage of low interest rate deals, but if your credit is bad, you can't."

"But what if you got no credit?" Devon asked.

"There are things you can do to slowly build your credit rating. Like get one credit card, use it, and make sure you pay it off every month."

Karen looked puzzled. "So you're saying that what we should do is—even if we have the money to buy something—we should use a credit card and then pay it back right away?"

"You just have to be careful," Liz said. "Don't let things slip up on you. And believe me, I speak from experience. When I was younger, I had the Fred Sanford approach to paying bills. I'd get a bill and just put it off and tell myself I'd pay it later. But that's a trap. It's a trap that the credit card companies want you to fall into."

Several students wanted to know what Liz recommended in terms of investment strategies, and she launched into a minilesson on the relative advantages and drawbacks of stocks, bonds, and mutual funds. Then she asked the class if they'd like her to invite a stockbroker in to address their concerns in more detail.

"Capitalist pigs!" declared Napolean, whose flared-out Afro was wider than it was tall.

"That's interesting," Liz said. "Why do you say that?"

"'Cause they're greedy. They're just in it for profit. They wanna make as much money as they can."

"Sounds good to me," someone said.

"Me, too," another voice called out.

As the discussion continued, I thought about how this impromptu lesson might, on its surface, seem a far cry from the sort of critical teaching Liz advocated. After all, if she really wanted her students to question and analyze their worlds, shouldn't she be pushing them to examine the excesses and inequities of capitalism rather than spending time on the dos and don'ts of credit ratings and investing? Shouldn't they be exploring alternatives to the present system? Wasn't Liz giving an implicit but ringing endorsement of the economic status quo?

I didn't think so. Liz was fully aware that capitalism creates a canyonlike economic divide between rich and poor in this country, and she understood that that gap widened most drastically along racial lines. She wanted to help her students understand the bigger economic picture and think about possible pathways toward change, but she also wanted them to be able to navigate the system as it is. "It's about survival for a lot of these kids," she told me later. "The unemployment rate for young black men—the demographic of my students and older—is probably 25 to 30%. That's not the rate you hear quoted, but that's the reality. And it really doesn't help them for people to sit around and talk about dismantling capitalism—because they're not eating! And because they're not eating, they're choosing all these underground economies to survive."

Liz said she walked a fine line whenever she talked about economic issues in class. "A lot of kids grow up with the message: Go to school, work really hard, make a lot of money, and move out of your neighborhood," she said. "I really get them to question that. We talk a lot about what the purpose of getting an education should be. But at the same time, I do think it's important for people to have access to capital because that gives them a better quality of life—*and* allows them to help their community. To make changes in any community, you need economic resources. The reason why I'm very specific about talking with my students about credit is because that's something that really debilitates black people and black communities. It kills us."

In one of her classes, Liz told me, her students had had an ongoing debate about whether they should try to redevelop their own neighborhoods. "This one kid would always say, 'I am never coming back. Why would I put money into this community? They'll just tear my stuff down.' And kids on the other side would say, 'But what's our responsibility?' So it got deep, and it wasn't just about making money and getting paid. We were asking questions like 'Can you be part of the capitalist system and be enlightened?' and 'What is your responsibility to your community?'"

She went on. "If the whole system of capitalism unhinges itself and we do have a more equal distribution of resources—well, that would be a wonderful thing. But that's not going to happen in the next 10 years without a whole lot of bloodshed, so in the meantime, what are we going to do to help these kids?" Some might find that a cynical or contradictory approach, but it made sense to me. Liz was teaching with one eye on a more just world, and the other firmly fixed on the world as it is. To teach her students well, she had to keep both eyes wide open.

············

"Let's go! Let's go! Let's go!"

In the hallway outside Liz's room a week later, a sea of teenaged bodies was in constant motion. It wasn't a chaotic scene—just really noisy and jam-packed with talking, laughing, flirting kids. As a couple embraced and kissed near an open locker, a sunglasses-wearing security guard blew her whistle—and blew and blew and blew it—in an effort to get students to hurry along. "Where's your ID, boy?" the woman growled to a slightly built kid in saggy jeans who was passing by with two companions.

"You heard that? She called him 'boy,'" one of the kid's friends said as they hustled past her.

"I don't see no man up in here," the security guard called after them.

On down the hall, a male student with a maze of braided hair stood face-to-face with a petite, dark-skinned female. It looked as if they were arguing, but I was too far away to tell for sure.

Suddenly, the guy turned to walk away, then spun on his heels and again faced the girl. "I'm through with your black ass anyway, you black burnt biscuit!" he yelled in a voice that drowned out even the whistle's squeal.

That comment lingered in my mind during Liz's next class, as her fourth-period students discussed the previous night's reading from *The Autobiography of Malcolm X*. Despite their earlier complaining, most of the kids had ended up either purchasing the book themselves or giving Liz the money to buy it for them. Her impassioned endorsement had surely swayed some naysayers to get with the program, and others had been persuaded by her no-nonsense bottom line: "Let me be real clear about this," she'd told all four of her Afro sections. "You will not pass my class if you do not read this book." For those students who hadn't been able to come up with the cash, Liz had created payment plans, giving kids the book on credit if they agreed to pay her back in weekly, one-dollar installments.

Sierra, not surprisingly, had been one of the most stubborn resisters of *Malcolm X*, and today she'd come to class without her copy of the book in hand. Liz noticed right away and made her way to the back corner to investigate.

"I can't read that book," Sierra said. "I can't even pick it up no more. It's garbage."

Liz's eyes narrowed but she kept her composure. "Have you read it?"

Sierra looked out the window. "I read enough of it."

"Well, if you haven't read it, you really can't critique it." The irritation in Liz's voice was impossible to miss. "But it's not garbage."

As Liz returned to the front of the room, Sierra mumbled to herself: "Why we need to know about this? How Malcolm X gonna help me in the real world? If somebody pull a gun on me, what I'm gonna say: 'Oh, I know Malcolm X'?"

I'd grown quite fond of Sierra in the short time I'd spent at Matheson. I enjoyed her witty asides during class, and I appreciated her lively spirit. But at that moment, I couldn't help feeling angry at her. I'd been in similar situations with students I'd taught—kids who seemed to be resisting for no other reason than to sabotage my lesson—and while I tried to remind myself to look at things from their perspective, their actions sometimes made that difficult. I felt sure Sierra could see that Liz was doing her best to make the class meaningful. Why was she so determined to be a thorn in her side?

"OK, who has a section from what you read last night that you'd like to read aloud?" Liz asked. "Something that spoke to you." The chapter they'd been assigned described Malcolm's first encounters with the bourgeois middle-class blacks in Boston's Roxbury section, and his initial experience having his hair "conked": a then-fashionable method, popular with urban blacks, of soaking one's hair in burning-hot lye in an attempt to straighten it.

Camilla volunteered to read an excerpt. "This is on page 54," she said, "right after he got his hair conked." She read:

> This was my first really big step toward self-degradation: when I endured all of that pain, literally burning my flesh to have it look like a white man's hair. I had joined that multitude of Negro men and women in America who are brainwashed into believing that the black people are "inferior"—and the white people "superior"—that they will even violate and mutilate their God-created bodies to try to look "pretty" by white standards.

"So what's Malcolm's message there?" Liz asked. "And by the way, as you read each chapter, underline the messages Malcolm is trying to teach people. This is a teaching book."

"He's sayin' don't conk your hair."

Liz nodded. "OK, but is it just a hair-management issue or does it go deeper than that?"

"He's saying we have no sense of identity and beauty as a race," said Camilla. "Most of what we call beautiful has something to do with what white people call beautiful."

"Like the contacts people wearin' now," Keisha added. "Everybody want green eyes or blue eyes or hazel eyes but not they own dark brown eyes."

Behind me, Sierra chewed on a safety pin, muttering under her breath. "Oh, my God. We wastin' time."

I wasn't sure if she really believed that or if she was just being her contrarian self, but Liz, I knew, didn't agree. She'd told me that jokes about dark skin and other forms of what she called "self-hatred" were all too common among some of the black students at Matheson. "In one of my classes last year," she told me, "they would make jokes about each other all the time—'You black so-and-so.' 'Wash your face off.' 'We can't even see you if we turn the lights out.'—just cracking up, you know? A couple of kids have done it this year, too. And when I challenge them on it, they're like, 'Why are you even bringing that up? We're just joking! We don't mean anything by it!' They think I'm way too sensitive, and that I address it too much. But I want them to think about why they're saying those things and what it really means."

If Liz seemed passionate about encouraging her students to identify and overcome buried feelings of self-hatred, it was largely because she'd spent years dealing with those same issues herself. And it started long before she first walked down Chalmers Upper School's lily-white halls as a ninth grader. "When I was younger," she remembered, "I really suffered a lot of black hate stuff. Being dark-skinned—it was real bad. My friends and I, we would sit and put our hands out and say, 'Who's darker?' 'Oh, you're darker. Too bad. Your life's gonna suck!'" She laughed, but the pain of the memory was plain to see. "So that really kind of affected me. I had the long hair, I did the whole perm thing, I had a horrible, horrible Jheri-curl—but only for a week!" Liz laughed again and touched a hand to her short dreads. "Oh, my God, it was the worst! I was, like, 11, and of course I didn't go to the shop—my mother did it at home. It was this whole kit. I don't know how my hair ever recovered from it. It was just, like, frizzy and wet. I mean, it was really traumatic. It was horrible."

Though Liz's parents and her all-black grammar school both communicated messages of African American cultural pride to her, she received quite a different message from the mainstream media, where white, Eurocentric norms were constantly idealized. "I was just part of that culture," she told me, "that idea of buying into the American dream of what you should be and what you should look like and what you should do. I got all of those images from television and movies. And it's really difficult to love your-self when you buy into those images."

As a teacher, Liz saw her students being seduced by the same standards of beauty—wearing light-colored contacts, for example, or dying their hair blonde or platinum—and she found it troubling. She regretted that it had taken her so many years to begin to work toward a healthier, more affirming self-definition, and she worried that some of her students might never get to that point without a caring adult prodding them along. "I think that's part of why I want them to be analytical about everything," Liz told me. "I want them to be able to remember something we read or talked about that will make them think twice about getting violet contacts or making a black joke." She paused. "It's difficult, though. So many of the self-hatred issues come from ignorance and a lack of exposure to things and a lack of critical reflection. You're talking about years and years of stuff that you have to unpack, and it takes a long time."

Of course, some would argue that that's exactly what's wrong with public schools: They're spending far too much time trying to raise kids' self-esteem and not enough teaching them how to read and write. But Liz didn't think it needed to be an either/or equation. She prided herself on setting rigorous academic standards in the classroom, on having high expectations for her students and insisting that they rise to meet them. But she also believed that a crucial component of her work with African American young people involved helping them to see themselves with more accepting eyes, and to value—yes, even to love—who they are.

· · · · · · · · · · · ·

"What do you think of when you think of police brutality?" Liz asked the students in one of her Afro classes the next day.

"Amadou Diallo."

"Rodney King."

"Abner Louima."

"I think about my sister's boyfriend," said Shanice. "Marcus Tatum. He got killed by police. They stopped him, and he was fixin' to get down, and they shot him."

"I've seen it right here at Matheson," Ebony added. "This boy got pushed into a locker by the police, elbowed in the face, and then *he* got suspended."

"The Chicago Police Department is one of the biggest gangs there is," said Kentrell.

Liz had chosen to put *Malcolm X* aside for the moment so her students could focus on a burning front-page news item: An unarmed 19-year-old black man had been shot and killed by a white police officer in Cincinnati, setting off 3 days of civil unrest and mandatory curfews there. This sudden change of gears in her lesson plan might not seem such a big deal, but it exemplifies a sense of teacher agency that's become harder and harder to find in public school classrooms. One of the many tragedies of the high-stakes testing craze in public schools is that the basic curriculum question—What knowledge and experiences are most worthwhile for my students?—either doesn't get asked by teachers, or, if it does, its answer seems all too obvious. When you're handed a booklet of state goals, loaded down with district-level require-ments, and told what sequence of lessons to follow, the above question can seem either beyond your purview as a teacher or entirely beside the point. Curriculum becomes not something you wrestle with or debate but something you unwrap: a social studies series called "Discoveries," let's say, that doesn't give kids the opportunity nor the inspiration to make any.

In her world studies and U.S. history classes, Liz struggled constantly to balance "coverage" of board-prescribed content and objectives with the kind of in-depth, thematic study she thought was more meaningful for kids. With African American studies, she had no district or state guidelines to follow, so she was free to call the shots on what direction the class would take. But that didn't mean making curricular decisions was easy. "One of my biggest struggles is deciding what's most important," she said. "I don't know how to fit it all in. Like, I could spend all year on slavery and slave rebellions, and it would be really valuable, and we could go really deep with it. But then I wouldn't get to the Booker T. Washington/W.E.B. DuBois debate and to the Harlem Renaissance and through to the Hip-Hop Renaissance, which is what I'm trying to do."

Today would be another detour of sorts, but Liz thought it was a necessary one. For her, African American studies wasn't just a study of the past but an opportunity to look at current challenges facing the black community and debate how they might be most effectively addressed. While most of her students already knew of the Cincinnati incident from TV news reports, she wanted to be sure they had some common background before initiating a discussion, so they spent a good bit of the period reading two short pieces: a magazine article recapping developments in the story and an editorial about racial profiling.

Liz's eyes scanned the room. "So are we all in agreement that police brutality is a problem?" Heads nodded around her.

"No," Sierra called out. "You just gotta learn how to fight back."

Sierra's answer sounded more like an attempt to derail the discussion than a genuine attempt to disagree. Liz didn't engage it. "OK, most of us are in agreement that police brutality is a problem," she said. "It happens a lot. So why did this incident lead to such a violent response?"

"Right here it say 15 people been killed by Cincinnati police since 1995," said Marquis, gesturing toward his paper. "And all of 'em black! People want revenge for that."

"Then why not go through the justice system?" Liz asked.

"'Cause it don't work."

"They gettin' vigilante justice."

"But this is a democracy," Liz argued. "Can't we work through the channels of government?"

"They sat in City Hall for 3 hours," Marquis pointed out, "and nothing was happening. They figured they'd get more response by doing something theyself."

"To me, living in society is like a partnership," Kentrell said, a hand on his chin in full philosopher mode. "If I'm gonna behave and act orderly, you gotta do the same thing. But if you act crazy, that kinda gives me my ticket to act crazy, too."

"Nah," said Ebony. "I mean, it's wrong what the cops did, but if you wanna protest, why you gotta be violent? Sometimes violence does get your point across, but pulling that white lady out of her car for no reason? That's not right. She didn't do anything."

The bell was about to ring, so Liz tried to bring some closure to the conversation. "So how can we resist?" she asked. "Tomorrow I'm going to ask you to come up with your own prescriptions for what Cincinnati can do. We've been learning a lot about old-school resistance, but I want us to look at how we can create some new-school resistance. What can we do in our own lives to resist injustices?"

I wasn't sure what Liz had in mind, but I knew she wanted to give her students more opportunities to do things that stretched beyond the school's walls. The lack of an integrated action component was, she believed, one of the weak spots in her teaching. "I haven't really moved my kids enough to the level of doing that," she told me. "I have a colleague who does that really well. His kids write Nelson Mandela, they've written Fidel Castro—they do active stuff. And that's the really empowering part: to move toward doing something instead of just looking at an issue and saying, 'Oh, this is what's happening—isn't that bad?' Because it can get depressing and overwhelming if you feel like there's nothing you can do."

Teachers, of course, sometimes feel that way themselves, and I wondered if Liz was beginning to reach that point with Sierra. I'd smelled the remnants of a smoked joint on her clothes as she'd come into class that day, and Liz apparently had gotten a whiff as well. When the bell sounded, she motioned for Sierra to stay behind.

"What's going on?" Liz asked after the other students had cleared out.

"Nothin'," said Sierra with a shrug. "Ain't nothin' goin' on."

"You have to tell me what I can do to help you, Sierra, because I think you know what my frustrations are." Liz waited for Sierra's eyes to meet hers. "Come back and see me during sixth period lunch. We need to sit down and talk."

••••••••••••

In a cramped room adjacent to the history department offices, Liz and Sierra sat face to face, separated only by a narrow table and Liz's bowl of cafeteria-issue stir-fry. Sierra held a backpack in her lap, her upper body slumped over it, her hands clutching it like she might've once latched onto a frayed but well-loved blanket. I sat a few feet away, feeling a bit more intrusive than I typically did in whole-class situations, even though Sierra had said it was OK for me to be there.

"I ain't tryin' to make an excuse, Ms. Kirby, but when your days like my days, you gotta get away from it. I can't deal with the stress like you can."

"How do you think I deal with my stress?"

"I don't know, but this school is depressing. Oh, my God. It's like the teachers come to work just to argue with you."

"So you're telling me you're getting high so you can have better relationships with your teachers?" Liz shook her head. "Come on, Sierra."

"I know I can't justify it," Sierra said, running a finger back and forth over her bag's zipper. "I know it's wrong." She put her head down on the desk.

"Look at me," Liz said. Sierra raised her head. Their eyes locked. "You could be the top student at this school. You are thoughtful and bright and you really question things. But it's your work ethic that needs improvement. I understand what you're saying, but you need to come up with some better coping skills. You're always going to have bad days."

Sierra looked away—past Liz, past me, past Matheson, her neighborhood, and the city beyond. "I just wanna get out of here and go to some small town where there ain't no problems."

Liz pushed her food aside and put both elbows on the table. She explained that her biggest concern at the moment was that Sierra not jeopardize her education. "You need to come to class. You need to do the reading. You need to participate."

"But what is *Malcolm X* gonna help me with?" Sierra protested, echoing her earlier objection. "How is that gonna help me in the real world?"

"One of the reasons I picked that book is because I think it shows that people can change," Liz said, her hands dancing in front of her as she talked. "Because he has this whole evolution, and to me that shows that just because you have a crazy lifestyle when you're young doesn't mean you can't one day have a big impact on the world."

Sierra thought it over. "I don't wanna tell you I'm gonna change and then I don't, 'cause then my word don't mean nothin'."

"You can change," Liz said. She leaned over the table to bring her face even closer to Sierra's. "Look—I'm not going to suspend you. But you cannot come to class high. Period. This isn't even about your participation in class, it's about what's best for you. And this is what's best for you."

"So what do you suggest I do to relieve my stress?"

Liz put forth a modest proposal. The next day, Sierra would report to her classroom instead of leaving school during her lunch period—which is when she usually smoked—and then the two of them would eat lunch together sixth period. If it worked out, they could make it a daily ritual. "One weed-free day," Liz said. "Let's try it."

As I listened to Liz's words, and watched the two of them sitting virtually knee to knee, I was struck by a powerful reminder: that good teaching, in the end, nearly always comes back to personal relationships. The challenging readings Liz assigned, the provocative lessons she taught, the creative projects, the politically conscious approach—none of that would mean very much, or perhaps even be possible, without the one-on-one connections she made with kids like Ebony and LeJohn, Charles and Racquel, Kevin and Sierra. It's a point that proponents of critical conceptions of teaching often underestimate: While seeing the bigger picture of systemic pathologies and schooling's social contexts is crucial, equally so is taking the time to see each student, to build trusting relationships, to let kids know that their lives have value, that you care.

Liz would take that one step further. She would say that for a teacher to be truly effective, she has to love her students. Some might balk at such a notion, writing it off as either quaint or exceedingly naïve, but Liz would argue that a love ethic must inform a teacher's work. "People have different definitions of love, I guess," she told me. "But for me, I have to have that sense of love to sustain myself. I really do care about my students—about what they know and how they grow and how they develop. I really, genuinely care. There can be kids you dislike as a teacher, but I think you have to care about where they're headed in the future, and how they're going to take what you're teaching with them. To me, that's love."

Sierra did show up as planned the next day—minus the scent of marijuana—but Liz knew there were no guarantees of long-term success. Such was the life of a teacher. "That's why a philosophy of love and hope is so important," she told me. "You have to believe that people and things can change for the better." Yet Liz's wasn't a passive hope; it was an active one, sustained not only by her belief in the capacity for goodness within every young person she taught but also by her commitment to working in practical ways toward a more decent, more just world for her students. "You can never underestimate your power as a teacher," she said. "You have the ability to profoundly affect people's lives. You don't always know what the return's going to be, or when it's going to come. But it will come."

Photo: Antonio Pérez

3

cynthia nambo

It was my first day in Cynthia Nambo's classroom at New Horizons, a brand-new, all-girls charter school, and she was giving me fair warning: "There's something I want you to know about me up front," she said. "I'm explosive. When things are going good, I can be explosive in a positive sense. When things aren't going so good, I can be explosive when I get mad. So you're going to see that whole range."

I was prepared for fireworks, then, when the 23 sixth-grade girls in Cynthia's second-period science class bounded in. Instead, Cynthia exchanged "Good morning" and *"Buenos dias"* with a few, received a hug from another, and said "That's beautiful!" when yet another student proudly showed off a sketch she had finished in art class. No fuses got lighted, nothing detonated. I relaxed.

Cynthia spent a little time settling the girls down, then told them they'd have the first 20 minutes of the period to discuss their homework with their groups. Twenty minutes to discuss homework might sound excessive, and it would be if it were the sort of assignment I often received as a sixth grader: odd numbers from 1 to 30, definitions of a chapter's "key words"—what's there to discuss? But this had been a meatier task, requiring the students to put themselves in the role of a funding agency to read, analyze, and evaluate brief scientific research proposals and decide whether each should receive financial support. Busywork this definitely was not.

The girls sat at tables of four—the kind of standard-issue, wooden-topped, steel-legged tables you might see at any Chicago school. But the chairs were a different story. They were the large, padded, rolling type—office chairs, maroon with black armrests— a donation to the first-year school, Cynthia later told me, from a corporate sponsor. They were comfortable, of course, but beyond that the chairs seemed part of an overall strategy to convey to these girls, in whatever way possible, an unambiguous message: You are important, you should dream big, and if you work hard and persevere, great things await you.

I listened in on a group as they weighed the merits of a proposed experiment that would determine "if increasing the amount of water consumed during a meal would help people lose weight." The plan was to conduct a clinical trial on "24 young, slim women," then possibly to test other groups in subsequent trials.

"They're only talking about women, that they're gonna do it on women," said Joya.

Bianca curled her lip and tugged on her Spelman College T-shirt. "That's sexism. It's not like women are the only ones who are fat. Men have beer bellies. Why would you wanna test it only on women? It's like they're saying, 'We want the entire female population to die before we test it on men.'"

"If you would read, it you would see that they were going to test women *first*," said Jenny, one of only three white students in the class, pointing to her copy of the proposal.

Bianca didn't appreciate Jenny's condescension. "Well, I still don't think we should fund this project," she snapped.

"Experiment," corrected Jenny.

"Whatever," Bianca said with a roll of her eyes, and suddenly I was reminded that I was in the company of sixth graders.

Off to the side, Cynthia was talking quietly with Lakeisha, whose shoulder-length braids hung down to veil her round face. "All you have to do is ask me," Cynthia said, hugging Lakeisha's head. "Just ask."

Meanwhile, noise from the class next door was seeping through the thin walls of Cynthia's room, and over the din I could hear a woman's voice: "Girls!" The rumble not subsiding, the teacher's voice became progressively louder. "Girls! Girls!! GIRLS!!!"

•••••••••••

During the 1990s, girls' performance in—and experience of—

elementary and secondary school garnered more attention than ever before. Catalyzed by the American Association of University Women's *Shortchanging Girls, Shortchanging America* study in 1991 and by the work of Myra and David Sadker, an entire body of research developed that inquired into the flagging self-esteem of many preteen and teenage girls, and the resulting negative effects on their academic confidence, school success, and career aspirations. Nowhere was this more evident, according to numerous studies, than in the areas of math and science, where girls showed a marked decline in feelings of competence as they moved into their teenage years. Instead of learning math and science, the reports suggested, girls were learning a hidden curriculum of compliance and submission.

While the definitiveness of these findings was questioned by some (and, in the last few years, has spawned a backlash of research which claims it's actually boys who are being short-changed in schools), it nonetheless caused many educators to sit up and take notice. Scattered school districts around the country began experimenting with separating boys and girls for certain classes. By the late 1990s, coalitions of concerned women in several states had taken that idea one step further, founding all-girls public schools, independent schools, and charter schools. New Horizons—with a student body that was 73% African American, 13% white, 9% Latina, 3% American Indian, 2% multiracial, and 100% female—was one of them. Like other all-girls public schools, it was separate but equal turned on its ear.

But simply removing boys from the equation didn't mean the sailing was always smooth. "I hate girls!" 12-year-old Raven Thomas blurted out one morning as she stomped into Cynthia's room and threw her book bag to the ground. "I can't stand bein' around girls all day! I wanna go back to my old school." When several other students followed behind her with pleasant greetings for Cynthia, Raven mocked them. "Good morning, Ms. Nambo," she mumbled, mimicking the singsong cadence of their words. "Y'all some lames. I can't stand this class!"

Cynthia motioned for Raven to come out in the hall with her. I couldn't hear their conversation, but whatever they were discussing, Raven didn't look happy. Later, Cynthia told me she'd pulled Raven aside to try to squash a problem she'd heard was brewing between Raven and another sixth grader, Marissa. Typical of the sort of soap-opera dramas facing middle school teachers everywhere, the chain of events, as I understood it, went something like this: Raven's best friend, Nadine, had been friends with Marissa. But Marissa started talking about Nadine behind her back. Raven sent Marissa an e-mail warning her to stop talking about Nadine and threatening to kick Marissa's butt if she didn't. Marissa then publicly confronted Raven with the "Who do you think you are, saying you're gonna kick my butt?" line, and the stage was set for a showdown. Cynthia's advice to Raven was to chill out and let Nadine fight her own battles. Raven's response had been only silence and gnarled eyebrows.

"Good morning!" Cynthia finally said to the class. The welcome—delayed a couple minutes today by the impromptu conference with Raven—was a daily ritual.

"Good morning, Ms. Nambo," responded some of the girls. Others continued their conversations, not noticing—or at least not acknowledging—that Cynthia was asking for their attention.

"Did you all eat a lot of sugar last night or what?" Cynthia asked, a not-so-subtle hint for the girls to quiet down. And they did. Sort of.

"The first thing you need to do is get your homework out and put it in your homework folder," Cynthia told them. As the sound of pages being ripped from spiral notebooks filled the room, a girl next to me fished through her backpack. After much huffing and puffing, she pulled out a paper that looked as if it had been through a complete wash-and-dry cycle and filed it away. At a table across the room, a hand went up: "Ms. Nambo, we gotta put our homework in our folder?"

Cynthia looked at the girl incredulously. "How many times do I have to say it?"

"Two," someone answered. I wasn't sure, but I guessed the someone might have been Raven.

Cynthia's classroom wasn't a place that screamed science. It was evident that scientific work went on there—around the room were a skeleton, a work table, live plants, a poster with "Fascinating Facts about the Human Body"—but it didn't have the antiseptic feel of a lab. Colorful *papel picado* decorated the area above a chalkboard. A reading area in a rear corner had two well-stocked bookshelves and a beanbag chair. Cynthia's desk, inconspicuous along the room's north wall, contained a laptop computer and a boombox amid papers, books, and framed photos of a niece and nephew. A copy of *Teaching With Love and Logic: Taking Control of the Classroom* was propped open on top.

Cynthia began to explain the activity she had planned—a role play about whether a girl with hepatitis C should take part in a clinical trial of a new treatment for the disease—but she wasn't more than two sentences into it when the noise level picked up at two of the tables. Cynthia stopped abruptly. "You know, it's getting ridiculous that I always have to talk while you're talking. I'll give you a minute to get yourselves together."

She'd told me that dealing with this sort of distraction was one of her biggest frustrations at New Horizons. "A lot of these girls like to push limits," she said. "And when I react to that, they'll say, 'You're just too strict!' But I don't consider it being strict. I push them—I mean, *really push them*—because I want them to have a baseline. I want them to understand that this is what I expect and I'm not going to expect anything less."

Listening to Cynthia, I was reminded of my own struggles with balancing freedom and control in the classroom. As a teacher I constantly wrestled with the contradictions between the ideals of an "emancipatory" education and the reality of needing to negotiate some sort of teacher-imposed order. I asked Cynthia how she reconciled the two. "I think it's actually a natural balance," she said. "You can only have freedom if you're disciplined in your thought. I don't think you get freedom by just doing whatever you want, by just making leisurely mistakes. When you do that, you're just all over the place. And the thing is, then you never have a clear sense of what you want to do. That's not freedom."

•••••••••••

Freedom was a concept Cynthia had begun thinking about in practical terms at an early age. At 15, she ran away from home to escape a verbally and physically abusive stepfather. "He was really mean," she remembered. "He wanted good things for us, he wanted us to study and go to college, but he was very hypocritical. He was Mexican, but he didn't believe in us knowing about our culture. He did everything he could to assimilate us. He wouldn't even let us speak Spanish—my mom would have to sneak and let us pray in Spanish when he was asleep." According to Cynthia, it was one of her mother's many quiet forms of resistance. "My stepfather brought us up with the idea that if you have an accent, you're dumb," she continued. "And that had a big impact on me. That's actually one of the reasons I went into education, and bilingual education in particular." She said she wanted Latino kids to be proud of their home language—not embarrassed by it.

Cynthia spent her grade school years in a neighborhood of steelworkers and recent Mexican immigrants on Chicago's southeast side. Her mother, who had come to the United States from a city in central Mexico at the age of 16, had two other daughters by Cynthia's stepfather. In their home, the man had the first and last word. "My mom didn't have any say in how we were raised," Cynthia told me. "She was dumb and stupid—that's what he would call her. In reality, my mom is very strong, very intelligent, very charismatic, very dynamic, very articulate, fully bilingual—all of our strength we got from her. She just didn't know how to deal with the situation. She wanted us to have a father. She didn't have parents—hers died when she was 9—so in her mind, she was giving us a family. And her image of a family was two parents."

As bad as living with her stepfather was, mustering the courage to leave wasn't easy. But when Cynthia finally did, her world changed. "Running away was a turning point," she said. "That's when I started discovering what I wanted—and I knew I didn't want to be around that kind of a man. That's also when I started discovering my culture—listening to the music, dancing the dances, eating the food." Cynthia stayed in the homes of friends from school and made occasional, unsuccessful attempts to reunite with her family. She also found refuge at a neighborhood Catholic youth center, where the codirectors helped foster her awakening consciousness. "Carlos and Altagracia helped me out a lot," she said. "Altagracia started giving me books on feminism, and we would talk about that, and about race and class and all kinds of issues. I would see the dynamics of other families—people I was living with—and I started to realize that I'd grown up in a really patriarchal home. And I started to question all that."

At 18, Cynthia graduated from St. Sebastian Academy—a north side parochial school that shuttered its doors the same year—and headed off to study psychology at the University of

Illinois' Champaign campus. There she got involved with several political groups—most of which worked to champion women's or Latino rights—and eventually cofounded her own, *La Fuerza*, which focused on the meaning of being a woman within Mexican or Latino culture. But while the feminist thread running through many of her chosen causes was clear, Cynthia never fully embraced the movement. She found its white, middle-class origins and its reluctance to embrace the perspectives of women of color off-putting. "I don't know what I call myself," she told me. "But I don't use the word *feminist*."

The deeper Cynthia got into her psychology major, the more research-focused the classes became, and the more disenchanted she grew. She'd always liked the natural sciences more anyway, but she felt too boxed in by labels to change paths: "I was Mexican, I was a woman. Back then I just didn't have the belief in myself." With gritted teeth, she stuck to her original plan, and returned to her home turf after 5 years with a B.A. in psychology in hand. By that point, the last straw with her stepfather had finally been pulled: After discovering that he was having an affair, one of Cynthia's sisters had tossed all his belongings onto the sidewalk, scratched up his car, filled his gas tank with sugar, and told him never to come back. He hadn't returned, and Cynthia couldn't have been happier.

Determined to use her university credentials to serve her community in some way, Cynthia accepted a job counseling students at Futuro Latino, an alternative high school and social service agency in Chicago's largest Mexican neighborhood. At first, it seemed like the perfect opportunity. It turned out to be both a humbling experience and a wake-up call. "At the time, I had this attitude that I now call 'compassionate superiority,'" Cynthia said. "I really cared about what I was doing, but I was also kind of presumptuous. I thought I had the answers, that I knew how to fix other people's problems. In college I'd been reading all this stuff and thinking, 'My community needs me and I've got to go kick some ass.' And then when I got there, they were like, 'What are you talking about?' I mean, the complexities of the problems—abuse, domestic violence—I didn't know where to start. So I started thinking, 'How can I really help?' That's when I thought maybe I should get into education."

After teaching third grade for a year, Cynthia decided she

needed more specialized training, so she enrolled in a master's program in bilingual education at a local university. But it was her students, Cynthia told me, who taught her the most important lessons. "Just seeing the kids' lives and having conversations with them made me see that being Mexican wasn't what I thought it was," she told me. "It's not a show. It's not something you wear on your sleeve. Waving the flag or whatever—you don't have to do things like that. I fell into stuff like that when I was in college. But being with the kids made me see the real essence of what it is to be Mexican."

When the opportunity to apply for a position at New Horizons came up after Cynthia had been teaching for a few years, she initially had mixed feelings about it. She'd been looking for a situation where she would be able to grow with like-minded people, and New Horizons seemed like a hand-in-glove fit. But the school had only a small number of Latina students signed up, and part of Cynthia felt that teaching there would be tantamount to abandoning her community. Still, the chance to be in on the ground-floor planning of a new school—one that sought to put into practice the sort of teaching Cynthia advocated—was an opportunity she couldn't pass up. She took the job and resolved to make bilingual issues and the recruitment of Latina students two of her primary areas of focus.

••••••••••••

"The fun thing about pastels," Roz Wagner, New Horizons' art teacher, was telling the girls in one of Cynthia's science classes, "is that you can blend them." She scribbled a few dark lines onto a piece of white butcher paper with purple and blue pencils, then pulled her thumb across the colors to create a fuzzy, vibrant fusion of the two. "You can use your finger and you can smear them."

Blurring the lines was exactly what had brought Roz to Cynthia's room in the first place. The two women had wanted to work together on a project that would merge their subject areas—a pair of disciplines that typically remained walled off from one another in middle and high schools. Even in schools where subject matter is thought of and organized in less traditional ways, the crossover frequently happens with language arts and social studies, or with math and science—combinations where the connections seem to make the most sense or create the fewest waves. Art and science, on the other hand, are commonly viewed as starkly different ways of seeing the world, and thus come to occupy different ends of the hall, different wings of the building, different universes altogether.

To help remedy that state of affairs, Cynthia and Roz had drawn up a 2-week-long study of the organs of the human body that would integrate science, art, research, and writing. The plan was to have students use pastels to draw and color a designated organ solely on the basis of what they thought it might look like, or from what they knew or remembered about it. For homework, the girls would dig for information on their assigned organ. The following day they would come together with other students and utilize their newfound knowledge to make a second drawing—one that was scientifically accurate. The next step would be to work as a group to construct and paint an oversized papier-mâché model of their organ. Each group would then write a haiku that explained their organ's role in keeping the body functioning smoothly, and the finished models and poems would be displayed in the school's foyer.

Of course, that condensed description of the project, tidy as it is, leaves out almost all of what would actually need to happen for the undertaking to be a success. It doesn't convey any of the thinking or gathering or purchasing or setting up or modeling or questioning or rethinking or prodding or starting over or guiding or brush-cleaning or decision-making or cheerleading or negotiating or putting away or setting up again that Cynthia and Roz would undoubtedly do at various points along the way. It also doesn't take into account the potential hitches: "But what if I don't know anything about the gall bladder?" "How am I supposed to do research when I don't have no computer at home?" "I can't work with her." "I can't draw." Project-based learning is easy enough to advocate, but one thing I learned as a teacher is that most worthwhile student projects turn out to be far more complicated and time-consuming than they originally seem.

"I don't wanna draw this!" whined Patrice, her nose wrinkling as she held up a card that read, OVARIES AND FALLOPIAN TUBES.

"She thinks it's disgusting," Regina whispered to me.

At an adjoining table, the word on Lena's card—LIVER—immediately stirred a personal connection. "The lady that lives in the apartment upstairs from me," she said breathlessly, "her liver, like, blew up and made her all yellow. It was gross. And now she's dying. She's an alcoholic."

Across the way, a white girl with her tongue still blue from a between-classes lollipop was whining to Cynthia: "I don't know how to draw an intestine."

"OK, let's think about it," Cynthia said, taking a seat next to her. "The small intestine . . . you know it has to do with what?"

"Digesting," said the blue-tongued girl.

"So where do you think it might be in the body? What might it be connected to?" One thing I'd noticed about Cynthia was that she seemed to enjoy engaging in extended conversations with the girls in her classes. She was not the type of teacher who circulated constantly around the room, popping in on discussions for a quick comment and then moving on to the next group. Instead, she'd frequently pull up a chair and get comfortable, looking as if she were talking to the girls in her own living room.

I moved to hover over another table, where I found two girls arguing over what the heart looks like. Though both were sixth graders, one looked as if she was about 9 years old and the other looked at least 17. The range in maturity of middle school kids— physical and otherwise—can be striking. "My mama's a nurse," said the smaller girl, dark-skinned with thick glasses, "and she gave me this book about the heart that shows how it is."

"You always think you know somethin'," the bigger girl said and left in a huff.

"She can get a little bossy sometimes," the smaller girl, whose name was Kenya, confided to me. "Here, I'll show you the correct way to draw a heart."

The girls in the class were energized—out of their seats, sharing drawings with each other, having a good time. Bianca skipped up to Cynthia and held up her interpretation of the human brain. "Wow, that's beautiful," Cynthia said. "You've got it in sections. What makes you think it's in sections?" Nearby, the blue-tongued girl was using a ruler to sketch out a highly angular rendition of the small intestine.

Suddenly, Patrice's raspy voice filled the room. "OK, I'm finished," she announced, holding up her drawing of the ovaries, fallopian tubes, and uterus for all to see. For a moment, no one commented. Then Brianna playfully snatched the drawing from Patrice's hand. "It looks like a chicken," she laughed. "Ms. Nambo, are we supposed to be making chickens?"

....

"I read about this research study," Cynthia was telling the 16 girls in her advisory group, "where they were trying to find out why certain students do well on standardized tests." The girls were all gathered around their teacher.

"They cheat," Brianna said.

"I gotta admit—I got a copy of the Iowa test at home," added Yolanda, referring to the annual assessment used by Chicago's elementary schools.

"Yeah, right," Cynthia said. "No, this is what they found: They found that students who score highest on standardized tests read on their own for at least 45 minutes every day." Today was one of two weekly "reading days" in advisory. "But it's not just about raising your test scores. Of course we want you to have the skills, but we also want you to have the power. There's a power there."

Denise balled up her fists and flexed her arm muscles. "Power," she repeated softly. Joya and Brianna, who were both sitting behind Cynthia, caressed her hair, pulling it into a ponytail as they listened to her. "Reading is so important. It's the key. That's why I'm trying to get more books in here, and that's why I'm trying to make the reading area more comfortable."

"Go to Ikea," Candice suggested.

Cynthia put an arm around her. "And one more thing: You know it's Women's History Month, right?" They all nodded. "One thing I want you to think about is that during Women's History Month, you see a lot of white women, you see a lot of black women, but you don't always see many Mexican women, many Native American women, Latina women. They're always left behind. And I think it's important for us, as human beings, to recognize the contributions all women have made."

"I've seen Latina women," said Joya.

"Like who?"

"Gloria Estefan."

"Well, it's good that they're recognizing our music, but there's a lot more to Latinas than that. Besides, she's Cuban, not Mexican."

"I saw a special about Selena on TV!" Candice added.

"Like I said, it's good that they recognize our music, but what about everybody else? What about Frida Kahlo and Sor Juana and Sandra Cisneros and Cherrie Moraga?"

"Who are they?" someone asked.

"See?" Cynthia said. "That's my point." I wasn't sure if the girls all got it or not, but I had a feeling that, before the end of the year, they'd know who all those women were. "OK, so go pick a book. Quickly. Or if you already have one, get it out. And remember, there are times to be noisy and times to be quiet. This is one of the quiet times. I want to read, too, and I can't focus when there's a lot of noise." She was holding a copy of Carol Lloyd's *Creating a Life Worth Living*.

For the next few minutes, girls plucked books from the shelves or their backpacks and then chose comfortable spots in which to read. It took a little while, but gradually the class settled in, their heads hidden behind such titles as *Inside the WNBA, Brain Surgery for Beginners,* and *The Diary of Latoya Hunter*. Within 10 minutes, the room was completely silent, 16 young women—and one somewhat older—lost in literary worlds both strange and familiar. Not a sound.

It lasted for about 45 seconds, and then an amplified voice blared from above: "COULD THE YEARBOOK COMMITTEE PLEASE MEET IN THE MAIN LOBBY? THE YEARBOOK COMMITTEE PLEASE COME TO THE MAIN LOBBY. THANK YOU."

So much for the magic moment.

....

The next day, second period began with Cynthia struggling to calm the class down. She'd already asked them to get into groups according to which organ they'd researched, but the transition was getting too loud and taking too long. "One . . .!" Cynthia called out, her face tightening. "Two . . . ! Three . . . ! Freeze!" The effect was less than spectacular. The girls slowed down, some came to a near halt, but it was nowhere near the sort of stop-action she was obviously aiming for. "Eye contact is one of the best ways of showing someone that you're listening," Cynthia said, a touch of irritation in her voice. Most of the girls got the hint and looked her way. Keisha smacked her lips. "I'm sorry—did I say smacking your lips?" Cynthia asked, staring directly at Keisha. "I meant to say eye contact."

Roz arrived a few minutes later with a cart full of pastels, watercolors, brushes, cans, and markers. "OK, take out your research," Cynthia told the groups. "Talk to each other, show each other what you found." I was sitting with the intestine group, where the blue-tongued girl—whose name, I had learned, was Molly, and whose tongue was now back to a more boring shade of pink—was showing off an old biology textbook she'd brought from home. The girls flipped straight past the digestive system to the section on childbirth. "Ugghh! I can't look at that," Diana moaned. As I glanced around the room, I noted that most of the students had brought in some sort of information on their assigned organ: a library book, printed pages from the Internet, an encyclopedia, handwritten notes. I was impressed.

In my early years of teaching, I'd occasionally assigned students research to do on their own, but the results had usually been underwhelming. Kids would explain that they didn't have a computer at home, or didn't have a ride to the library, or that their families didn't subscribe to a newspaper—all legitimate reasons, I thought, for not completing whatever task I'd given them. Eventually I all but stopped assigning such away-from-school research because I thought my students simply didn't have the resources to get it done. Yet here was a class full of city kids proving me wrong.

From what Cynthia had told me about the socioeconomic mix of her students, I knew it was likely that a number of these girls had more available to them at home than my students had. New Horizons was attracting the daughters of professionals—both black and white—who'd long ago written off public schools. Still, I wondered if the heightened expectations at the school challenged all the girls, no matter their background, to demand more of themselves, to be more resourceful. My guess was that Cynthia and other teachers at New Horizons were finding ways to traverse one of the fine lines that "progressive" white teachers like me have trouble with: understanding the forces that constrain students and showing compassion to their situations, yet at the same time insisting that they push against those constraints with everything they've got.

Near the computers, the stomach group was debating which shade of green they should try to achieve with their watercolor mixture. "It has to be, like, throw-up green," insisted Felicia. Back in the reading area, Joya, Gaby, and Bianca were deciding how best to paint the human eye. They were also bouncing to some music that was audible, if just barely, all the way at the front of the class. Hearing it, Cynthia's ears perked up and she immediately headed toward them. "You know what?" she said. I was sure she was going to lay down the law. "Why don't you turn it up so everybody can hear it?"

Joya raised her eyebrows as if to say "Are you sure?" waited for a half second, then spun the volume knob. The opening verse of Christina Aguilera's "What a Girl Wants" suddenly filled the room. Nearly all the girls—black, white, and Latina—knew the song, and gradually heads started bobbing and lips began mouthing the lyrics. Candice applied brush strokes to the beat. By the time the chorus came on, practically the whole room was singing out loud: *What a girl wants, what a girl needs, whatever makes me happy and sets you free.* Patrice had left behind her group's painting and was doing a full-fledged dance routine, borrowing steps from the song's music video. As Keisha joined her, Cynthia began chanting, "Go Keisha! Go Keisha!"

If the jubilance and spontaneity of the scene were palpable, so was its apparent irony. Here were these bright, ambitious young women—budding scientists and artists, engaged in serious academic work—taking a break to revel in the lyrics of a commodified pop princess. Sure, Aguilera nodded toward female independence and empowerment in her song, but her protagonist ultimately finds happiness—and her identity, it seems—in the arms of a guy. Hearing the students in Cynthia's class sing along, I was reminded how persistent the pull of popular culture can be, how ingrained the messages about what a girl should want and need. But the more I thought about it, I realized that what struck me most profoundly was the freedom the girls in Cynthia's room seemed to feel. It was not only a freedom to be smart and inquisitive, or creative and expressive, but a freedom simply *to be.*

Sometimes that meant delving into the mysteries and wonders of science; other times it meant singing along with the newest MTV sensation. In either case, it meant being in a place where—with the occasional exception of an intruder like me—they were safely outside the gaze of males, a place where they could think purposefully about the wants and needs they really did have, and begin, however tentatively, to define themselves as young women.

•••••••••••

Who defines whom and who speaks for whom were questions that had troubled Cynthia since her undergrad days, so when I first approached her about the possibility of working together on this project, she was hesitant. At the time, we were only casual acquaintances—introduced through her husband Alfredo and a few mutual friends—and she was reluctant to entrust even part of her story to a guy she barely knew. The fact that I am white didn't help my cause any.

Not that Cynthia dislikes white people. To put a spin on a familiar line, a couple of her best friends are white. But she tired of "progressive" white educators who were seemingly oblivious to their own privilege, and it pained her to read article after article about Latinos told through a white author's eyes. She had read my memoir about my work with predominantly Mexican American students, and while she thought the book had its merits, its existence still rankled her at times. "You're white, and you've published a book on working with people of color," she told me one day after school. "And maybe it's my own bias, but it's always—if you're white, you can do these things. You can go into a situation and be progressive and be respected and everybody says, 'Oh, what a wonderful job you're doing.' And the people of color who are doing that work are not recognized. Not that we're doing it for recognition, but our stories need to be out there. So I get frustrated. I'm frustrated by the fact that you can do that but we can't. It's a struggle every step of the way when we want to tell our stories."

Cynthia and I talked several times about the project, and she went back and forth about whether or not she should take part. It was a decision she believed shouldn't be made lightly. On one hand, she thought that her story, if published, could help fill the void of Latino voices in educational literature, and perhaps open the eyes of non-Latinos to see teaching through a different lens. On the other hand, she wasn't sure I was the best person to tell that story. She believed I had good intentions, but good intentions, she pointed out, weren't always enough when placed against a history of misrepresentation and silencing. "It's just so hard to deal with," she told me, and while I thought I understood what she meant, I knew I didn't understand it the same way she did. And that, of course, was the root of the dilemma.

After thinking it over for several weeks, Cynthia finally made the decision to participate. The advantages, she ultimately concluded, outweighed the possible drawbacks. Even so, her reservations about taking part never fully subsided, and conversations about race and representation, power and white privilege, became an ongoing feature of our working relationship.

Negotiating relationships imbalanced by race and power dynamics was nothing new for Cynthia. She believed her voice was often ignored or overshadowed by well-meaning whites who claimed to know what was best for children of color—the very silencing, Cynthia said, that Lisa Delpit (1988) describes. In workshops and conferences and at the schools she'd worked in, she'd felt dismissed on numerous occasions by white educators who considered themselves allies in the struggle for social justice. Even in the area of bilingual education—which Cynthia not only studied extensively but to which she also had an intensely personal connection—she had seen her opinions disregarded by whites who seemed to believe they had a clearer understanding of the needs of Spanish-speaking students.

A year before joining the staff at New Horizons, Cynthia had taken a freelance consulting position with a nonprofit organization to assist in developing programming and curriculum for Latino teens. But it didn't take long before she began to feel shut down by the "compassionate superiority," as she called it, of her mostly white coplanners. "Any organization has to look at the way they communicate," Cynthia told me. "You have to go through a process of changing how you talk to people or else it's just a hierarchy. But these people weren't listening to me, and I was getting really frustrated. I'd come home and talk with my husband about it—because he's my sounding board—and he'd just be like, 'The whole world is like that so we just have to keep going.' And I'd tell him, 'Why am I going through this struggle with these people when they don't really want to see it?' You think the director of the project, who is a progressive woman and feels she is not racist, really wants to go through the process of me saying, 'You are being racist because you're not listening to me?'"

It seemed clear that this hadn't been an isolated incident, that the frustration Cynthia was expressing was cumulative. She continued: "I'm not one of those militants—well, I can be militant, but I'm not one of those militants who says, 'You know what? Forget white people. If you're going to work in our community, you have to be us.' We can all work together to make social change. It's just that—I've been teaching for 5 years. I was a counselor in my community for 2 years. I've done a lot of research, I've done a lot of study, I have a lot of experience in the community. Yet there are people who don't have the experience that I have and they are listened to. They don't even have the life experience that I have, and they're listened to."

What seemed to distress Cynthia most was that the educators she'd felt stifled by weren't closed-minded conservatives—they were "progressive" men and women, whites who were outwardly committed to issues of educational equity and social justice. But their vision became clouded, Cynthia believed, when it came to examining their own limited experiences and how they unwittingly continued to support the status quo. "They don't know how it feels to be compared to white students all the time, and then to go home and see white people on TV, with the blue eyes and the blonde hair," she said. "They don't know what it feels like to be a secondary citizen all the time, and to scrape together whatever you can to give yourself some dignity to keep on going. They don't understand that. They can see it, they can agree with it, but they can't really understand it. Yet they get heard. And when I'm written off, it feels horrible. It's not about recognition, it's not about me—it's about people *like* me!"

•••••••••••

What Cynthia had originally called explosiveness, I came to see as an intense passion. What she believed in, she believed in deeply—not just on an emotional register but on an intellectual one as well. That point was worth noting, because the last thing

Cynthia wanted was for her concerns to be dismissed as those of a disgruntled Latina. "People use that as an excuse not to listen," she told me. "When a person of color gets upset about some kind of injustice, they'll say, 'Oh, she's too emotional' or 'She's overreacting' or 'She's exaggerating.' But I don't just go off about things for no reason. I read about issues, I study, I think, I use my intellect."

Cynthia felt morally obligated to stand up and speak out when she believed something wasn't right, and as a teacher, she urged her students to do the same. She talked openly with the girls in her classes about the systemic and institutional barriers that stood in their way as women and people of color. But she also returned frequently to the theme of individual responsibility and initiative—on both the macro level of society and the micro level of the classroom. "These girls go through so many things—sexual abuse, physical abuse, discrimination," she said. "So I let them know that they have to believe in themselves. I tell them, 'You will get justice, but you have to have self-discipline and you have to have faith and you have to have passion.'"

Part of the reason for her explosiveness, Cynthia told me, was that she wanted her students to be more aware of their situations and how they were affected by societal inequities. "Sometimes I want to light a match under them," she said. "Because I do feel that's part of the process. I think in terms of political consciousness, that's a key: to get angry about the injustices that have happened, and then to take that anger and do something with it—to try to bring about change."

Cynthia's students had once joked that if she had a child of her own, she'd be spanking it and smiling at the same time. What they meant, I thought, was that while they saw Cynthia as rigid, maybe even overly strict at times, they also knew that she believed in them, and they could feel her genuine concern and affection for them as individuals. That mixture of toughness and tenderness, of high expectations combined with genuine caring, is a characteristic Judith Kleinfeld (1975) noted among the successful white teachers of Native Alaskan children she studied. She dubbed them "warm demanders," a term I think fits many of the effective Chicago teachers I know—particularly teachers of color.

But casual observations in such classrooms can be deceiving. While the toughness is easy to see—Cynthia's repeated disciplinary lectures and her refusal to compromise on behavioral standards come immediately to mind—the tenderness often manifests itself in less obvious ways, far from the bright lights and roaring crowds of whole-group instruction. One way it was visible in Cynthia's classroom was in the amount of physical contact between her and the girls: Hugging, hands touching, and arms draped around shoulders were all familiar sights. Cynthia appeared so comfortable with these intimate interactions that I'd assumed it was simply an extension of her personality. But she told me it was an openness she'd learned from several of the African American girls in her classes.

"I'm very much a person of distance," she said. "With adults, it's just shaking the hand and that's it. And with my Latino students before—this is kind of sad, actually—but there was never hugging, never touching. Then I came here, and these girls were hugging me all the time. At first, it was hard for me to adjust. I've never been a touchy person. They'd come really close and put their head right here on my chest—and at first it was freaky to me. But now I'm used to it, and I like it. I never thought it would feel so good that they have the confidence in me to do that. Students who I never thought would do something like that come up to me and hug me. And it feels good."

The closeness went beyond hugs, though. Whenever Cynthia and I talked about particular students, it was clear that she'd made conscious efforts to get to know each of the girls in multiple ways, to view them as complex, three-dimensional beings, to push beyond simplistic labels to see the children underneath. There was Ada, who Cynthia said had "so many problems she just doesn't know what to do with herself. She comes in class like a spectacle all the time—she's loud, she doesn't know social cues. But she's also so intelligent and so articulate, and there's such a kind side to her. She really tries hard to be liked by the other girls, but at the same time, she irritates people, she agitates."

Then there was Joya, precocious and outgoing, who often pushed Cynthia's buttons in class and whose mother was a counselor at another school. "She's very smart. Brilliant, I would say. I wish she would show her brilliance a little bit more, but it's that kind of thing. She really amazes me sometimes. She tries you, and she tries you in a very, very calm way—I love it! I wish I could be like that. She makes these quick commentaries and she knows how to manipulate situations. I hardly ever pull her aside for her behavior but, when I do, I tell her, 'You have to start learning to distinguish when you can say things, and when you can't.' Her mom doesn't just side with Joya—she gives her a lot of support, but she also knows how her daughter is. It's kind of cool, actually."

Of all the girls in her classes, Cynthia had developed perhaps the closest bond with Lynette, whose shy smile was rarely contained when the two were together. Between classes, Lynette's head invariably popped through Cynthia's doorway, whether her next class was nearby or not. "Ms. Nambo, you going to our basketball game today?" Lynette asked one morning after bounding into the room. "It's at 6:30 at McDowell Park." After thinking through her afternoon responsibilities, Cynthia agreed to go, but Lynette was already back at her desk, scribbling something onto a Post-It. When she'd gone, I went back to see what it said.

game

6:30 tonight

McDowell Park

Remember Ms. Nambo!

"I really like her," Cynthia said of Lynette. "She's the one that challenges me all the time about culture. Like at the beginning of the year, she said, 'You're white, and all white people are evil.' I'm like, 'OK, first of all, let me clarify something—I'm not white. And not all white people are evil.'" Cynthia laughed at the memory. "We've had discussions about being gay and how she thinks that's wrong. And now it's just an ongoing battle. She sends me all these cute little notes saying, 'I love you, Ms. Nambo.' I'm like, 'Wait a minute, I'm an evil devil.'" More laughter. "So I always mess with her. She really challenges me, and she's really fun."

Cynthia told me that she and Lynette communicated via e-mail on a regular basis—not just to say hi, but to have debates and delve into serious issues. "At first, I didn't give them my e-mail because

I'm not used to giving my personal information out," she said. "It can be overwhelming. But little by little I've been doing it, and my list of e-mails from Lynette is about this long." She spread her arms as wide as they'd go. "They're short notes, but they're really profound sometimes." Lynette had once asked Cynthia if she got offended when people referred to Mexicans as "chalupas"—a word taken from the menu at Taco Bell. "She told me a Mexican student had told her the term didn't bother her," Cynthia said. "And I said, 'Well, some people don't get mad. But I do.' I said I was offended by any word that gives a one-dimensional view of a complex culture. But she really is genuine when she asks those questions. That's why I like our relationship."

Watching Lynette when she was around Cynthia, I could see that she valued their relationship as well. But not surprisingly, she wasn't as comfortable expressing her feelings about it with me. When I pulled her aside to talk about Cynthia one day, her comments were measured, her enthusiasm contained. "She nice," Lynette said of Cynthia, her eyes avoiding mine. "She run the class good, and she explain things good. If I have a problem, she'll give me advice." It was guarded praise at best, but a few days later, one of Lynette's friends shared with me what she claimed was the real deal: "They have their differences sometimes, but Lynette, she love her some Ms. Nambo. That's her best teacher. She can say what she want, but the truth is she love her some Ms. Nambo. That girl can talk about Ms. Nambo for 3 hours straight."

・・・・・・・・・・・・

"This is a crazy mess today," Cynthia said as she closed the door behind me. I was back after a 2-week absence, and not at all surprised to discover that the "organs of the human body" project had fallen behind schedule. It was part of the nature of project-based learning, it seemed: Things always took twice as long as you thought they would.

One of the reasons the schedule had gotten thrown off was that Cynthia had been out with the flu for the past 3 days. "I've never missed more than 2 days of work in the past 5 years," she told me between coughs. A red nose and watery eyes indicated that she still hadn't fully recovered, but she'd been forced to hit the ground running: Roz had called in sick this morning, so Cynthia was flying solo on her first day back.

"Hey, where have you been?" Gaby asked me as I set down my book bag.

"We missed you," added Felicia.

"I didn't," Candice said with a smile.

Around the room, models of organs were in various stages of completion. An eye with painted red-tube veins sprouting from the back looked almost done, as did a brain lined with Styrofoam packing peanuts, painted a glossy pink. A cardboard-tubing-and-papier-mâché large intestine, on the other hand, sat neglected on the floor, looking as if it had been through a bungled colonoscopy. All of the tables were covered in plastic with blobs and dribbles and smears of paint here and there. On one, cafeteria trays full of papier-mâché goop sat next to a pile of old button-downs, which the girls were using as protective overshirts.

As they all got busy, I noted the myriad questions that were thrown Cynthia's way—some scientific and focused on the work at hand, others from left field, right field, and center.

"Should the esophagus connect to the stomach like this?"

"Ms. Nambo, you ever seen a ghost before?"

"Did you see *Temptation Island* last night?"

"Blood is blue, not red—right, Ms. Nambo?"

"Is it true that your soul can't rest 'til you find out who killed you?"

The groups were more or less on task, but as the period moved along, the noise meter, as usual, began creeping into the red. "Girls!" Cynthia called out. "I've asked you to quiet down twice already." I could tell her patience was thin today.

"We know," Patrice said. "The noise bounces off the walls."

A couple of groups were now working on haikus, and the constant counting out of syllables was contagious. "These—things—help—you—breathe.   Don't—smoke—or—they—will—turn—black." I caught myself measuring every syllable that was uttered, whether it was haiku-bound or not.

"What's this, a vagina?" Six. A girl was holding up an unfinished lump of papier-mâché.

"That look like a vagina to you?" Nine. One of the goals of the project, Cynthia had told me, was to help the girls become more comfortable talking about their bodies using scientific language, and at that it had evidently been a success.

A train rolled by on the elevated tracks outside, its low bass rumble momentarily filling the room. Nicole, whose group had already finished painting and begun working on their haikus, counted off syllables on her fingers. "It—helps—di—gest—food. That's five," she said. I asked her how she liked New Horizons compared to her old school. "It's easier to concentrate here," she told me. "When boys around, they be buggin' you and touchin' you and stuff. Here you ain't bein' judged by what you say. Over there, you make a mistake and people make fun of you. Here, they say, 'That's OK. Try it again.'"

"But they's some racist people in this school, too," Lynette pitched in.

"They's racist people everywhere," countered Nicole.

Lynette didn't back down. "Most of the black girls don't like the white and Mexican girls," she said. "In the lunchroom, the white girls sit by theyselves. And the Mexicans, too—they stick together more. Black people ain't like that so much. Blacks be killin' blacks."

Yvonne, who, like Lynette and Nicole, was African American, shook her head. "Every culture likes to hang out with their own kind. There's nothing wrong with that. But girls should stick together, no matter what the race. Girl power is very strong."

It wasn't the first time I'd heard one of the girls mention racial tension among New Horizons' students, and while their comments undercut, to some degree, the "strength in diversity" language of the school's marketing material, they really came as no surprise. Many of these sixth graders had come to New Horizons from neighborhood elementary schools that were essentially segregated spaces, so working with students of another color was something new. Before any real bridges could be built, questions needed to be asked, stereotypes needed to be debunked, prejudices needed to be confronted. It made sense that such discussions should happen, or at least begin, in the classroom, but past experience had taught me that many teachers avoid racial issues for fear of stirring the pot, or of not knowing how to respond—especially in schools where several racial groups are represented. That's why I'd been so impressed when I walked into an empty lunchroom at New Horizons one afternoon and saw the following questions printed on a left-behind piece of newsprint:

- Why do some students sit only with their own ethnic group?
- Why do we tease each other about our accents?
- Is ignorance better than knowledge?
- What did Martin Luther King mean when he said, "Whatever affects one directly affects all indirectly?"

Here, it appeared, race and racism were on the table—and not only to be referenced in the past tense, as they had affected some faraway people in some long-ago time, but also as they impacted these girls, the halls they walked, the lives they lived.

Race and culture had long been important lenses through which Cynthia viewed her work with children. But coming to New Horizons had forced her to reexamine her assumptions, to both broaden and sharpen her focus. "At my other school, I was around just Mexicans, so I felt really clear about my purpose," she told me. "And then I came here and I had white students—and that was a challenge for me. I had always said that they have privilege—so why was I working with them? And with the African American community, I felt that they had a lot of resources, and that they had a large middle class that helped the situation." Cynthia said she still believed those things to some extent, but that she didn't let it affect how she treated her students. "I always have in the back of my mind the distribution of power and all that, but I feel that justice also means fairness. So whatever culture a student is from, as a teacher, I have to give her my all."

It was economic differences, rather than racial ones, that provided Cynthia with her biggest "culture shock" at New Horizons. A third of the school's first-year students had transferred from Catholic schools, and over 40% failed to qualify for free or reduced-price lunches. That didn't mean they were rich, but their situations, Cynthia said, were far removed from those of the poor and working-class immigrant families she'd known during her first 5 years as a teacher. She'd had a hard time adjusting to the realities of some of her new students' lives—and to their accompanying attitudes, which she described as "spoiled": "A lot of them are middle class, and in terms of values in their homes, there is this value on money—you have to have clothes from American Girl, you have to have a swimming-pool party. I mean, these girls have their birthday parties at hotels. Personally, it's hard for me to deal with." Of course, Cynthia was now part of the middle class herself in some ways, but she made conscious efforts not to be sucked in by it completely.

Back in the classroom, Cynthia's voice suddenly rose above the room's dull roar. "Janelle! Move to another table!" I wasn't sure what had provoked her reaction. Janelle looked at Cynthia but didn't budge. "Now!" Cynthia demanded, and punctuated it with a hoarse cough.

"I'm moving!" Janelle snapped back.

"Stop! Right there!"

"But you told me to move!"

"Is that how you speak to me?"

"I said, 'I'm moving.'" Janelle's tone was slightly less abrasive this time.

Cynthia's wasn't. "Is that how you speak to me?"

Janelle repeated herself once more, this time without the attitude, and took her things to a different table.

"You know what? I'm not dealing well with this noise today," Cynthia told the class. "Let's just be quiet for 10 minutes. Just do your work. No talking, no murmuring, nothing." The girls did as they were asked, but it didn't take long for someone to break the silence. "I said quiet! Qui—et!" Cynthia yelled. This time they got the message. "See, unfortunately I have to yell for you guys to listen to me. That's ridiculous."

After class, Cynthia vented more of her concerns to me, reconnecting to themes she'd touched on before. The discipline issue, she felt, was commanding far too much of her time and attention, and she saw it as a worsening problem school-wide. "The leadership here wants to have an open, free environment," she said, "but I think there has to be more structure. There's too much chaos, and the more these girls see chaos, the more they will replicate it. It's like I told you earlier: To really have freedom, you have to be disciplined in your thoughts and actions."

While Cynthia went out in the hall to corral her next group, I stayed behind to review my notes. On my way to retrieve a fresh legal pad from my book bag, I noticed a homemade card sitting open on her desk:

Dear: Ms. Nambo

Hey Ms Nambo how are you. I know I have not been the perfect student but I try my best. You should not get upset so much because your so cute and you don't want to mess that up. I am just trying to say I will start being on task because the stuff you tell us do get to me and have me thinking. Also you are the first best teacher on my list. I know you are sayin to yourself this girl is telling a story but I am not.

Sincerely,
Nicole

············

On a sunny Saturday morning just after 9:00 a.m., Cynthia and her husband Alfredo sat around a table with six somewhat bleary-eyed seventh-grade girls in a decaying annex of San Mateo Catholic Church. A paper taped to the door read MEETING ROOM, but otherwise the pale yellow walls were bare. An empty coat rack sat in a corner next to a globe stand minus its globe. Four naked fluorescent bulbs burned overhead. On the table, as if to enliven the somewhat drab surroundings, Cynthia and Alfredo had laid out a spread of food: bananas, churros, and an assortment of Jumex juices.

"OK, before we begin, I have a *chiste*," Alfredo said. "Why didn't the vampire drink the blood of the clown?" The girls looked at each other but no one took a stab at it. "Because it tasted funny," Alfredo said to a smattering of laughter. "That's an original joke from one of my sixth graders."

If Cynthia occasionally expressed regret about being torn from her community to teach at New Horizons, the truth was that she'd never really left. Every other Saturday for the past 18 months, she and Alfredo had come to San Mateo—strictly as volunteers—to meet with this group of girls, all of whom had been students in Cynthia's bilingual classroom 3 years before. It was about maintaining connections, Cynthia said, about providing the girls with a support system. "We want to help them become truly bilingual and confident in who they are: Mexican young women," she told me, saying she saw the work as part of her life's larger purpose. "The reality is that I do want to help my community," she said. "That *is* my goal: to help my community succeed—somehow, some way. Whatever little I can do, I'm going to do it and I'm going to do it well."

Two weeks before, the girls had taken disposable cameras around the neighborhood to document life in the community. Cynthia asked a couple of them to talk about what they'd photographed. "I took a picture of the church," Zury said, nervously sliding a nameplate charm back and forth on her necklace, "'cause it's like the center of everything for Mexicans. We go there when we're sad, when we're happy, when we're thankful for something. And there we don't fight with each other, 'cause we respect the church."

Chela's mother had taken her camera to her job. "She took it to her factory and took a lot of pictures of Mexicans doing heavy work. And then she took it to the office and took pictures of people who weren't Mexican working in the office."

After discussing the photo project and talking briefly about their next endeavor—a trip to Borders to see how many Latino authors were represented in the young adult section—Alfredo explained today's assignment. The girls were to write for 10 minutes on one of the themes listed on the board—*leyendas, tradición, sobrevivimos, violencia domestica*, racism, and others—or come up with one of their own.

Next to me, Maribel thought for a while before starting to write. She looked ready to disappear underneath a black hoodie and an overflow of hair that cascaded down past her eyelids. But as she started putting words to paper, she sat up straighter, pushed her hair back, and gradually became more and more visible:

> A lot of latinas get descrimenated because they say that latinas in school get pregnet at 15 years that they don't have a future that they don't go to college. That we are only here to work in factories and have babies. Well some of us are going to prove them wrong.

Cynthia seemed more at ease here than in her classes at New Horizons—not more comfortable, just more relaxed. Part of that, it seemed to me, had to do with the fact that she'd built longer and stronger relationships with these girls, that they were fewer in number, that she had another caring adult to work beside. But another part was that this *wasn't* school—there were no discipline problems to worry over, no attendance book to fill out, no bell schedule to be slave to, no standardized tests to cast menacing shadows over everyone. There were only children and adults around a table of food, coming together to create a curriculum from their lives.

Toward the end of the meeting, a few of the girls started reminiscing with Cynthia about their time in her classroom. "Being a bilingual teacher is the best thing that ever happened to me," Cynthia told them. "You guys taught me a lot."

"How?" Zury asked.

"Sus conversaciones, sus sueños." Your conversations, your dreams.

"But we gave you a lotta headaches, too," said Angelica.

Cynthia smiled. "Well, that's what love is, no?"

············

Back at New Horizons a few days later, Lynette and Joneisha were hyped up. Their words tumbled out in bunches, each sentence chasing off the one before.

"We're gonna do a trial!"

"Yeah, we're gonna be lawyers."

"We're gonna act out this play and try to decide if somebody was under the influence of alcohol."

"We gotta figure out all the evidence."

As the rest of the class excitedly hurried in, Cynthia handed me a copy of the text she used, *Science & Life Issues,* opened to a section called "Under the Influence." The activity in the book featured a fictionalized court reporter's record about a case involving an alcohol-related automobile accident.

"Don't both attorneys ask questions?" Jayla asked Cynthia. "'Cause I was watching *The Practice* the other day and both attorneys were asking questions."

"Yeah, they do," Cynthia said. "But you're getting ahead of yourself. We're not there yet. And remember what I said yesterday: I don't want a play that is just focused on making everybody laugh." She was talking to the entire group now. "If you can make everyone laugh in the process, great. But that shouldn't be the focus. Your play should be based on what?"

"Evidence."

"Right. So that's what you need to focus on right now—getting a good understanding of the evidence. And to do that, you're going to need to make inferences." On the board, she wrote INFER. "That means from information, you are able to assume something."

"I don't get it."

Cynthia thought for a moment. "OK, from what you know about me, what will I wear to school next Thursday—a skirt or pants?"

"Pants!" It was unanimous.

"But how do you know that?"

"'Cause that's what you always wear!"

"But how do you know that's what I'll wear next Thursday?"

"Just 'cause—you always be wearin' pants."

"OK, so you can infer that based on what you know about me. You don't know it for sure, but you can make an assumption based on the information you have. You infer it." Cynthia passed out a worksheet and explained that each group should first go through the court reporter's record, listing both the direct and inferred evidence it contained. They were then to categorize the evidence according to whether it supported or contradicted a finding of guilty against the defendant. After everyone had a solid understanding of the evidence, they would divvy up the parts and plan for a semi-improvised mock trial.

Cynthia let the groups talk on their own for several minutes, then sat down at one of the tables and crossed her legs. Two pens were stuck like harpoons through the bundle of hair gathered behind her head. "So what have you come up with so far?"

"I think Mr. Kline probably wasn't paying attention to the road," Sarah said.

"Why do you say that?"

"'Cause it says his passengers were rowdy so he was probably paying attention to them."

"OK, so which part of that is direct evidence and which part is inferred?"

"It's evidence that they were rowdy."

"And we can infer that he wasn't paying attention," Jayla added.

"Ms. Nambo!" Joneisha called out from across the room. "I got a theory! I think Mr. Kline is from Europe."

Cynthia cracked up. "I want to hear this." She got up and went to sit with Joneisha's group. "OK, why do you think he was from Europe?"

Joneisha tried to put on a serious face. "Well, I think he was here visiting, and he was used to driving on the left side of the road, and he just forgot and drove on the wrong side."

Cynthia laughed some more. "But is there anything in the court reporter's record that leads you to infer that?"

"Mmmm—well, the witness, Jaime Lopez, said Mr. Kline was driving kinda crazy."

"His name is *Jaime*," Cynthia said, emphasizing the Spanish pronunciation.

"That's his name?" Joneisha asked. "Well, I'm gonna say 'Jamie.'"

"His name is *Jaime*," Cynthia repeated. "How are you going to change somebody's name? Should I call you Janoosha?"

Cynthia didn't let the girls forget that she was bilingual, or that she was Mexican—or that she was fiercely proud of being both. She frequently employed Spanish phrases, telling the girls things like *"Déjame en paz,"* or *"Ándale, chica,"* or "I have a piece of *consejo* for you." She also used her facility with the two languages as a teaching tool. Once, when a student trying to identify the human body's different systems said that the lungs were part of "the breathing system," Cynthia had reminded her that the Spanish word for "breathe" is *respirar*. "That's what I meant!" the girl then exclaimed. "The respiration system!"

While her students continued working, Cynthia passed out completed evaluation rubrics for their most recent writing assignment. At New Horizons, there were no grades—a poorly done essay received a "not yet." Teachers were encouraged to give written feedback on assigned work, and twice each trimester they wrote lengthy narrative assessments for each student. It was time-consuming, Cynthia said, but in the end she got a better sense of how each student was doing. "Sometimes I think, 'God, I wish we had percentages,' because then I could just have a running tally, put the grades in a computer program, and that would be my grade. But I have more fun with this. I really do read their work, and I really do try to understand what they're trying to say."

Students I talked with said they appreciated the more person-
alized approach. "With grades, it's like when you're getting A's
and B's, you might wanna brag about it," said Candice, who had
legs so long it didn't seem as if the rest of her would ever catch up.
"And when you're getting D's and F's, it makes you feel bad. But
'Not yet'—that just means you're not there yet. You could still
improve." Candice talked me through her paper, explaining what
a placebo is, what a clinical trial looks like, how to set up a double-
blind study. After a few minutes I was convinced that she understood quantitative research methods about as well as I did—
maybe better. "Science is my favorite subject," she told me. "I've
learned a lot this year. At my old school I never did this much science. We'd only have it once a week, and most of the time we
wouldn't even do anything." She slid her assessment rubric care-
fully into a folder and then put the folder in her book bag. "So I can
show my momma," she said.

············

"Who wants to make a difference in this world?" Cynthia
asked her third-period girls the next morning. "Who feels you
have a responsibility to make this world brighter and better?"

Most teachers I know—even those who are not the least bit
egocentric, and who understand that good teaching does not cor-
relate with being always in front of the class—have their moments
on the soapbox, or in the pulpit. These can be occasions for empty
rhetoric, of course, or time-fillers, but other times they're more
substantive. Occasionally, it's as if the teacher feels a sudden need
to be explicit about why she shows up every day, to say out loud
what the meaning of it all is—if not to remind her students, to
remind herself.

"I want you to look at our government," Cynthia continued.
"Are there enough women or women of color in our government?
In leadership roles all over the world? In science, math, and technology? The reason we created this school was not for this"—she
sat down and meekly folded her hands—"for girls to just be quiet
and listen. We want you to be free. But with freedom comes the
responsibility to realize that your actions affect others, not just
you. Community isn't just about where you live, it's about what
you build. We can have a community here at New Horizons, but
we have to work at it." I wasn't sure whom Cynthia was trying to

convince more with that last statement—the students or herself.

The girls were a rapt audience. Even Raven was listening with both ears. "You know, my mom used to always try to talk to me, to give me advice," Cynthia said. "She used to tell me, 'Listen, *m'ija*—'"

"What's mita?" a lone voice asked.

"*M'ija*," Cynthia repeated. "It means daughter. In Spanish it's a term of endearment. And my mom would always say that— 'Listen, *m'ija*'—she'd try to tell me things, but I didn't want to listen. I thought I knew it all already. So I know how it is to feel like somebody's lecturing you. But when I talk to you like this, it's not about lecturing. It's about caring. I care about what happens to you, and I want you to be able to reach all the goals you have set for yourself, all your dreams. Since you're women, or women of color, you may have to work twice as hard as other people—even three times as hard—to achieve those dreams. But you can do it. I want one of you to be President of the United States one day. Or just to be a good mother who instills good values in her children. You can make a difference that way, too. You have the power—all of you do. It's in your heart, it's in your soul, it's in your mind. Use that power. Don't let anybody take it away from you."

It seemed like a perfect time for the music to swell and the credits to roll, but this was a real classroom, not a movie. Life, after a genuine but brief silence, went on. "OK, let's get in your groups," Cynthia said. "I know that's kind of a harsh transition, but we need to rehearse these plays."

Her impassioned speech notwithstanding, Cynthia had been feeling uncertain about her future at New Horizons. Discipline in her classes continued to be a major issue. She hadn't found the time to do significant long-range curriculum planning, so she was forever playing catch-up, struggling to stay one day ahead in her lessons. And she still hadn't sat down with the school's directors to discuss transitioning into a bilingual support role for the upcoming year—a position she thought would allow her to spend more time doing what she'd hoped to do when she signed on: recruiting and advocating for New Horizons' Latina students. Like other conversations at the young school, Cynthia said, it had been put on a perpetual back-burner.

"Ms. Nambo, can we do a ghetto court case?" It was Raven, smiling broadly.

"You can do a ghetto court case if the evidence is there. But if you get up there and all people do is laugh and they don't hear your evidence, then we miss the point."

"I'm not doing no ghetto thing," Aliyah said. "That's not my style. You people wanna do ghetto, go ahead, but I'm not gonna be in it."

"Me, either," said Kim, modeling the black hooded sweatshirt and cape she planned to wear for her role as the judge.

Raven glared at her disapprovingly. "Girl, you look like a TeleTubby. You look like a black TeleTubby." She glanced down at her notes. "OK, so you the judge, I'm the prosecutor—who's gonna play Jamie Lopez?"

"*JAIME!*" the entire class yelled at once.

"The way I see it," Cynthia had told me, "is that whatever I can do to secure justice—and not the way the government defines it, but just pure, simple justice—onto any human being, to afford them the opportunities that are within their rights, that's why I do my job." While one of her goals was to help her students become more socially aware and politically conscious, she was equally determined to push them to think through issues for themselves, to set their own political agendas. "I don't want them to do what I'm doing. I want them to do what they feel is the right thing—to understand that there are inequalities and when something's wrong to do something about it."

I wondered if Cynthia ever felt as I sometimes had as a teacher: that the steps she was taking were too small, the road ahead too steep. I asked what she thought of the idea, put forth by many critical theorists in education, that schools only serve to reinforce and reproduce societal inequities, and that efforts by teachers to stem the tide will be essentially meaningless unless more fundamental changes are made. "A lot of radicals—both academic and grassroots—say, 'We have to overthrow this, we have to overthrow that,'" she said. "And I agree that we have to transform the system. As it is, our schools are definitely not doing a good job of serving students of color. But that transformation can happen on many levels. It can happen one person at a time or one conversation at a time. Because that can lead up to something much bigger. The conversation you had with *that* child at *that* moment may be the difference."

Photo: Antonio Pérez

4

freda lin

I'm drowning.

Freda Lin said the words, then paused from her flurry of activity to allow them to hang in the air for a moment. Though it was barely nine o'clock on a cold winter morning, Freda was perspiring. She hurriedly filled both arms with folders, class schedule forms, her attendance book, and a large bottle of water, then surveyed the piles of stuff she was leaving behind. "I'm drowning in paper," she said, motioning with an elbow to a towering stack on her desk. "I have all these to grade. And these." She shook her head. "I think that's my biggest downfall in teaching. I cannot get things graded on time."

Freda headed for the door, straightening a few desks and retrieving a wad of paper on the way, and I followed close behind. Second period had just ended, and we were on our way to her division, a 20-minute session where Freda would take the day's official attendance and handle other school business with her 16 student advisees.

"How are you doing?" I asked once we hit the hallway. It was the first chance I'd had to squeeze a word in since my arrival an hour earlier.

"Busy," she said without breaking stride. Dumb question.

We rounded a third-floor corner from Freda's room, 311, and proceeded along the building's east wing toward room 342, where her junior-level division met. For Freda, the trek was a daily ritual. One of the realities of the overcrowded conditions at Warren G. Harding High School was that some teachers had to vacate their rooms during planning and lunch periods so that "traveling" teachers—who bounced from classroom to classroom throughout the school day—could use them. Veterans with the most clout didn't get bumped; newer hires like Freda, who at 28 was in her third year at Harding, had assigned rooms but were forced to abandon them during so-called free periods. Those lowest in rank—rookies and the unlucky veterans who found themselves in disfavor with the school's principal—spent their days as Harding nomads, packing and unpacking papers and materials as often as their students did.

We arrived at room 342 and Freda went in. I lingered in the hallway to watch the passing crowds—a multiethnic, multinational, multilingual mix of kids. I heard sprinklings of Spanish, Polish, and maybe Hindi and Vietnamese in nearby conversations. A black girl with braids and a Jamaican accent leaned against the wall next to me, talking with a friend and spreading cream cheese onto a bagel. A flyer taped to the wall said, "Islamic Club, Room 201, 8th and 9th period Wednesday. Everyone is welcome!"

Across the hall, a teacher and a male student stood on either side of a doorway. The kid was digging in his nose.

"Could you not pick your nose?" the teacher said.

"I can't help it," said the kid.

"You know who that reflects on when you do stuff like that?" asked the teacher.

"Who?"

"Your parents."

"But why? It's my nose. It's my own personal nose."

The teacher was not amused. "Don't give me that grade-school stuff. You're supposed to be in high school, not fifth grade."

"Oh, yeah," the kid said. "I keep forgetting."

Inside 342, Freda unpacked her things and took a long drink of water. Today she was scheduled to help her advisees program their course selections for the next school year. She'd been through the process before, and even with today's extended division period of 60 minutes, she knew it was going to be a rush job. She also knew that she'd probably come out of it feeling guilty—about not spending more time with each kid, about biting her tongue instead of challenging ill-informed choices, about not knowing some of her students well enough to really help them. A self-described perfectionist, Freda second-guessed herself as a matter of course, and was rarely satisfied with her efforts, whether inside the classroom or out of it. "I'm trying to get better about not being so hard on myself," she told me. "But it's difficult. I've always been that way."

A recording of the National Anthem, which opened with a long drum roll, crackled through the intercom speaker. The students all stood up—as was required by school policy—but there were no hands over hearts and no one sang along. One girl pulled out a mirror and applied a fresh coat of deep brown lipstick. The girl from out in the hallway took another bite from her bagel while reading Toni Morrison. "Somebody farted, Ms. Lin," the nose-picker called out as soon as the final strains of the anthem had faded away.

Freda didn't even look up. "Open a window," she said.

············

Freda Lin's parents were born into well-educated families in Taiwan, and both came to the United States in the late 1960s to further their own scholastic pursuits—Matthew to complete a medical internship, Audrey to obtain a master's in chemical engineering. They met and married in northern New Jersey, then moved for Matthew's residency to New Orleans, where Audrey gave birth to Freda. A few years later, the residency completed, the Lins, now with Freda and a younger son in tow, headed back north, settling into an upscale suburban section of Long Island.

Other than the Lins, the new neighborhood was almost all white, and Freda spent much of her time in grade school and high school trying not to stand out. "I didn't have many other Asians around me, so I was very isolated," she told me. "I was just trying to fit in as much as possible. I was definitely not in tune with my identity. In school, I remember feeling embarrassed about my culture. Teachers never really did anything about cultural awareness, so I kept the Taiwanese part of me at home." The desire to assimilate was so strong, Freda said, that when a high school friend told her "I always forget that you're Asian," she was flattered. "I remember feeling so good that she didn't think of me as different. I went home and wrote it down in my journal. I guess back then I was what other Asians would call a 'twinkie'—yellow on the outside, white on the inside."

Freda never actually heard the term "twinkie" until her freshman year at Northwestern University, when a few politically
inclined Asian students pinned her with the label. Hurt and con-
fused, she gradually began to question her ethnic identity, and to
learn more about the discrimination various Asian American
groups had suffered. The more awareness she gained, the more
involved she became, and by her senior year she was serving as
vice president of Northwestern's Asian American Advisory Board
and leading campus protests to demand an Asian American studies program at the school. The political awakening led Freda not
only to question her own schooling experiences but also to redirect
her plans for the future. "I realized that I'd had a totally
Eurocentric education in grade school and high school," she said,
"and that the things I was being introduced to in college should
have been taught to me back then. That got me excited about curriculum reform, and through my interest in curriculum I got
inspired to go into teaching."

After graduating from Northwestern, Freda landed a part-
time teaching fellowship at a boarding school just north of
Chicago, where she taught a history class, developed curriculum,
and organized a cultural diversity club. Her experience there
convinced her that she needed more formal training in education,
so she enrolled in a master's program at Brown University. While
at Brown, Freda taught in a summer enrichment lab for high
school students and completed several field-work assignments in
the public school classrooms of Providence, where she became
increasingly intrigued by the challenges of teaching in an urban
setting. In 1998, her MAT in hand, she returned to Chicago,
where she accepted a position at Harding teaching U.S. history
and Asian studies. She had offers from other schools, but
Harding's sizable Asian American student population gave it the
edge. Freda hoped to help Asian students examine their identities and avoid the sort of cultural denial she'd gone through as a
teenager.

Finding the time to do such mentoring, however, had proved
more difficult than she'd imagined. Today's extended division
period—also known as "advisory"—was a once-a-week session
that board of education policymakers initiated as a partial antidote
to the impersonal experience common to many large, overpopu-

lated high schools. It should be a time, they'd said, for teachers to develop personal connections with students, to participate in small-group discussions, to plan service projects, to build a caring school environment. The fine print said that the time could also be used to "develop test preparation strategies" or "improve study skills," but those goals were said to be secondary. At its heart, the advisory concept was supposed to be about bringing teachers and students closer together, building and nourishing relationships, making big schools feel smaller.

Freda said it mainly just made her feel tired. "I feel like it's an extra burden they put on us," she told me. "I mean, it's a good idea, but where are we supposed to find the time to plan for it? It's like an extra lesson plan we have to do." If I hadn't spent time as a public school teacher myself, this might have sounded like so much random bellyaching. But I knew that top-down reforms, regardless of the soundness of the reasoning behind them, often came in the form of decrees, and were too rarely accompanied by support structures that might help teachers put them into practice in a meaningful way.

As a group of male students huddled around the sports pages at the back of the room, Freda conferenced with Marie, a Polish immigrant. Marie needed to choose one more class—something that would fulfill a science requirement. She looked over the list of courses and finally pointed to one.

"Physics?" Freda asked. "Are you sure?"

Marie nodded and looked away. Freda opened her mouth, then eyed the form one more time. I thought she was about to suggest that Marie reconsider her choice.

"OK, sign it right here," Freda said. She looked at her watch. "Jason, you're next."

· · · · · · · · · · · ·

As is the case in many of the city's aging public school buildings, the thermostat at Harding is erratic, and on cold days the monstrous basement boiler tends to overcompensate. On this day, the sidewalks outside were covered with newly fallen snow, but Freda's third-floor room was hotter than July. All the windows were flung open, their upper panes frosted over completely with condensation. A kid stood in front of one, leaning out and waving his arms inward, apparently trying to convince the colder air to come inside. From my seat across the room, where I was already roasting in a wool sweater, I couldn't feel that his coaxing was making much of a difference.

Freda paced a wide aisle that spanned the length of the room and separated short rows of desks on either side. She spent much of her time during classes navigating this open space—working the crowd, moving closer to kids who were losing focus, going to the board to refer to an outline or chart. After a few quick announcements, she told the class they'd have the entire period to work on their History Fair projects. The school-wide event—which Freda was helping to orchestrate—was coming up, and she'd made it a requirement that all of her students do a project, even if they didn't plan to exhibit their work at the fair.

Evidence of Freda's beliefs about teaching and curriculum was all around. On the walls, hand-lettered posters encouraged students to make their voices heard. WHERE DO YOU STAND? called out one. GIVE US OUR RIGHTS! demanded another. "I try to be student-centered in the classroom," she told me. "I try to hear their opinions, and to connect the content of whatever we're studying to current issues or their own lives so it's engaging for them. I think that's really important: for them to interact and really learn—not only content, but to learn to think through things and develop their own opinions."

On a nearby bulletin board, a student-made bar graph showed the various religious affiliations among Harding's student body: Muslim, Hindu, Catholic, Buddhist, Protestant, Jewish, atheist. On another board, editorial cartoons done by Freda's U.S. history classes commented on Nike's use of sweatshop labor in poor Asian countries—an outgrowth of a unit on U.S. imperialism. One drawing depicted a woman on a leash underneath the Nike swoosh. "Nike—women and children are our favorites," the caption read.

"I try to teach about issues that might be controversial or disturbing so that the students can be more sensitive and more aware about things," Freda said. "Sometimes I worry that I'm too anti-American in my teaching. I mean, almost everything I teach has a negative twist to it about what the U.S. did to other people. But you know, it's true, so I feel like I need to teach that. It's something

I didn't learn and I feel like it doesn't get focused on in classes. So when I teach about imperialism, I make connections to modern-day imperialism. Or when I teach about expansionism, and the fact that a lot of our land used to be a part of Mexico and was taken away, I emphasize that people are still fighting for that, that it's not just a thing of history."

Yet Freda often wondered how much of what she was trying to get across was really sinking in. "Sometimes I feel successful only with individual students," she told me. "And then sometimes there'll be a really engaged, active class. Like my first year I had this awesome fifth-period U.S. history class, and whenever we talked about any issue, we had these long discussions about it. With that class, I felt like I really struck a chord in many ways, and I think some people might have stepped out of there with some ideas. That's one of the most important parts of my philosophy— to make my students more active citizens, to get them more engaged and more aware and more excited about issues."

As students gradually got busy, Freda went to talk with Javier, who walked in with no books, no book bag—nothing at all in the way of materials. He was sitting on a heater vent, looking out an open window. Freda asked what he'd gotten done so far on his project.

"I was gonna do research on Michael Jordan, but he's not in your encyclopedias," Javier said. He was right. The Britannica set in Freda's room was published in 1988, before Jordan had reached household-name status.

"Well, there's other interesting things you could work on," Freda suggested.

Javier turned back to the window and I noticed the artwork on his T-shirt: an air-brushed rendition of praying hands holding a rosary in front of a wooden cross. Below were the words, *RIP Junior. We'll miss you.* "Ain't nothin' I like in here," he said, pointing toward an encyclopedia on a nearby desk. "I ain't interested in this stuff. I wanna study Larry Hoover." Hoover, I knew, was the jailed leader of one of the city's largest street gangs. "You know about him?"

Most of the students had chosen to work in twosomes, and I traveled from pair to pair, listening in on conversations, watching kids at work. According to History Fair guidelines, their topics had to be city-focused, but other than that, the students had free rein to choose subject matter. A pair of African American girls—Danielle and Ayanna—was researching former Chicago mayor Harold Washington. "We wanted to study him 'cause he was the first black mayor," Danielle told me. "If he was still alive, things would be a lot better. 'Cause we still don't really have that many black people in office." She was interrupted by Leon, who out of nowhere plopped down in a chair directly across from her. "Why you all up in my grill?" Danielle demanded. "Gimme some room! Don't you got somewhere to go?"

Across the aisle, Freda was conferring with Isaac, a witty, burly Puerto Rican kid whose productivity, Freda had told me, was as unpredictable as his moods. He was hot and cold with her: engaged and pleasant one day, disruptive and belligerent the next. She'd learned it was best not to be confrontational with him—it usually only made matters worse. Still, she knew he was a smart guy, capable of high-caliber work, and that made his on-again, off-again routine all the more frustrating.

On this day, he was off again. "I left it at home, Ms. Lin. I don't got it." Isaac had been telling Freda he was putting together a project on journalist and antilynching crusader Ida B. Wells, but so far she'd seen little tangible progress.

She turned to the group. "This is the last class time you're getting to work on these, everybody. We can't spend any more time on this." I sensed from her words that the familiar inner debate of depth versus breadth, quality versus quantity, project-based learning versus "coverage" of material, was gnawing at her once again. For the most part, she liked what she'd seen of the kids' History Fair efforts, and she believed it was helping bring the various topics to life for them, but she also felt the CASE demons breathing down her neck. The CASE—the Chicago Academic Standards Exam—was a locally created test designed to assess district goals in the core subject areas. Most high school teachers I knew despised it, but since CASE scores were part of the criteria the central office used to evaluate principals, the pressure to keep them high—or, at schools such as Harding, to raise them—could be immense. Teachers like Freda felt their feet put to the flame. "I know the way my principal operates," she said. "On every CASE bubble sheet, the teacher's name is on it, and I know he's watching me in that way. That shouldn't have a bearing on how I do things, I know, but it does."

In her more insecure moments, Freda feared that any class time spent on projects like the History Fair would be time lost on something else—something that could easily show up on the CASE. "One thing I always feel pressured against is time," Freda told me. "Time to get to the CASE, time to finish a unit, time before the bell rings—whatever. So a lot of the class discussions that I could make more inclusive or involved, I feel like I can't— I have to just get them done. I consciously hear myself telling my students, 'OK, we have to get through this discussion really quickly because we have to get to this next.' And I'm very torn about that."

The high stakes surrounding the test had led Freda to grudgingly accept the fact that no matter how great a lesson might be going, no matter how engaged a class, she would always have a nagging voice whispering in her ear: *Hurry up, Freda. The tests are coming. You need to move on.* It was the same whisper teachers in school districts across the country were hearing with increasing frequency. "There's a lot of pressure to cover a certain amount of material," she said. "But I do want it to be meaningful. Doing projects takes more time, but I've found that kids really remember things we do projects on, whereas when it's just notes on the board, they're just memorizing for the test. But then again, they have to take the CASE, and I don't want them to feel like failures when they take it. So that pressure kind of gets to me. I'm one of these people who wants to please everybody. But you can't please everybody. You have to pick something."

•••••••••••

"Ms. Lin, I'm gonna freak out!" May said as she burst into the room. "We're not ready! We don't even have all our props!"

When I returned to Harding a few days later, Freda's sixth-period Asian studies students were in a mild panic. For several days, they'd been writing, rehearsing, and making props for "mini-plays" about India's fight for independence from British rule, and today they were scheduled to perform them. The skits would count as their final project grades for the unit they'd just finished.

"That's OK. You can do it," Freda said reassuringly as she opened a locked cabinet and pulled out a camcorder.

Seventeen of the 20 students in the class were of Asian descent. Some had arrived in the United States only recently from their home countries, while others were native-born. Many of the kids traced their roots to India, Vietnam, or the Philippines, but there were also those whose families had come from Korea, Pakistan, China, and Cambodia.

As Freda readied the camcorder, the groups rehearsed their lines. The anxiety level was high, but I couldn't decide if it was because the students were being graded or because they were being recorded. Either way, May wasn't the only one freaking.

"Judy, come on, this is serious! You don't have time to be looking at no magazine! We need to practice!"

Judy, whose family were Hmong refugees, flung a copy of *VIBE* across her desk. "OK, just calm your horses down!"

Freda saw herself as a role model of sorts for students like May and Judy. "I think having an Asian American teacher they can talk to helps with their own identity development," she said. "They ask me about my experiences, they want to know if my parents were as strict as theirs—that kind of thing." Freda also used her influence, she told me, to encourage Asian students not to accept discriminatory treatment—from others or from each other. "Some of them will call each other 'chinky,'" she said. "Or I had this one Korean student, and all her white friends called her 'soy sauce,' and she said it didn't bother her. So in situations like that, I try to talk to them. I say, 'When they're calling you that, do you realize what it means?' I try to get them to understand that there's a lot of history behind it."

Freda made antiracist teaching a priority in her classroom, and took steps to make it more than a black and white issue. "I've seen how Asians get left out of discussions about race," she said. "We have this stereotype as the model minority, and, yes, there are Asians who are doing really well. But there are also a lot who aren't: refugee families, people from Southeast Asia—a lot of the kids at this school. Historically, too, there was a lot of racism toward Asians, and it bothers me that people don't recognize that.

A lot of times, we're kind of put in the middle. I consider myself a person of color. I identify with that. But I know other people don't always see me that way."

The Asian studies course had been Freda's baby, a curriculum she'd developed pretty much from scratch over the preceding 2½ years. "It's a difficult class to teach," she said, "because you have these supersmart honors students and then you have a lot of ESL students. I mean, they're smart, too. They're all really smart. But I'm constantly having to slow down for the ESL students because of language issues. So finding a balance is really hard. I go back and forth: Sometimes I think I'm expecting too much from them, and other times I ask myself if I should be expecting more. But I do want it to be academically challenging. I don't want it to turn into an Asian support class."

She also didn't want the class to be just another jewel in her principal's crown. According to Freda, he was a man who'd always been concerned more with appearance than substance, more with how things looked at Harding than how they really were. Because the school had a relatively large number of Asian students, Freda said, her principal was especially conscious of reaching out to that population. But from her vantage point, his efforts seemed superficial at best, and at worst insincere and self-serving.

Freda didn't want to be part of her principal's "Asian showcase." She didn't want dignitaries being paraded by her room to be impressed by the young Asian teacher and her Asian studies class. "I don't want to make the school look great when I disagree with the way the administration treats the teachers and students," she told me. "What's the point of making it look great if it isn't actually great, you know? What does it really mean?"

At the moment, however, those concerns were taking a back seat to a more pressing one: Freda couldn't seem to get the video camera to cooperate. Its batteries had long ago lost their juice, and now the power cable wasn't functioning.

"I think it's broke, Ms. Lin," Tommy said.

"Guess we'll have to wait 'til tomorrow," added May, looking up at the clock. Only 20 minutes remained in the period.

"No, you're going today," Freda told them. "Get your props ready. As soon as I get this camera working, we're doing it."

In her assignment of the project, Freda had encouraged her students to make their plays as creative and entertaining as possible—as long as they were based on accurate historical information. So she didn't complain when one group's script included three references to the number of positions in the *Kama Sutra*, when another mixed in character names from *The Simpsons*, or when a third continually referred to Gandhi's loincloth as a diaper. Her main concern was that the students demonstrated a grasp of the material, which included not only facts but the larger issues as well—imperialism, nationalism, and nonviolent resistance as they related to India's struggle for independence.

"We only got 15 minutes left," protested Tommy, shaving at least 4 minutes off the clock's time. "We might as well just go tomorrow. We timed ours and it's longer than 15 minutes." Freda said nothing but the look on her face let Tommy know she wasn't buying it. "Seriously," he insisted. "We did."

Just then, the camera whirred to life. "OK," Freda said. "Let's go."

"Aw, Ms. Lin." May, Tommy, Judy, and the rest of the group moaned and groaned their way to their spots for the skit's opening scene. They tried to stall—fumbling with props, returning to their desks multiple times—but Freda called their bluff. "In your places, everybody. I'm recording in 10 seconds. Audience, don't forget to put comments on these assessment forms. And don't just put a plus or a minus—I want to know why you put it. Give the students you're watching some comments."

The kids scurried to their positions. A couple minutes later—10 seconds is rarely 10 seconds for teachers—the camera's red light flashed on.

> *Narrator:* Five students were given a project to do on India—
> the country that their teacher knew would screw them up.
> They all hesitated, but they had no choice, for their lives
> depended on the grade.
> *Kenny:* Gandhi was dope. He got a beat-down and took it like
> a man.
> *Tommy:* Damn, if I was him I would've stood up and busted a
> cap in them asses!

May: He said Gandhi took the beating like a man. I guess
you're not a man then.

The skit continued in this fashion—ironic and self-referential, a
project about a project, a postmodern mishmash of information,
humor, and opinion. Details about India's struggle against the
British were woven throughout, though not, I guessed, as expertly
as Freda would've liked. Still, she couldn't help but smile when,
with the play's closing line, the kids got in a dig at her expense.

Narrator: Tommy, May, Judy, Ben, and Kenny all presented
their project to their teacher. They didn't get an A but they
did pass. And they all learned never to take a history class
ever again.

·············

On our way to the faculty room for lunch, Freda handed me
a thick binder. The cover announced "Certificate Renewal
Manual" in bold letters. It was the guidebook for the state board
of education's new professional development program, which
required teachers to obtain a certain number of continuing education credits in order to keep their certification current. I'd
heard teachers complain about the program ever since it was
unveiled, and paging through the binder's six sections and ten
appendices with Freda, I began to see why they might be feeling
intimidated.

"I would like professional development," Freda said as we
went in, "but I don't like it forced down my throat. Did you see all
those forms in there? And I'm supposed to come up with a plan in
the next month to say how I'm going to accomplish all this? They
call this education reform?"

At one of the tables, a teacher with graying hair was reading
*The Five Love Languages: How to Express Heartfelt Commitment to
Your Mate.* A younger male teacher was sound asleep on a couch,
his head tipped back and his mouth hanging open. Freda took
three small Tupperware containers out of a cloth lunch bag and
put one in the microwave. Most other teachers were eating school-
issue lunchroom fare, but not Freda. "I'm very picky about my

food," she said. Every Sunday she spent a few hours cooking enough for the coming week and packing it into Tupperware.

We sat down at a table with Phil, a first-year English teacher, and Dave, a drafting teacher who'd been at Harding since the early 1970s. Freda had told me that she made a conscious effort to sit with different groups of teachers during her lunch period because "you always have these little pockets of people—the cliques." I looked around and noted the groupings: mostly white male teachers by the windows; older women of color at the table nearest the door; a younger, gender-mixed crowd on the couches in between. "I'd rather not be associated with any one group," Freda said. "Plus, I like hearing what different people have to say."

On this day, Dave was glad to oblige. As soon as Freda introduced us and told Dave what I was working on, he launched into a wide-ranging critique-cum-venting session about everything from budgeting to teacher accountability to school leadership. "Oh, I've seen this school change," he said. "It's all this accountability stuff—which basically means, 'If there's anything wrong, blame the teachers.' It's all on the backs of the teachers. Am I right?" Dave looked to Phil for confirmation. Phil nodded.

"Years ago, it was up to the teacher," Dave continued. "You made decisions. There was no structured curriculum, no CASE exam. But now . . . " He adjusted his oversized glasses frame. "I don't think this microscopic inspection—always leaning on us, always watching over our shoulders—is good for anybody. There's a lot of tension. Teachers are stressed. Relations among faculty are much worse now," he said, looking around the room. "*Much* worse."

I asked Dave what he thought could be done to improve the situation. "A lot of it comes down to leadership," he said. "People are afraid of the administration. We feel like we're being spied on—because we are!" He laughed. "We used to have a principal who had a lot of good ideas, and she did such a good job of convincing you they were good that you ended up thinking they were your ideas. That's real leadership. Now, it's more like, 'Do this or I'll kill you.' And then there's the money issue. They give us $1.50 a year per student to teach drafting. So either it comes out of your pocket or you do worksheets. Before, we had a bigger budget, and we charged a fee to students and went out and bought things.

Now we don't even have a storeroom to store the materials if we had them! I'm sounding a little angry, I know. But it's more a matter of survival now than trying to teach something."

Freda hadn't been around nearly as long as Dave, but 3 years of working under an administration that she described as bordering on dictatorial had already taken a toll. "Whatever the principal says, you have to do," she told me later. "If you in any way challenge his authority, he writes it in his mental list—or maybe he has a physical list, I don't know—and he remembers it, and there's the possibility it could turn into a little vendetta. I've seen that play out—my first year here, there were maybe six teachers that left because of pressure he put on. He would change their schedules around, make it uncomfortable for them—things like that."

A wide range of things bothered Freda about the principal's administrative style—his lack of communication with most classroom teachers and his Orwellian monitoring of the staff being two of the most egregious. But what made her most angry were the once-a-year formal evaluations she received. "I'm all for observation," she insisted. "I wish people observed me more and gave me some constructive feedback. But the way he does it is that he has a little checklist. He walks in the classroom whenever he feels like it—not necessarily at the beginning of the period—and the main thing he looks for is the attendance book, to make sure it's done well. He has his little calculator, and he starts punching in all the numbers to make sure that they're all tabulated. Then he goes through his checklist: Does she do this? Does she do that? Does my lesson at that minute coincide with my lesson plan? Do I have all my lesson plans written out on those sheets? Maybe a little bit about interaction with students. Check, check, check. And then whenever he feels like leaving, he just leaves."

Based on that single observation—maybe twenty minutes, maybe a half hour—and on her attendance record and her students' test-score averages, Freda would be evaluated for an entire year's work. "He doesn't talk to you about it," she said. "He just gives you the papers, lets you look at them, and then you have to sign the papers and immediately leave. No questions. I asked him one question once because I was marked down for 'needs improvement' in relating well to other faculty members. So I asked him a question about it, and he just gave me this very trite answer that didn't really answer my question. He kind of pushed me out the door—not literally, but with his words and the tone of voice."

The whole evaluation process was a big charade, Freda thought, perpetuated to create the illusion that the principal was abreast of what was going on in the school. But she knew differently. "How can you tell me how I teach or what type of teacher I am when you don't even know what goes on in my classroom?" she wondered aloud. "He stays in his office most of the time, and if he goes around the school, it's to make sure people have their hats off and their jackets off in the classroom. There's no positive interaction that I see. So who is he to tell every teacher in the school who they are? On one hand, I don't really care, but at the same time, it makes me very upset. The fact that a person like him is allowed to be a principal is just—I don't understand it. And there's no accountability at all. The Local School Council loves him. No one ever looks at the quality, they just look at the numbers. And that bothers me."

············

As soon as Freda stepped into her room after lunch, Isaac was in her face. "I'm proud of myself, Ms. Lin," he said, holding his History Fair display board in front of him. It was an eye-catching mix of text and photos on a blue background with a heading that read: IDA B. WELLS—A TRAILBLAZER FOR A NEW ERA. "You gotta grade this right now," Isaac gushed. "This is an A project. This is exemplimentary work." Clearly, it was an "on" day for Isaac.

"Wow," Freda said, admiring the board while resisting the urge to call attention to Isaac's invented vocabulary. "That looks great." Even more impressive was that he was finished a day early.

Isaac turned excitedly to Danielle, his foil in many antagonistic classroom exchanges. Just the day before, at the end of a heated back-and-forth, she'd called him an "ugly creature," and the week before it was "Daddy Longlegs." But this time, Isaac seemed to be genuinely seeking Danielle's approval: "This is my first project I ever did on a board like this."

"How come you ain't never do no project before?"

"'Cause I never had a chance."

"It look nice," Danielle said without fanfare.

Isaac set up his display board on a heater vent and I went over to check it out. When I asked him why he chose to research Ida B. Wells, he explained that her story was important but largely over-looked. "You don't usually hear that much about her in school," he told me. "You get some black history, but it's mostly Martin Luther King and Malcolm X and that's about it. Ida B. Wells was a strong woman, a powerful woman. She didn't stay in the corner and be quiet about things she thought was wrong. She was like, 'If you're gonna go for it, go big, or don't go at all.' She wanted equality—for black people, for women. It wasn't that she hated men, but she wanted to be equal with them."

Freda made her way to the blackboard where the day's agenda was listed. "Very impressive," she said to Isaac as she passed.

"Everybody know it look good, Ms. Lin. You don't gotta whisper."

After a brief review of the previous day's lesson, Freda hand-ed out a study guide she'd prepared on the U.S. annexation of Hawaii, then told the class to read it—along with the correspon-ding section from the textbook—and answer the questions that fol-lowed. She knew she was repeating one of the worst pedagogical clichés—"read the chapter and answer the questions at the end"—and it wasn't the way she normally preferred to teach. But it was eighth period, it had been an unusually draining day, and she was worn out. She had no energy left to lead a class discussion, espe-cially not with this lively bunch.

In previous conversations, she'd told me that—more so than her other classes—this group took the ball and ran with it. "We have really interesting discussions," she said. "One of them that I remember the most is when we were talking about the cold war and communism and Castro. I was talking about how the U.S. used to support Castro when he was first trying to overthrow the former dictator, because the former dictator only favored the upper class, and Castro was this revolutionary who had high ideals of equality and all that stuff. And then somehow once he came to power, he lost sight of it. And then, of course, once he embraced communism, that's when the U.S. completely wrote him off. So Leon said, 'What's up with the U.S. and communism? So what—if he's trying to change things for the better.' You know, they see the hypocrisy in things. They really pick up on the hypocrisy of the U.S. I don't even need to play devil's advocate with them—or I play it in a different way."

Grumbling rose up from around the room about the silent reading assignment. "I don't know how to read, Ms. Lin. I'm illiterate," Danielle joked. Freda tried to ignore the protests, but doing so went against her democratic impulses. After a few minutes, she caved.

"OK, there are some proposals from people in the class who would rather read this together than on their own," Freda said. "So let's take a vote. Who wants to read individually? How about together?" All but two of the students voted to read as a group. Freda took a deep breath, called on someone to begin, and dug down to find 30 more minutes worth of fuel.

"In 1886," Mayra read from the handout, "American business people, planters, and traders in Hawaii formed the secret Hawaiian League. Its sole purpose was to overthrow the monarchy of Hawaii and persuade the U.S. to annex Hawaii. League members wanted to get rid of the ruler of Hawaii so that the U.S. could control Hawaii instead."

Danielle looked up from the reading with a snarl. "Wasn't there any other countries tryin' to take nothin' over? 'Cause I'm about sick of hearin' about the U.S."

"The U.S. always takin' somethin' from somebody," Leon said. "I'mo kick the U.S.'s ass."

Another student picked up the reading, which summarized the Hawaiian League's strong-arm tactics to force Hawaiian King Kalakaua to sign a new constitution—one that restricted the monarch's role to figurehead status and limited native Hawaiians' rights to hold office in their own country.

"They told that king, 'Sign it or die,' right?" asked Leon, who had his white headband pulled down around his neck.

"I don't know if it was that harsh," Freda said.

"Yeah, it was. You know the U.S. You know how they is. They ain't gonna tell it like that in the book, but that's how it was."

"What were the Hawaiians thinking about all this?" someone asked.

"That's a good question," Freda said. "What would you have been thinking if you were a Hawaiian?"

"I'da been thinking it was dumb," Isaac responded. "How they ain't gonna be able to hold office in they own country?"

"Yeah," added Danielle. "What's the sense of them being the king or queen if they ain't gonna be ruling over nothin'?"

The reading moved on to Queen Liliuokalani's fight to regain rights and power for native Hawaiians, and the United States' eventual takeover of the country in 1898. With 10 minutes left in the period, Freda got inspired. Instead of having the kids do the chapter questions as she'd planned, she decided to do an alternative assessment. She asked the students to make a drawing or sketch that showed what they'd learned from the reading and discussion.

"Huh?" Leon looked at Freda as if she'd asked him to turn himself inside out. "How we 'posed to draw the U.S. taking over?"

"This ain't art class, Ms. Lin," added Danielle. "Why you got us drawing?"

"Because it helps you connect things," Freda said in a line straight out of a progressive teaching manual.

Leon's eyes darted up from the sketch he'd just started. "Well, somebody need to show me how to connect these lines, 'cause my stick people look like they on drugs."

•••••••••••

A week later, Freda's posted agenda in her Asian studies class listed only a single item: "Put together textbook." Her students had been working in small groups to create self-designed "textbooks" about one of the Southeast Asian countries they'd studied. The projects were due by the end of the period, but few of the groups looked ready. As they went about their business, Freda was bombarded from all sides by questions and requests.

"Ms. Lin, where's the scissors?"

"Is this good for a political cartoon?"

"What's *criteria* mean?"

"You got a highlighter, Ms. Lin?"

"Can we put aliens in our textbook?"

Freda developed this textbook-creation assignment both as an alternative means of assessing what her students had learned and as an implicit critique of textbooks themselves. She'd pointed out to her students that no Asian studies textbooks for high school students even existed—or if they did, she hadn't found them. As they crafted their own minitextbooks, she wanted them to think beyond the way textbooks were to the way they could or should be. But that was proving easier said than done.

"Where's your section seven?" Freda asked Kenny's group.

"Oh, we didn't really understand what to do for that part— 'Section of Your Choice'?" he said quizzically, reading from the assignment sheet.

"It's a section you think should be in textbooks but isn't."

Kenny looked at Freda blankly. "I still don't get it."

Freda went to retrieve a battered copy of *Rise of the American Nation* from a shelf. "Look," she said, placing the book on a desk in the middle of the group and flipping through its pages. "This book has charts, summaries, key events, timelines, factual information. But what does it not have? What's getting left out here? Is there more to history than just this?"

Across the room, Joshua, one of only two white kids in the class, sat with his group, but his shaved head was resting on his desk, the hood of a yellow sweatshirt almost covering it.

"Joshua, why don't you help?" asked Lilly, the group's demanding leader. She was looking through a stack of photocopied articles that she'd downloaded at home the night before.

"'Cause I don't feel like doing any work," said Joshua, lifting his head to reveal a face and neck full of red blotches.

"What are you doing in school then?"

"Breathing," Joshua said.

"You think you're gonna get graded for breathing?"

"I hope so."

When I asked Freda about Joshua, she informed me that he spent most of his day in a self-contained special education class. But her frustration with him was evident. "I don't want to say I've given up on trying to get him to do anything," she told me, "but I'm close. I'll say, 'When are you going to start working?' And he'll say, 'Tomorrow, tomorrow.' I tried other things at the beginning of the year, but nothing's really been effective. I'm kind of at the end of my rope with him." She paused for a few seconds and then her voice softened. "It's hard," she said. "I know he probably needs more attention, but I can't just sit with him the whole period. What about everybody else?"

••••••••••••

It was lunchtime, but we were on our way to the main office so Freda could pick up her absence bulletin, a document issued by the school's attendance office each day around noon. It was a double-sided sheet with three columns of student names on each side and, at the bottom, a list of the divisions with perfect attendance for the day. Freda retrieved today's edition—along with a stack of announcements, flyers, forms, and catalogues—from her mailbox and gave it a once-over. Two hundred and twenty-eight of the school's 1600 students were absent, and of the 66 divisions at Harding, only four had perfect attendance. "Wow, four out of 66," Freda said. "Great job." Then, as we continued on to the teachers' lounge, she added, "You'll notice that I'm very sarcastic."

"More than you used to be?" I asked.

"I didn't have enough energy to be sarcastic my first year. I was too stressed out."

Freda would spend her lunch period today working on the monthly attendance summary for her division—counting up and totaling tardies, cuts, and absences for each of her 16 students. The summary form was due in the main office by day's end, and Freda knew she'd have no time to work on it after lunch: She still had to teach another U.S. history class and then lead a student council meeting after school. So it was now or never. "I have to get some food first, though," Freda told me as we climbed the stairs. "I'm dying. I've been dying since I got here this morning."

The hallways were humming with activity. I overheard a security guard explaining to a teacher that he was searching students' bags because a book had come up missing from another teacher's classroom. "Well, it wasn't the students," the teacher said, and I was relieved to hear an adult advocating for the kids. Then she continued: "They don't steal books. They don't read."

Freda and I squeezed through the throngs on our way to the faculty room. "We're supposed to help get these kids to class," she told me. "That's part of our responsibility. But I just don't have the energy. I think I'd have a nervous breakdown every day if I tried to do that." But just then, we approached a kid in a white puffy coat who craned his neck to view a girl who'd just walked by. "Baby! Got! Back!" he said with more enthusiasm than three exclamation points can effectively convey.

"That's not a very respectful way to talk," Freda told him. The boy shrugged and moved along.

I asked if sexual harassment by male students was common. "Yeah, the girls tell me about it," she said. "And I call students on it a lot. I definitely stop the behavior. I tell them, 'Don't touch that girl the way you just did. If she says no, that means no.' And typically the guy will say, 'Oh, she didn't really mean it.' So yeah, there's definitely that issue." Later, I learned that the topic hit closer to home with Freda than she'd initially let on. Protecting her female students from groping and verbal harassment inside school was only part of the story. She'd had battles of her own to fight.

"There were three men I had incidents with," she told me. "Three male teachers. One guy kind of hugged me from behind, and that was really uncomfortable. I told him so right when he did it. I said, 'Hey, I don't like this. What are you doing?' And he was cool with that. Another guy, he was always friendly and everything, and he wasn't really flirty, but basically what he did to me was—he tickled me. Right at the copy machine, right in front of other teachers. Not that everyone was watching, but I just felt like he was treating me like a little girl. I told him, 'Don't do that, please,' and it was really awkward, because I was just so shocked. I was thinking, 'Do men not know how to interact with women? What's their problem?'"

While the first two men had stopped once Freda told them they'd made her uncomfortable, the third teacher—I'll call him Carl—didn't get the message so easily. "He's in his 40s, he's never been married, and he's like a gigolo type," she told me. "I've seen him touch other women—the back of their neck, lower back area, shoulder—everything, you know? And they have no problem with it, obviously. I don't know why, but they don't. They just say, 'That's the way he is, there's nothing you can do about it.' But I'm not like that. It's not like I can't be touched or anything—but I think there's a line."

The first time Carl crossed the line with Freda, he'd touched his hand to her head. As she'd done in the other instances, she immediately told him it was inappropriate, and asked him not to do it again. For awhile, he complied and everything seemed fine—so much so that Freda agreed to play tennis with him a couple times. "I guess he thought that gave him the green light to do whatever he wanted," she told me, "because he started touching me again. One morning he came up to me while I was signing in and he kinda grabbed me on the elbow. And it was very uncomfortable. I just don't like the way he does it. It's just so slimy." Freda didn't say anything to Carl at the time because she thought she'd already made herself clear on the issue, and she didn't think she should have to tell him again. Her strategy became one of avoidance, of dodging any possible contact with Carl. But that only worked for so long.

"One day I was at my locker," Freda remembered. "I was squatting down, getting my stuff out, and he was walking by with a student. And he brushed his hand across the top of my head. And I just made this very violent movement—just made it very obvious that I didn't like it. I was like, 'What the hell?' you know? I saw him down in the office right after that and I confronted him right there. I said, 'You know how I feel about this issue. Why are you still touching me? What is your problem?' And he says, 'Well, you know, I can't help it.' So I said, 'Well, I have certain borders, and I have certain limits, so please respect them.' And that was it." Until the next day. That's when Freda filed a letter of complaint with the principal.

She hadn't really intended the letter to go any further than that, but the principal—always concerned with doing things by the book—immediately turned it over to board of education officials. Before Freda knew it, she was telling the entire story to a sexual harassment officer. A few days later, Carl also got called in for questioning, but the board ultimately decided that there wasn't enough evidence to discipline him. "They said it didn't rise to the level of 'egregious behavior'—that was the quote," Freda said. "At first I was mad, because at that point, since I was going through the process, I wanted him to be found guilty and I wanted him to get in trouble. I mean, some people might consider the things he did to be subtle things, but the fact that I said no and he didn't comply makes it sexual harassment to me. I mean, that's the law. That's what it says."

Carl was given a warning by the board and told not to have any further contact with Freda. It was a small victory, she thought, but it didn't give her the sort of closure she'd hoped to achieve. "Ultimately I'm glad I did it," she told me, "but I just wish there had been someone in authority who could've sat in between the two of us to kinda talk it out. I'm all for communication, and there was no communication whatsoever. There was no apology from him, and I don't know if he even feels any remorse. I know I can't change people's behaviors overnight, but I feel like he needs to know why I reported him, and he needs to respect that. I would've liked to hear that from him. And I never got to hear it."

I'd heard stories of sexual harassment by male coworkers from other teacher friends, but I didn't know any who'd followed through on reporting it to the extent Freda had. One woman told me that, during her student-teaching experience, the principal of the school where she was working had touched her several times in ways that made her uncomfortable. But she was too intimidated to say anything at the time: She doubted herself, thought she must have been making too much of it, wondered if anyone would believe her.

As a man, I'd never had to deal with anything like that. Just as I didn't have to worry about my competence being called into question because of my race, sexual harassment had never been so much as a blip on my radar screen. In fact, being a man had seemed to work in my favor from the moment I decided to become a teacher. At just about every school at which I interviewed, I was given the red-carpet treatment, and what seemed to impress the hiring squads most was not any qualification or credential I had— at the time, I had few—but the fact that I was male. One might think that in elementary schools—one of the few professional places of employment where women far outnumber men— "unearned male advantage," as Peggy McIntosh (2001) calls it, would be somewhat nullified. If anything, though, it seemed more exaggerated. On the basis of my experience, I concluded that a man needed to demonstrate little more than the ability to breathe to be considered a prime classroom recruit.

············

Considering that they had been salvaged from another school's garbage heap, the textbooks Freda used with her U.S. history classes were in pretty good shape. Two years earlier, Betty Linder, the chairperson of Harding's history department, had heard that a neighboring high school was getting rid of some of its outdated texts. Strapped for funds and in desperate need of books for her teachers, Linder made a trip to the school one afternoon and loaded her car with close to 200 copies of *Rise of the American Nation.*

To say that one school's trash is another school's treasure would be overstating the case. The text was clearly outdated—the copyright was 1982—and from my cursory examination, it looked to be beset with many of the weaknesses common to U.S. history books: It was transparently pro-American, dryly written, and favored breadth of coverage over depth of analysis. Still, Freda appreciated having the books. "With my Asian studies class, it's hard because I don't have a textbook to give me ideas. I have to come up with everything," she said. "With U.S. history it's so much easier because at least I have a starting point. I see the textbook as a reference, as one resource. You don't read the whole thing cover to cover. You pull out things and analyze them—is there some type of central question in there, like 'What is power?' or 'What is leadership?' or 'What can we learn from history to help us do something different today?'"

As eighth-period began, Freda was asking herself that last question. The day before, the class had been up for grabs, and now she was wondering how she'd get the group back on track. The climax of events the previous day, Freda told me, had been her verbal skirmish with Isaac, who she said had pushed the limits of disrespect one too many times. "I kept saying, 'Isaac, watch the line. You're crossing the line,'" she remembered. "And he was like, 'Da-di-da-di-da.' He always has to have the last word in, and yesterday that just got to me. I gave him two detentions because I felt I was being too soft and lax with people. That's an issue I've come up against a lot. Sometimes I feel like I'm too strict, and then sometimes I feel like I'm not strict enough."

Freda ended up kicking Isaac out of class and sending him to the office—something she rarely did with any student—and meeting with him, his grandmother, and the school's disciplinarian later in the afternoon. Isaac apologized for his actions in class, but said he thought Freda had escalated the situation. "You didn't have to yell," Isaac told her. "I don't like it when people yell at me." Freda explained that the only reason she'd raised her voice was because Isaac had refused to listen when she'd tried to reason with him.

Earlier, Freda had told me she wasn't even sure Isaac would show up today—she thought he might be serving some sort of in-school suspension. But just before the bell rang, he walked in, crossed the room, and spread his long legs and wide body in his usual seat.

"Did you grade our tests yet, Ms. Lin?" two girls asked in unison.

"No, not yet. Sorry," Freda said. I looked over at her desk, hoping for her sake that the ever-present stacks of ungraded papers had somehow magically disappeared. They hadn't.

"So who killed this archduke?" Freda asked, flipping a page in her notes and pulling down a retractable chalkboard. "Where were they from?" On the board, Freda had written CAUSES OF WORLD WAR I.

Next to me, a kid leaned forward and whispered to a fellow student, "Yo, you was here yesterday?"

"Nah. You?"

"Nah." That was the last I heard out of either of them for the rest of the period.

"They were from Serbia," someone called out.

"They were Serbian Nationalists."

"I got a paper cut," said Danielle, looking at her finger. During earlier visits, I'd observed that Danielle said aloud pretty much anything that came to her mind. Often her comments were on-point and perceptive. Other times, they were stream-of-consciousness and completely unrelated to what was being discussed.

"And what's a nationalist?" Freda asked.

"A person just out for their country no matter what. They feel like their country's the best." The words came from Isaac. He was participating. A good sign.

"And besides nationalism, we talked about how a lot of these European countries were also imperialists," Freda said. "They were competing with each other for land, right? Kind of like gangs do. They fight, and then they mark their territory."

"It ain't all about territory with gangs," observed Danielle. "It's about rocks."

A skinny white kid on the back row raised his hand. "Ms. Lin, I got a question. How come it doesn't have the names of the guys who killed the archduke?"

"Probably because it's a U.S. history book," answered Freda. "Did you learn about this over there?" The kid nodded his head. I later learned that his name was Alexis and that he'd grown up in Serbia. "Yeah, I know this is taught much differently over there," Freda added. "They go into much more detail about the assassination."

"Then I'm goin' to Serbia," said Danielle, "so I can get me some real U.S. history."

"They had a right to kill that guy!" Alexis announced to the group, making no pretense of hiding his passion. "He came onto their land. That's trespassing! He was trying to take over and they didn't like it."

"See, all these people, when they don't like something, they start a war," said Danielle. "So why didn't black people go to war with the plantation owners?"

"That's a good question," Freda said. "Why do you think?"

"They was scared."

"They were poor," someone else added.

"It's the same thing with Puerto Rico," said Sandra, whose family was from the island. "They've been talkin' about independence for so long—why don't they rebel? 'Cause they're stupid, that's why. They don't know what they want."

"Well, it's complicated," Freda said. "Rebelling against powerful people isn't easy." She continued reviewing the early stages of the war with the class, and eventually they got to the British naval blockade of Germany.

"So the Germans were the first ones to invent the submarine?" asked Isaac.

"Yes," Freda said.

"But Germans aren't that smart." Isaac grinned, knowing the comment would provoke a reaction from his teacher.

"Isaac, do we need to review what we talked about yesterday?" I could feel the class get tense. Most of them had witnessed yesterday's showdown.

"Nah, I can say that—I'm part German."

"But that statement is—"

"I know. Prejudiced."

"And anytime you say that everybody in a certain group is one way—"

"It's a stereotype. I know, Ms. Lin. I was just kidding anyway. But I *am* part German."

"Part German Shepherd," said a boy a few seats away.

The class blew up. Everybody was laughing. I looked to Isaac, waiting to see what his response would be. "OK," Isaac said. "You gonna play like that? Just wait." But as he turned back to Freda, he was chuckling, too. "Ms. Lin, I got another question. How Hitler gonna try to lead Germany when he not even German?"

"People adopt identities," Freda answered. "Look at Eminem."

Isaac snickered. "Black people don't even like Eminem."

"He just got some rhythm, that's all," added Danielle. "He still white, Ms. Lin."

············

I was a few minutes late arriving for the Asian American assembly, which Freda was coordinating for the third straight year, so I tried to slip in a rear door as quietly as possible. I got about two steps down the aisle when a man in a pea-green suit stopped me and asked why I was there. When I told him I was visiting Ms. Lin, he reluctantly let me pass. "But put your visitor badge on so we don't call the police on you," he said. Appreciative of the warm welcome, I took a seat next to two lunchroom workers who had come in to watch the show. I was only mildly surprised when I realized later that the man in the pea-green suit was Harding's principal.

I spotted Freda near the front of the auditorium, conferring with the student emcee. She looked frazzled. A few days before, she'd told me that planning the assembly always raised her stress level a few notches, and that this year it had manifested itself in nightly bouts with insomnia. Still, it was an extra responsibility

Freda willingly shouldered. "The thing I really enjoy about it every year is that the students are excited to show their dances. They really want to do it," she told me. "I think it's great for the other students to see how proud these kids are of their cultures, because there are definitely a lot of stereotypes at Harding, a lot of assuming different things about people. Students will laugh at Asian names, or stuff like that, because they really don't know anything about them."

Watching the first few performances, I suddenly felt the spotlight shining on my own ignorance of things Asian. The printed programs had all been handed out by the time I arrived, so as each act took the stage, I was left to my own devices to try to figure out what country or culture was being represented. A group wearing what I thought was traditional Indian dress danced to music that I also identified as Indian. But as soon as I'd made that determination, I wondered why. What made it "Indian" to me? It could've just as easily been from Pakistan or Bangladesh or somewhere else entirely. Wherever it was from, a black teacher behind me was out of her seat and grooving to the rhythm, doing her best to follow the dancers' moves. The bass was heavy, and the woofers rattled as if they might blow any second. It was as if we were all crowded into the back seat of a low rider made for 500 people.

"I think it helps to dispel the stereotypes a bit," Freda told me during our conversation about the annual show. "At least it gives other students and teachers exposure, gives them a different perspective. But it never seems to be enough. This year I wanted to have poetry and skits in the assembly, too, to address some of the stereotyping issues directly. But I never followed through. It's just . . . I don't know. I just haven't planned everything out as much as I should have."

If that was true, you'd have never known it by the audience's reactions. Screams, squeals, and loud applause followed each performance, and when the bell rang to end the assembly, I heard favorable reviews from those around me. Two corn-rowed black girls fought against the flow of the crowd to hug a Filipino friend who'd danced. "It was great!" one of them said. "We were cheering you on from the back row." An older woman I'd never met turned to me on her way out. "Seeing things like this," she told me, "is one of the fringe benefits of being a teacher."

While I waited for Freda, I struck up a conversation with Mateo, one of her Asian studies students from the previous year. I asked about his experiences at Harding. "There are some good teachers," he said. "Some of the younger teachers seem like they want to resolve problems more than ignore them. But then some of the teachers—it's like 'zero tolerance' in their classes. They come down really hard on kids, so then the kids get really demoralized and don't want to do the work and they end up failing. And then they get so frustrated at failing classes that they drop out. It's a cycle I've seen throughout my high school career. It's really negative."

Mateo, who described himself as "Filipino in every way," wore a necklace pendant that featured an outline of his homeland wrapped in barbed wire. "The barbed wire is supposed to symbolize the struggle of the people there," he said. "Seventy-five percent of the people in the Philippines are below the poverty line." He told me he thought Freda's efforts to raise awareness about Asian cultures and issues at the school were important. "There's a lot of racism against Asians here," he said. "One time I was failing a class and this teacher asked me, 'What kind of Asian are you?' Another time I was walking to the lunchroom and this guy says, 'Look at that Chinese. Ching-chong-ching-chong, Bruce Lee.' The thing was that this guy was Latino—a person who's also oppressed because of his color—and he's coming at me. That's messed up. But it's an experience that's shared by lots of Asians."

Having the Asian studies class at Harding, Mateo told me, was one way to combat such ignorance. "Even a lot of the colleges in Chicago don't have an Asian studies program," he said. "So to have something like that at the high school level is really important. It's a great opportunity to make people more aware." The ultimate goal, said Mateo, was for more Asian youth to become politicized: "We need to start standing up for ourselves as Asians. Our culture sometimes tells us just to keep quiet about things. But we need to speak out."

Mateo and I made our way to the front of the auditorium, where Freda looked more relieved than satisfied. "I was having a heart attack up here," she told me, her face still damp with perspiration. "Everybody was telling me to calm down." Around her, a group of students was gathered—hugging, laughing, congratulating one another. Onstage, a kid beat out a rhythm on a wooden drum, and two girls improvised dance steps. For this moment at least, the tide seemed to be receding, Freda's head bobbing just above the waterline.

············

"I don't know how I'd label myself as a teacher," Freda said when I asked her to define her work. "Ever since college, I'm very wary of labels, or of calling people certain things. I think I'm trying to change things, and I think you could say that I'm an activist teacher in that I'm trying to put things out there for my students, so that hopefully they can take that and do something good in the world. I want my students to be able to identify social injustices— whether it be racist, sexist, classist, or just plain unfair—and to care about changing them and hopefully to try to make a difference."

For Freda, teaching for social justice wasn't something she explicitly mapped out in all of her lesson plans. Rather, it was a natural extension of who she was and what she believed as a person. "I believe that people should be treating each other in certain more compassionate and fair ways," she explained, "and that there shouldn't be so much inequality in the world. I think people need to be more caring and try to change things rather than accept the status quo and be passive. And I think that because I'm that type of person, those things have to come out in my teaching. They come out when I talk with my students, in the way I interact with them, in my lesson plans, in the discussions that we have, in the material that I focus on—in all kinds of ways. It's part of who I am."

The bell rang to start class, and a girl who'd barely beat it shuffled across the room and sat down next to me. She placed her red-stained fingertips into her mouth one by one, sucking away the residue of the Flamin' Hot Cheetos she'd just finished off as a mid-morning snack.

"Can we learn from history?" Freda asked, holding a legal pad in one hand. "And if so, how?"

"Yes and no," Linda said. "Some things we learn, but some things we don't. Like racism. People are still racist. It's still there. We haven't really learned."

"Yeah, like Ms. Lin," Victor added. "You're a racist. You don't pass us 'cause we're dark-skinned." Seeing his grin, Freda let the comment pass.

"Nah, but some people think like that," Linda said, trying to steer the conversation back in a serious direction. "People think Mexicans are alcoholics 'cause we go to soccer games and people drink beer."

"That's true." The words came from Jerrell, whose tightly braided hair and neatly pressed plaid shirt and jeans made him look as if he'd just been unwrapped. He was the only black kid in this class. "If you ask other African American people, they just think Mexicans eat burritos and ride around in trucks full of oranges."

"You're being racist, bro," Diego said, crouched forward in his seat. His thick laces were untied and his ankle-length shorts defied their name.

Jerrell looked surprised by the comment. "C'mon, little man, I'm not trying to be racist," he said. Freda intervened, explaining that Jerrell was merely acknowledging that such stereotypes exist, not saying that he believed them. "Yeah, I'm just trying to express myself," Jerrell said. "I'm saying that some black people *who are only around other black people* think that all Mexicans like bullfighting or something. It's ignorant stuff. If one Mexican does something, they think that every single Mexican is like that."

"But why do people think that?" Freda asked.

"They just do," said Linda, swinging her long ponytail over her shoulder. "You can't change the way people think."

As much as Freda hated to hear cynicism like that, she couldn't deny occasionally feeling it herself. She'd chosen a life in the classroom with the notion of "making the world better through teaching," but now she sometimes wondered how much of an impact she was really having. "I mean, I know it makes some difference," she said, "but I know there are more direct things that could be done to help immediate situations. I feel like teaching can be kind of hit or miss. Maybe you'll get somebody who will connect with something and then actually do something about it later on. But with most of the students I teach, I don't know if that's going to happen. Maybe I'm being too hard on myself, but I don't know if I'm being that effective in turning them all into social activists by the time they leave high school."

Still, she tried not to let the doubts overtake her. Maybe she'd allowed herself to become more pessimistic on the surface, but deep down, she still held on to her belief in the possibility of teaching for change. "So are you saying that we can't create a less racist society through education?" she asked the class. "It's not possible?"

The kids were quiet. "There's still gonna be problems," Linda said finally.

"You guys are pretty cynical today," Freda observed as she crossed the room.

"It's not our fault," Diego said. "History is racist."

"Yeah, it doesn't really help us," added Angel.

"But can't we learn from the bad things that have happened so that they won't happen again?"

Silence. Then more silence. "Maybe," someone finally said. The discussion continued until the next bell, but Freda moved the class no closer to outwardly acknowledging that they could indeed be agents of change, that creating a better world was possible. An unenthusiastic *maybe* was all she got. For Freda Lin, on this day, that would be enough.

Photo: Kevin Horan

5

toni billingsley

Early on a slightly overcast morning on Chicago's west side, in the basement of a 97-year-old school building, it was already showtime for Toni Billingsley. Around her, 19 seventh graders who'd only rolled out of bed an hour or so before were crawling on all fours, following her command to meow like lost cats. Toni chuckled. "OK, on the count of three, you will no longer be hypnotized," she told them. *"Uno! Dos! Tres!"* This was Spanish I, Toni Billingsley-style: part introduction to the language, part aerobics workout, part improvisation workshop, and part standup comedy routine.

"Señor Jones, levantate!" she called out a few minutes later. A thick kid with a gray hoodie and plaited hair stood up. *"Salta y tira la pelota como Miguel Jordan,"* Toni told him. I used my decaying Spanish to translate the sentence in my head: Jump and shoot the ball like Michael Jordan. Señor Jones reluctantly raised one arm in the air and stretched the other out behind him in a halfhearted approximation of Jordan's celebrated dunking pose. *"No es como Miguel Jordan,"* commented Toni, who then took a flying leap across the room and slammed an imaginary basketball through an imaginary hoop. "Eso *es como Miguel Jordan.*"

Without missing a beat, Toni turned her attention to another student. "Señor Hill," she called out, and a boy with a short Afro and reddish skin tone sat up a little straighter. Toni went to him and held out a pen in one hand and a pencil in the other. *"Toma la pluma,"* she commanded, and Señor Hill, after a momentary hesitation, took the pen from her. *"Ahora, toma el lápiz."* He took the pencil. *"OK—la pluma besa el lápiz."*

119

"What you say?" asked Señor Hill.

Poker-faced, Toni said it again, enunciating each word distinctly. Señor Hill, whose name I later learned was Derrick, screwed up his face. He looked around at his classmates, seemingly to confirm whether or not he'd heard his teacher correctly. They were all smiles. "*La pluma besa el lápiz*," Toni repeated again.

Derrick quickly touched the pen to the pencil and made a soft smacking sound with his lips.

"No, no, no," Toni said. "*Un beso muy sexy.*"

Derrick shook his head in disbelief, then again pantomimed the pen kissing the pencil—this time with a louder smooch of his own to accompany it.

"*Muchas gracias, Señor Hill*," Toni said, then turned to the class. "And that's the only sex scene you'll ever see here in *la clase de español.*"

Clever puns, corny one-liners, sly references to black popular culture, outright slapstick—they were all part of the program for Toni. While fun may be overrated as a condition for children's learning, in Toni's classroom it was an indispensable ingredient. "I think the learning experience has to be fun for both the teacher and the student," she told me. "If I'm bored, I'm not going to be teaching my best. If the students are bored, I'll get frustrated, and I won't be teaching my best then, either. So if I see the class is going the wrong way, I'll crack a joke or something. They get most of them, but sometimes you hear the crickets in the background, and then you cough into the microphone." She laughed. "Most of the time, we have fun."

Toni next led the class through a physically exhausting and deliberately bizarre Simon Says routine that incorporated past vocabulary words ("Stand up! Sit down! Run in a circle! Kiss your hand! Scream like a crazy person!"), then told a simple story in Spanish about a boy eating a meal of catfish with hot sauce. After several students retold the story in English, she passed out a napkin, a plastic fork, and several gummi fish to each student, and together they reenacted the tale. Later, the class played Bingo with the new words they'd learned. "Whoever gets five words first will be the winner," Toni told them. "But remember," she added with a cheesy smile, "all of you are winners in the game of life."

The entire class period was a blur of activity, Toni a whirling dervish at the center of it all. "I'm the star," she told the class at one point. "Look at me." She was kidding, but the truth was that it was hard not to focus on her. She was all over the place: pacing back and forth, jumping around, leading exercises, gesturing, teasing, making faces and sound effects, her voice rising and falling. The only thing that amazed me more than her stamina was the realization that, as soon as these kids left, another group would come in, and it would be showtime all over again.

....

Watching Toni the performer, I saw how easy it was to get lost in the laugh-a-minute razzle-dazzle of that small, albeit gripping, part of her persona. But there was far more to Toni—both as a teacher and as a human being—than just that. Her days typically began at 6:00 a.m., when she'd get dressed, gather together everything she needed for school, and then wake up Corey, her 2-year-old daughter, to get her changed and fed. At around 6:30, she'd walk Corey down the block to her aunt's house for babysitting, then set out on a 35-minute car trip—north on Lake Shore Drive, west on the Eisenhower Expressway, and then another mile or so past the fast-food joints, storefront churches, and resilient graystones of West Garfield Park— to the Technology and Communication Arts Charter School, better known as TCA.

Before class began at 8:00, Toni would make copies, organize her lessons, squeeze in a bowl of cereal from the school cafeteria, and, if time permitted, sneak upstairs for a quick chat with her friend Lamayra Dixon, who taught sixth-grade language arts. In addition to her first-period Spanish class, she'd have a 50-minute reading class, another 90-minute block of Spanish, a 40-minute working lunch, a half hour of recess duty, a 90-minute planning period, and an hourlong student advisory—with informal student counseling sessions crammed into any spaces in between. School would end at 3:30, but Toni would usually linger an hour or so later to tutor students, give kids extra computer time, or sell candy to raise funds for a planned student trip to Mexico. She'd battle the traffic back home, pick up Corey at around 6:00, try to spend some quality time with her, rest a little, and then begin getting her head together for the next day. She'd give Corey a bath at 8:00 and put her to bed about an hour later. Her own bath would come at 9:30, and sleep wouldn't be too far behind.

"Being a teacher and the single parent of a toddler—it's rough," Toni told me. "I'm sure it'll get easier, but right now it's rough." Toni was thankful that Corey's father was a presence in the girl's life—he took care of her one night a week and every other weekend—but there were still times when she felt isolated. "You're with kids all day, and then you go home to a baby, so you don't have much adult interaction," she said. "At times, I've felt like I was going crazy. It's tiring and it's draining. And I was 25 when I had Corey, so I can just imagine what some of these young girls are going through."

Raised for several years on the same south side block where she and her daughter were living, Toni attended Chicago public schools from kindergarten through 12th grade. As a young girl, she'd been labeled "the smart one" by family members—her older sister was "the pretty one"—and she came to view her time in the classroom as a respite from some of the hardships she faced outside it. "When I was a kid, my biggest struggle was my home life," she told me. "It wasn't school. I had no problem with school. Clothing, bus fare—those were my main issues." During Toni's formative years, her mother spent 3½ years in jail and continually battled drug addictions after being released. Her father, too, was an addict. Neither parent was a consistent presence in Toni's young life. "On and off, I saw them," she said, "but I pretty much raised myself. My mom would come in and out of my life, and I would move around a lot, here and there."

Eventually, Toni found a semipermanent home with her grandfather, a man who became a constant source of strength and support. He reinforced for Toni the importance of education, and taught even more important lessons, she told me, by the way he lived his life. "See, he was not my mother's biological father," she said. "But he treated her as his own child. And *never* did I feel that he wasn't my grandfather. He didn't treat his biological grandchildren any different than he treated me. So for a long time, I didn't know that he was not my mom's biological father. I learned from him a spirit of caring and giving and kindness, regardless of whether you're family or not. You treat people kindly. You do good unto people. And good will come unto you."

Toni knew that it wasn't always that simple. She understood that societal and institutional forces continued to conspire to limit the life chances of too many black people—no matter how kind or good they might be toward others. She'd seen it happen to her own friends, her own family, the kids she taught. But there was still some truth, she believed, in her grandfather's message, and her own twist on it provided a mantra she frequently repeated: "My main thing is, if you live your life without harming other people, then you're OK. As long as you don't hurt anybody else, do your thing, y'know?"

·············

Through the windows of Toni's basement classroom, I could see the bottom portion of several iron scaffolding frames and the dirtied boots of two construction workers walking past. The ceiling of TCA's aging building, which for decades had housed a parochial grammar school, had sprung a leak, and further examination had revealed that the entire roof needed to be replaced. Since charter schools were responsible for raising their own capital funds, TCA hadn't been able to appeal to the central office for financial assistance. Instead, the school's leaders had been forced to scramble to find money in a budget that was already tighter than tight.

Inside, students were revising assignments for inclusion in their COW, or collection of work, a portfolio by which all TCA students were assessed at the end of each year. Toni sat with Shalisa, a chubby girl in a camouflage shirt, talking over an essay she had written.

"They was unhappy with the way things was going," Shalisa said. A butterfly-shaped hair clamp was clipped to the collar of her shirt.

"What things?" asked Toni.

"Like the way the system was."

"What system?"

"The caste system." Toni's Spanish II class had been studying New Spain, the name used between the 16th and 19th century for what is now Mexico, comparing and contrasting the race-based caste system there with the racial and economic stratification in contemporary U.S. society.

"And why did that make them unhappy?"

"'Cause they wasn't being treated right. The darker you was, the worse off you was. The Indians, they got it bad. And the blacks got it worst—just like now."

Trying to help her students see their own worlds with new eyes—and simultaneously look out on worlds previously unknown to them—were big parts of what Toni considered good teaching. She implicitly embraced the metaphor of curriculum as window and mirror put forward by Peggy McIntosh and Emily Style (1999). In her Spanish classes, kids examined the devastating impact of AIDS in Latin America as well as in their school's community. In her reading class, students read letters to President Bush written by teenagers in other parts of the country, then crafted their own messages to the President that highlighted the most pressing issues in their neighborhoods.

Helping her students make connections, Toni believed, was a vital part of her work as a teacher. After all, she'd seen firsthand how powerful such learning can be. As a young girl, she'd grown up breathing in the homophobic air that swirled around her: An aunt who helped care for her insisted that gay men and lesbians were hell-bound sinners, and most of her family and friends thought the same. Television and movies amplified the message—minus the religious fervor—and by the time Toni went off to college, she thought her mind was made up on the issue.

When one of her college professors offered extra credit to those who attended a meeting of the Gay and Lesbian Alliance on campus, Toni balked. "At first," she remembered, "I was like, 'I'm not going to that meeting because somebody's going to see me coming out of there and they're going to think I'm gay.' But I ended up going, and at the time they were talking about whether gays should be allowed in the military. And as I listened, I realized that a lot of the reasons people wanted to keep homosexuals out of the military were the same reasons they used to keep African Americans out of the military—and they're completely unfounded! So I made a connection. And just by making that connection of me and them being discriminated against for some of the same shit, something just clicked and I was like, 'That's not right.'"

Back in her Spanish II class, Toni looked up at the clock. "One more minute on the computers," she called out to a group who'd been working there for nearly 30 minutes. "And then you four need to let other people on. If you're not finished, you can come back after school. I'll be here 'til 4:30." She turned back to Shalisa and pointed to the second paragraph of her paper. "OK, one thing you need to work on here is writing more about why things were the way they were. Not just what happened, but why."

Watching Toni now—low-key, subtle, patiently helping students think about their work—she almost seemed a different person from the showstopper I'd marveled at in Spanish I. But that only served to confirm what I'd suspected already: that the jokes, the grandstanding, the look-at-me posturing—they weren't so much about ego as they were deliberate interventions she thought would help kids learn. When they were appropriate, Toni used them—and she had a ball doing so. But just like any good teacher, she had other tools in her kit.

At 27, Toni was in her fifth year in the classroom. She'd spent the first two of those years at William Henry Harrison, an all-black high school on the city's south side, before being lured to TCA by two former Harrison teachers, Sarah Howard and Michelle Smith, who were the fledgling charter school's codirectors. They hadn't had to give Toni the hard sell to convince her to come to TCA. Harrison had been put on probation by the board of education because of low test scores, and then reconstituted—a polite way of saying it had been taken over—which Toni said had created an atmosphere that was both oppressive and depressing. Teachers would spend hours in meetings with administrators and board officials talking about changes that needed to be instituted, only to watch the reforms fall by the wayside a short time later.

"Judging from that experience," she told me, "I would say that the Chicago public schools are not doing a very good job of educating African American kids. But it wasn't just the board's fault, it wasn't just the administration's fault, it wasn't just the teachers' fault, it wasn't just the parents' fault. Everybody should be held accountable. When I taught Spanish there, we had one class set of books, so the kids couldn't even take books home. We could only make 300 copies a week, so if you had a roster with 150 students, they'd get two handouts a week—unless you were paying. Field trips were a big hassle, getting money was a big hassle, classrooms were overcrowded—one year I had 40 students in a Spanish class." By the middle of her second year, Toni said, the pressure was becoming unbearable. She was feeling run down, even physically ill, and she knew she had to make a change. "When Michelle called me, I didn't care what the school sounded like—I was like, 'OK.' But when I came in, I liked what I saw. I liked that you could create your own curriculum. I liked that nobody was breathing down my back saying, 'You must do this in this way.'"

By most demographic and statistical measures, the student populations at Harrison and TCA were not much different. At both schools, the student body was over 97% African American, over 90% qualified as low-income, and average scores on standardized tests were well below state averages. One important difference, however, was size: Whereas Harrison had nearly 1,500 students, TCA had just 270 in grades 6 to 12.

Deborah Meier (2000) has written of the "crisis of relationships" that plagues large schools such as Harrison, and Toni had experienced that reality up-close. She believed that TCA's smallness made an immeasurable difference in terms of encouraging more meaningful teacher–student interactions. "At Harrison, I would be nice to kids, and they would ask me why, because they didn't expect it," she said. "But it's different here. The kids expect you to be nice. They expect you to go above and beyond the call of duty. I'm just a run-of-the-mill, average teacher compared to the other teachers here."

TCA's smaller size, Toni said, also made for a more respectful, reciprocal relationship between teachers and administrators. "At Harrison, I had to make an appointment to see the principal," she remembered. "Here, I can just walk into Sarah and Michelle's office any time. When they come into my classroom, I love it. They're not intrusive, and it's not an evaluation—they just come in to see how things are going. They're very supportive, and that's important for a teacher." At Harrison, Toni said, it had been a different story. "You had to have a scheduled observation, and my first year there, my principal never observed me," she told me. "When I went into his office to get evaluated, he asked *me* what kind of teacher I thought I was. So me, being modest, I said,

'Oh you know, just average.' And that was my evaluation: average. Had I known that was going to happen, I would've said I was superior."

From what I'd seen, Toni was anything but an "average" teacher, with its implication of bland mediocrity. As she continued to meet with students one-on-one, I wandered around the room, looking over shoulders, listening in as kids went about their work. After a few minutes, I sat down with a group of three boys—Marcellus, DeShawn, and Jeremy—whose conversation caught my ear.

"Why the janitors and the security guards got better cars than the teachers?" DeShawn asked. A portable CD player was sticking out of his bag, and his 'fro was dented in from constantly wearing the headphones.

"Yeah, Marvin got a drop-top," said Marcellus, referring to one of the school custodians.

"And Ms. Taylor ride the bus to school every day," observed DeShawn. "She gotta be makin' enough to buy a car."

I didn't know Ms. Taylor, but I figured she probably had a good reason for her choice of transportation. I decided to put in my two cents: "Maybe it's more convenient to ride the bus. Or maybe it's quicker."

Marcellus cocked his head. "Oh, no. I ride the bus every day. And let me tell you—it is *not* convenient, and it is *not* quicker." So much for my grad-school analysis. I went back to taking notes.

Marcellus looked down at my legal pad and read some of what I'd written. "You ain't gonna make us look bad, is you?"

The question took me by surprise. Since this was my first visit to this particular class, Toni had introduced me at the beginning of the period and asked me to explain my project. I'd tried to lay it out in terms that were understandable but honest, telling the kids I planned to observe and interview several young teachers to try to understand what being a teacher means to them. I said I'd be taking a lot of notes because it would help me remember what I'd seen and heard when it came time to write about it. I added that I hoped the project might become a book someday.

At the time, none of the students had asked any questions, but now Marcellus was tossing one my way, and it wasn't a softball: *You ain't gonna make us look bad, is you?*

"Uhh . . . I'm not planning to."

"I didn't like that awkward pause," Marcellus said. "After I asked the question, you had to think about it for a second."

I explained that I hoped to tell as much of Ms. B's story as I could without romanticizing the positive or overemphasizing the negative. "I can't ignore the bad things," I said. "But that's not what I'm focused on."

Apparently satisfied with my clarification, Marcellus turned back to Jeremy and DeShawn. "He's writin' down what I'm sayin'. I'm gonna be in his book."

DeShawn shrugged. "I don't wanna be in his book. I don't know him. I don't trust anybody I don't know."

"You know who I don't trust?" Jeremy said. "George Bush."

"Him, neither," said DeShawn with a sense of finality. "I don't trust nobody that's a Republican."

•••••••••••

While I hadn't been thrilled to be mentioned in the same breath as George W. and his Republican cohorts, I could understand how, in DeShawn's mind, there might not be a whole lot separating me from them. I could also see how Marcellus might be concerned that I would portray him and his classmates in a negative light. I figured they'd both probably had their share of oppositional encounters with white people: white cops harassing them; white landlords collecting rent but doing little to keep buildings livable; white shop owners watching their every move. Why should they think I would be any different? I'd gone to court with numerous former students facing charges on everything from disturbing the peace to attempted murder, and the racial divide in the courtroom—those supposedly upholding the law on one side and those who'd allegedly broken it on the other—was always striking: mostly white faces in front shuffling papers, mostly black and brown bodies shuffling in and out as their cases were called. With experiences such as those providing a backdrop for DeShawn and Marcellus, it shouldn't be surprising that they were somewhat suspicious of an anonymous white guy coming into their class with a notebook and pen. It would be more surprising, really, if they weren't.

"Race is a big issue for these students," Toni told me one afternoon following TCA's weekly faculty meeting. "And it affects their attitudes toward new teachers when they come in." School, of course, is the one place where many poor African American and Latino kids do have day-to-day contact with white people. According to board of education figures, nearly half of the teachers in Chicago's schools were white in 2001–2002, even though over 87% of the system's students were black or Latino. At TCA, the faculty was about evenly divided between blacks and whites. "I think the fact that I'm an African American female helps me relate to my African American students," Toni continued. "I don't know if it's respect or what, but I think it makes it a little easier. I've seen some teachers who have had some wonderful lesson plans, who would be outstanding teachers, but one of the things that hurt them in the classroom was that they were white."

The problem hadn't been simply a difference in skin color, Toni explained, but rather a clash of expectations. "One guy had a lot of liberal ideas that the kids were not used to," she said. "Same thing with this other female teacher. She was a wonderful teacher, but she came in and was all about the students making decisions about the curriculum, and they could not understand that. They saw her as a pushover. In their minds, they're thinking, 'You're the teacher. You're supposed to come in here and say: We're gonna do this, this, this, this, and this.' You know, with an iron fist." The teachers had apparently expected to be viewed as authority figures simply by virtue of their position and title. Their students, on the other hand, had expected them to earn their authority by showing they knew how to exercise it. It was a distinction many beginning white teachers in urban schools failed to fully grasp. I certainly hadn't figured it out during my first few years.

But Toni pointed out that a number of white teachers at TCA had built strong, mutually respectful relationships with their students. I asked what she thought made them different, why they were able to succeed where others failed. "Because they hang in there," she said. "From Day One, you can tell that they care about the students, and they stick in there. See, with these other teachers, after a year, they left. And to the kids, it's like, 'Oh, you're another white person who's abandoning us. You're trying to save us, you think that it can't be done, and then you leave us. You're not willing to stick with us.'" According to Toni, the white teachers who succeeded at TCA were also distinguished by a keen ability to be empathetic. "With them, it's like race just doesn't matter, because they *feel* where the students are coming from. But even some of them have talked about how they have to work a little harder to earn the respect and build a relationship with their students, because their skin's the first thing they see. So I think being African American makes it easier for me when I put my foot in the door. But does it automatically make me a better teacher to these kids? I can't honestly say that."

Toni thought it was important—crucial, even—for African American kids to have good black teachers, especially black men, in their lives. But she believed having teachers from other racial and cultural backgrounds was necessary as well. "How else are we going to learn different viewpoints if we don't learn from some-body else's perspective?" she wondered aloud. "I think it's a good thing for African American students to have African American teachers—but not only African American teachers. It's a good thing for Latino students to have Latino teachers—but not only Latino teachers. You bring something different into the classroom as a teacher than I bring into the classroom. Black kids need a teacher who cares, and if that teacher happens to be black, fine. But you can learn from whoever teaches you."

Nevertheless, Toni recognized the value of being able to connect on a personal level to her students' lives. As a young girl, she'd struggled against many of the same obstacles they were facing, and she'd seen up-close how an alienating school experience could have devastating consequences. "Too many of my friends didn't have a good experience with school, and so they didn't finish," she told me. "I don't know if their teachers related to them or not, but I can hon-estly say that most of my teachers didn't relate to me. Not many made an effort to get to know me. So I want my students to have a good experience with school. I don't necessarily want to be the stu-dents' friend, but I do want them to know that there's somebody outside of their family who cares about them, somebody who's been through some of what they're going through. I want them to know that they have somebody they can talk to."

············

It was Toni's planning period, but instead of finishing her stu-dent progress reports—which were due by the end of the day—she was sandwiched between two scowling seventh-grade girls, trying to get to the bottom of the static between them. Sweatshirt sleeves pushed up to her elbows, arms folded in front of her, hair pulled back in a short ponytail, Toni looked at one of the girls, then the other, her blank expression giving away not a hint of what she might be thinking. Both girls looked away, refusing to make eye contact—with each other, with Toni, with me, with anybody.

The problem had flared up just as recess was ending. The two girls, Angela and Unique, had exchanged words, and when their verbal jabs turned to threats, Toni and Lamayra had stepped in and brought them to the faculty room to talk things out. Disagreements among students were not an uncommon occurrence in the school, and in an effort to address such incidents before they escalated to physical fighting, TCA had adopted a conflict resolution program as part of their disciplinary strategy. Three staff members, including Toni, had volunteered to attend formal training sessions and then share what they had learned with their colleagues. According to school codirector Sarah Howard, Toni was a master mediator.

"You've been talking about conflict resolution in your advisory, right?" Toni asked the girls.

"Yeah," they both muttered.

"So you know what's about to happen."

"Yeah," Angela said. "Conflict."

"No, we're talking about resolution, about resolving this thing."

Before trying to discuss what had happened, Toni asked the girls to spend 5 minutes writing about the incident. "We need you to write about how you feel, and what you need to make you feel better," she told them. "Sometimes writing it down helps take away a little bit of the anger." Angela, at least two sizes smaller than her bulky St. Louis Cardinals jacket, and Unique, in loose overalls and sporting Afro-puffs, both looked as if they had their doubts.

When the girls had finished writing, Toni went over the ground rules with them: Use "I" statements, only one person talks at a time, no interrupting. She then gave each girl a chance to explain what had happened from her perspective. Angela went first: "We was in the gym, and she was—"

Toni stopped her cold. "No, no. I'm already hearing too many *she's* and not enough *I's*. What did *you* do?"

Angela started over and ran down her side of the story. Unique rolled her eyes. Unique then had her turn, and Angela let out several exaggerated sighs. There were a few points of contention in their accounts—who said who was gonna beat whose butt first being the main one—but Toni tried to help the girls understand that they might have to agree to disagree on exactly how events transpired. "We can't change what happened," she told them. "It happened. It's over. What we want to do is find out what we can do to make you feel better about it."

"I need to not talk to her," Unique said.

"I need an apology," countered Angela.

After 10 minutes more of Toni's careful back-and-forth peace-making, the two girls—who had entered the room ready to box—finally agreed to put the matter behind them. They apologized to one another, shook hands, and promised to come back for help if things got stirred up again. As they turned to go, Toni called after them. "Are you sure you're OK?" she asked. "Because I still feel some anger from you." They both assured her that they were, and as I watched them leave, I marveled at the patience Toni had demonstrated throughout the process—her delicate choice of words, her calm and deliberate manner, the respectful way she talked to each student. I was thinking I'd just witnessed one of those rewarding, feel-good, this-is-what-makes-it-all-worthwhile teacher moments.

But as soon as the door closed behind the girls, Toni slammed her open palms down on the table. "I hate this conflict resolution shit!" she said with a serious scowl of her own. "It doesn't work. They lie to me. Last time I did it, these kids were telling me, 'No, Ms. B, I didn't have any Pokemon cards. I don't know what you're talking about.' Ten minutes later they had the damn Pokemon cards in the bathroom."

While part of Toni might have been yearning for the seeming simplicity of old-school disciplinary approaches, the bulk of her frustration, it seemed to me, was coming from a different place. She'd learned early on that teaching is hard work, and that teaching beyond the accepted, beyond the "as is," beyond right or wrong answers and one-size-fits-all solutions, is exponentially harder. Mediating conflicts—and trying to teach kids to do the same—requires considerably more emotional and mental energy than dumping off an unruly student at an assistant principal's office or writing up a detention referral. Still, Toni didn't mind putting in the extra effort. Well, maybe she did sometimes—especially when she had a stack of progress reports waiting to be completed—but she recognized that it was all part of reaching toward something better for the kids she taught. "If you just come to work, teach your class, and go home," she'd once told me, "then you're doing maybe a tenth of your job."

What frustrated Toni at times wasn't so much the work itself but the uncertainty that accompanied it, the realization that whatever you did, however fully you invested yourself, you did so without guarantees. One of the most painful ironies of teaching with the intent of making a real difference in children's lives is that, as often as not, you're tempted to conclude that you're making no difference at all. When idealistic visions meet hard realities, the short-term results are often imperceptible, impossible to measure, and any rewards or payoffs—metaphorically speaking, of course—are indefinitely delayed. Philosopher Thomas Merton (1978) has written that once you get used to that idea, "you start more and more to concentrate not on results, but on the value, the rightness, the truth of the work itself." I'd found solace in those words as a teacher but, like Toni, part of me had still longed to see tangible outcomes, to get a more visible sign that what I was doing mattered. Maybe that was shortsighted, but it was real.

What was real for Toni at the moment was that she had only 5 minutes left in her planning period and a slew of progress reports yet to be done. She'd foregone her regular lunchtime again today to sell taffy apples in the cafeteria. She was determined to take a group of her students to Mexico this year if she had to sell a truckload of apples and M&Ms to do it. A planned trip the year before had been scrapped when fund-raising efforts came up short.

"I wish I could find the kid who stole my damn grade book," said Lamayra, reentering the room. "That's the source of my crankiness right now."

"All I know is I'm not taking any school work home this weekend," offered Thaddeus Dennis, TCA's algebra teacher and an all-but-dissertation doctoral candidate in mathematics.

"How late were you up last night?" Toni asked him.

Thaddeus removed his glasses. "I got 1 hour of sleep. I'm surprised I'm functioning as well as I am."

"I was reading essays until midnight," added Lamayra.

There weren't enough hours in the day, they all agreed, but as the only one of the three with a child of her own, Toni was particularly vulnerable to the time crunch. She wanted to be a good teacher to students like Angela and Unique, as well as a good mother to Corey, but too often she ended up feeling as if she'd shortchanged one or the other. The challenge, she understood, was to find a healthy balance between the two without losing herself along the way, but there was no time to think about that now. Advisory began in 1 minute. Toni quickly gathered her things, blew out a long breath, and headed to the basement.

············

Monday mornings typically weren't high-energy times for the middle schoolers I'd taught, but either Toni hadn't had the same experience or, if she had, she didn't let it dictate her routine. Early on this Monday, a kid named Mizell was standing next to her, trying to keep up with her Spanish commands: "Pick up the potato. Put the potato on your head. Put the potato on the table. Bark like a dog." After Mizell obeyed her last edict, Toni turned to the class. *"Él es Lil' Bow Wow?"* she asked jokingly, and then, before they could respond, answered the question herself. *"No, él es Snoop Perro Perro."*

After putting several more students through the paces with the props she'd brought in—a loaf of bread, some potatoes, plastic utensils, a toy cash register, a stuffed dog—Toni reviewed a list of vocabulary words she'd written on the overhead. Each word had a movement associated with it: *"pone,"* for example, which means "put," was symbolized by one hand placing down an imaginary object. As Toni called out each word, the students performed the corresponding movement. Later, she would spin a wildly imaginative tale about music icon Ike Turner shopping for potatoes and bread at a local discount grocery store—a story that would not only include nearly all of the targeted vocabulary but would have her students roaring with laughter as well.

The proceedings sometimes seemed like random silliness, but Toni's techniques were actually drawn from a beginning language instruction method known as Total Physical Response Storytelling, or TPR-S. Unlike the "listen and repeat" format common to many introductory language courses—and which Toni herself had used until this year—TPR-S, according to its advocates, puts the initial focus on aural comprehension through kinesthetic involvement. Students learn vocabulary through associating words with specific movements, through physically executing spoken commands, and through hearing words used in high-interest stories, which are in turn acted out. Eventually, they transition to using the language themselves, retelling the teacher's stories in both written and oral form, and creating original stories of their own. Proponents of TPR-S say it allows students to participate actively while the teacher continually provides "comprehensible input"—the foundation of Stephen Krashen's (1985) input hypothesis of language acquisition.

Toni had decided to try TPR-S after being introduced to it at a workshop the previous summer. She'd become frustrated with traditional, grammar-based approaches to teaching Spanish and was excited by the possibility of making her daily lessons more interactive. Though she'd always incorporated hands-on projects as part of her teaching, she believed her students often found the direct instruction portion of the class dull. But not anymore. "Most people learn better kinesthetically, so if you get them moving, then they're learning," she told me. "And it's working. I've had more success this year than I've ever had as far as kids understanding the language and retaining it." The best thing about TPR-S, Toni said, was that even though it was a structured approach, it wasn't overly scripted or rigidly sequenced. It allowed her to put her own unique stamp on lessons, and judging from what I'd seen, I could affirm that she took full advantage of the opportunity. I doubted there was another teacher using TPR-S anywhere in the world that morning who had woven both Ike Turner and Snoop Dogg into her storytelling.

Yet as much fun as Toni had with her classes, she was decid-
edly serious about her motivations for teaching Spanish to the
kids at TCA. "I'm a product of Chicago public schools, and I
always wanted to come back," she told me. "In college, when they
would ask me why I wanted to teach in the inner city, I would
always say that I wanted my people to be able to speak another
language. So I definitely wanted to come back and teach African
American kids, or minority kids, because they were the ones who
were not as privileged."

Most of the city's public school students, Toni knew, weren't
exposed to language study until high school, and even then the
majority never progressed beyond introductory courses. In that
context she'd been one of the lucky ones. In middle school she'd
had the chance to participate in a special program that bused a
select group of students across town to a magnet school for weekly instruction in French, German, and Spanish. She became enamored with German, but when she got to high school it wasn't
offered, so she chose Spanish because of its practical value. Her
Spanish teacher—a stern, uncompromising African American
woman who Toni remembered not for her classroom technique but
for her insistence that her students not sell themselves short—
turned out to be one of the few educators who made a lasting
impression. "She stands out because she was such a powerful person," Toni said. "I'm not knocking her as a teacher—I'm not saying she was the best teacher, either—but she was very powerful,
she was very demanding. She may not have been the nicest person
in the world, but she did expect a lot out of us."

The high expectations, combined with Toni's intelligence and
hard work, landed her at Illinois State University, where she
double-majored in Spanish and psychology while simultaneously
getting certified to teach. She was one of only two African
American undergraduates in the Spanish program, and during her
junior year she was the only black student from ISU to travel to
Mexico for a semester of study in the mountain village of Taxco. In
her education courses, too, Toni was surrounded by white students—most of whom had grown up in nearby small towns—and
the lack of an urban perspective sometimes left her feeling isolated. "I had this curriculum and instruction class, and this teacher's
approach was to scare us. 'Are you sure you wanna do this? Let me

show you this video—in this video, this woman tells her students to shut up 120 times!' He just tried to scare the mess out of us. That was his approach. He brought us to some 'inner-city' schools, and we got to sit in on some of the classes that were 'overcrowded.'" She traced the quotation marks around *inner city* and *overcrowded* in the air with her fingers.

"There were a lot of white students in our class," she continued, "and I think what he was trying to do was to show them the reality of it. They may have had the idea of being saviors and going into this wonderful profession and not having any problems. I think he scared a lot of those students away from teaching in the city. A lot of them applied for jobs near ISU—there's a lot of really small towns there. As a matter of fact, they tried to get me to work there. When I told them that I wanted to work in Chicago, it was always, 'Why? Why do you wanna do that?'"

Part of the reason was familiarity. Just as many of Toni's fellow students felt more comfortable seeking teaching jobs in or near the towns they'd grown up in, Toni was drawn to return to the place she knew best. But it was more than just that. For Toni, teaching in the city's public schools was an attempt, as Ruth Behar (1996) puts it, to "drive a wedge into the thick mud of business as usual" (p. 166). Toni wanted to do her part, however small, to chip away at some of the severe inequities of educational opportunity, to give her students a measure of hope along with the tools to have a fighting chance, to *not* be just another brick in their wall. She knew— despite the xenophobic rhetoric of "English-only" advocates—that language is power, and that a second language would open doors for her students that might otherwise be closed to them. "I want my students to be able to acquire a second language," she told me, "not just have an experience with it. I want them to be able to have conversations on many different levels, and hopefully to love the language so much that they'll continue on with it."

Toni also wanted to give some of her students the opportunity she'd had to travel abroad. Spending time in Mexico had opened her eyes to a much larger world, and she knew that her students— like any kids—would benefit greatly from such an experience. "A lot of kids in urban areas don't have the opportunity to get outside of their neighborhood, let alone travel to another country," she said. At Richland High School, located in a wealthy suburb just north of the city, groups of as many as 30 students routinely took 3-week summer excursions to such far-flung places as Spain, China, Italy, France, and Japan. The trips—which included language classes—could cost up to $2,500 per student, but the school did no fund-raising: If a kid wanted to go, the parents footed the bill. The families of Toni's students couldn't provide even a fraction of that kind of financial support, so she spent much of her supposed "free" time at school selling candy or taffy apples with her kids, organizing raffles, planning talent shows, or scheming other ways to raise money. If they were going to get to Mexico, it would be by nickels and dimes.

During her first year of teaching at Harrison, Toni told me, her students had initially been skeptical of her knowledge of Spanish. She guessed they'd never seen an African American who spoke the language; they thought she couldn't possibly be their teacher. "They asked me if I was mixed," she said. "They didn't expect an African American coming from where they come from to be able to teach Spanish." It didn't take the students long to realize that Toni was for real, but the fact that they'd had doubts at all continued to fuel her fire. The world Toni was working toward was a world in which, when a black woman walked into a classroom full of kids to teach them another language, no one would be the least bit surprised.

············

"Next week we're going to have a book club," Toni was telling her reading class. "Just like Oprah. You know—sit around a table, eat, talk about our book. So I need to make a list of what food everybody can bring."

Kids began excitedly shouting out suggestions: "Rib tips!" "Cornbread!" "Macaroni and cheese!" "Flamin' Hots!"

"Please," Toni interrupted, "no Flamin' Hots—not at 9:30." The students collectively whined. "C'mon, now," she continued. "How elegant is that? Sitting around a table munching on Flamin' Hots at 9:30 in the morning?"

"Aww, Ms. B," Raymond muttered.

Toni redirected the conversation. "I'll bring a cake. Strawberry or lemon, I'm not sure which. But keep in mind I don't have a lot of money, so I won't be able to buy a real fancy one. I may turn into Betty Crocker between now and then."

"Betty Crocker?" Loretta asked, squeezing out some lotion to put on her hands. "Who's that?"

Toni's reading class was composed of a mixed-age group of struggling readers: mostly sixth graders along with a few seventh- and eighth-grade students. Like all of TCA's reading classes that year, it was grouped by ability level. Though the school's codirectors and most of its staff were philosophically opposed to tracking, chronic low test scores had prompted them to take drastic action. A recent story in the *Chicago Sun-Times* had fingered TCA as one of the city's poorest performing charter schools in terms of standardized test scores, and while the school's staff could provide convincing arguments as to why that was an unfair measure, they knew that, in the end, it would be a large part of how their success or failure was gauged. With the school's 5-year review just a year away, the stakes couldn't be higher. A lack of improvement in student test scores could give the central office cause to pull the plug on TCA for good.

For Toni, it was an especially distressing development. The squeeze of test-score pressure had already chased her from Harrison, and now she could feel the claw closing in on her once again. She wasn't considering leaving TCA, but she did worry that the good work the school was doing might not be recognized by the powers that be. "Our kids are improving," she said when I asked about the *Sun-Times* article, sounding only a little defensive. "Most of the students here improve a grade level every year. But when they come in several grades below level—which a lot of them do—even if they increase a year, they're still way behind. So the numbers don't look good, and it's frustrating. But what do you do? Do you stop everything to try to get the test scores up? Do you exclude some students from coming here so that our scores look better and we can stay open and continue doing the wonderful things we're doing?"

There wasn't a trace of sarcasm in what Toni said. She really did believe the school was doing important work, and most of the other teachers I'd talked with at TCA seemed to share that view. But the low-test-score dilemma had put them in a theoretical and practical bind. They wanted to stay true to their vision, to hold firmly to their beliefs about how kids learn best, to continue to dance to their own funky rhythm—and they definitely didn't want decisions about what and how they taught to be driven solely by concerns over raising test scores. But they also recognized that if they couldn't find a way to boost the school's averages, none of those considerations would matter. Toni had told me that it sometimes seemed to her like a losing battle. It wasn't hard to see why.

Still, as Upton Sinclair wrote, it's the difference between being defeated and admitting defeat that keeps the world going. Toni, Lamayra, Sarah, Michelle, and the others weren't about to just throw in the towel. The staff had decided to make a concentrated effort to raise the school's reading scores, even if some of their efforts to restructure—like ability grouping—had well-documented downsides. Reading class sizes had been reduced—Toni had 16 students in hers—and teachers had agreed to do more instruction in targeted skill areas and with specific reading strategies. In the past, TCA's reading program had been built almost exclusively around quality literature: Shelves in the faculty room had classroom sets of such titles as Chinua Achebe's *Things Fall Apart*, Jacqueline Woodson's *From the Notebooks of Melanin Sun*, Ji-Li Jiang's *Red Scarf Girl*, Sherman Alexie's *Reservation Blues*, and James McBride's *The Color of Water*. Teachers were still using high-interest novels—Toni's book club discussion would be centered on Lynne Ewing's *Drive-By*—but they were also devoting more time to explicit preparation for the tests, emphasizing subskills they knew would show up on them. It sometimes felt like a deal with the devil, but what other choice did they have?

Toni had described herself as a "crappy" reading teacher, but as I watched her kneel on the hardwood floor to talk over a passage from *Drive-By* with Yashika, I couldn't help thinking that she, like so many good teachers I know, was excessively self-critical. I'd seen her use all kinds of resources with her class—from fairy tales and ghost stories to hip-hop lyrics and newspaper articles—and she was keenly aware of the obstacles her students faced as developing readers. "Vocabulary is a big issue," she told me, "because a lot of the vocabulary that they use at home, or even at school, is different from what they see on standardized tests. I don't feel qualified to say the tests are culturally biased, but the vocabulary is a problem. It all depends on which culture you're in, right? A kid who's been exposed to the vocabulary on the test is going to do better, because that's one less obstacle, one less hoop for them to jump through."

But that factor wasn't widely enough acknowledged, Toni thought. Instead, when kids in struggling communities scored poorly on standardized tests, teachers became scapegoats for what in reality was a much larger failure. "If we're not meeting the goals that have been set," she explained, "then we have to blame somebody. And who's with the kids every day? The teachers, right? So if the students are not doing well on the test, it must be the teachers' fault. But you have to think—well, as a parent, what am I doing to reinforce what goes on at school? As a politician, what am I doing to ensure that the students have the resources they need in school? As a community member, what am I doing when I see little Johnny out on the street corner when I know he should be in school? So it's not one person—it's everybody. It's everybody's responsibility."

Toni was not one to shirk her share of the load, but she expected others to do their part as well. As reading class ended, she appealed to her students to make sure they came ready for next week's book club discussion. "Please, please, *please* read what you're supposed to read. Be prepared—or we won't eat." She paused for a beat. "Well, I'll eat, because I'm going to be prepared. But you won't."

"I'll be ready," JoJo assured her amid laughter from the others. "And Ms. B, just so you know: I eat a lot."

....

Charter schools may not be able to escape being shackled to test score results, but they do enjoy several freedoms not available to regular public schools. One of the most highly prized is the freedom to set their own calendars and schedules: Since they aren't bound by board regulations or union rules, charters can experiment with longer school days, different vacation periods, and special hours for teacher workdays. Since today's workday followed a staff party the night before, and since TCA parties were notorious for continuing into the wee hours of the morning, Sarah and Michelle had scheduled a later start time—ten o'clock—for the opening faculty meeting.

Despite that consideration, at 12 minutes after 10:00 teachers were still straggling in. Most looked a little rough around the edges—unshaven faces, rumpled clothing, baseball caps covering ungroomed hair. Toni had left last night's party early, so she looked fresh and rested. She plopped down a copy of *Hispanic* magazine to thumb through and opened a carton of milk to pour on a minipack of Apple Jacks.

"OK," codirector Sarah Howard said after most of the teachers had trickled in, "let's make a circle so we can all look at each other." At most schools, such a statement would be ludicrous: A circle big enough for the entire faculty would have to be formed in the parking lot. But at TCA, it was possible for everybody to sit around a few tables and have a real conversation. There were 16 teachers present—about equal numbers black and white, male and female—and they all looked *Boston Public*-young. I guessed that, at 38, I was probably the oldest person in the room.

After quickly taking care of a couple bureaucratic details, Sarah went straight to the day's topic of focus: school climate. "What we're talking about is how the kids talk about the school, how they treat each other, how we treat them, are they taking ownership—how do you guys think it's going?" Sarah was obviously in charge, but her blue Michigan ball cap and gray sweatshirt, along with her relaxed demeanor, were anything but intimidating. Michelle, her codirector, was several months pregnant and was taking a needed day off.

"What exactly do you mean by ownership?" The question came from Carrie Carson, who'd taught science at TCA since it opened.

Sarah sat back in her chair. "Like, are students proud of the school? Are they saying 'This is *my* school?' or are they saying, 'I go to this bootleg school TCA?'"

Toni jumped in. "We have a lot of kids who don't want to go home after school, so that's a good thing."

"And I think the COW process is definitely becoming more a part of the culture of the school," Carrie said, referring to the cumulative portfolio assessments. "That's positive."

"The hallways are better," added Kate Surhoff. "Tardies aren't as much of a problem."

Toni recounted an incident from a few days before in which one of her female students had come to class late because she was having her period. "She told me she'd been late because her administration was coming down," Toni said, and the room rolled with laughter.

A first-year teacher I hadn't met mentioned a hole that had been punched in the wall between the boys' and girls' bathrooms as a worrisome sign. If the kids were taking ownership, he said, they'd take better care of things. "Or maybe they just want a unisex bathroom like us," Lamayra laughed. She was referring to one of the most visible signs of the closeness of TCA's staff: There was only one bathroom for adults, shared by the entire staff. The only rule was to knock before you entered. "No, really," Lamayra continued, "I've told the kids, 'When you put a hole in the wall, I can't buy art supplies because we're spending all our money on dry wall.' And I think a lot of them are starting to make that connection between taking care of the school and having some of the good things we have."

Sarah, who'd been taking notes but hadn't said anything since kicking the topic off, took a few minutes to review what had been discussed so far, then tried to refocus the group. "This is what I want us to try to think about," she said, holding up a paper that read I AM A TCA STUDENT at the top. The sheet contained first-person statements such as *I expect to be challenged and I know that I will rise to those challenges*; *I am caring, compassionate, and forgiving with myself and others*; and *I am a positive communicator and I speak thoughtfully*. "In what ways are we explicitly communicating the climate that we're after?" Sarah asked. "We can't just put it on a sheet and put it in their handbook. To date, we've sort of worked by osmosis: If we do our thing, and we're really good people, they'll kind of pick up on that." She paused, surveying the faces around her. "And they do. They do pick up on it. But I think we could do a better job."

She went on to give examples of efforts other charter schools had made to engender a positive, caring, academically rigorous climate among their students. At one school, Sarah explained, everything is based around the idea of students as scholars. They're even addressed as "scholars" by the school's staff.

"Oh my God," said Najia, a middle-school science teacher. "That's like the Nubian brothers saying, 'Queen, how you doin'?' I know I'm a queen, but I don't need to hear that every day."

Toni suggested having the students produce public service announcements to be shown on the school's closed-circuit TV system that would promote the values on the "I AM A TCA STUDENT" sheet. Dan Verleen brought up the idea of creating some sort of school-wide ritual. Chad Zemke thought the staff should encourage student leadership by training more student mediators for conflict resolution.

"But then wouldn't we just end up with a hundred mediators?" a first-year teacher asked.

"What's wrong with that?" Chad said. "We'll have all mediators and nobody to mediate."

At that, Kate threw a fist into the air. "Don't hate—motivate!"

"But we need to make sure that the mediators aren't just kids who never get in trouble," Chad added.

Lamayra agreed. "I think the ones who get in trouble the most should be the first ones to get trained." I was pretty sure I heard an "amen" to that.

Toni had told me that one of the things she appreciated most about TCA was that there was always open discussion among the faculty before decisions were made that affected the school. Now I could see what she meant. This was nothing like so many of the staff meetings I'd sat through, where a hundred teachers piled into a gymnasium and fidgeted while someone talked at them. This was genuine dialogue about the really important questions all good teachers ask themselves: How are we doing? What's working here? How can we be better?

Sarah wanted to return to Dan's idea about creating a ritual— a regular time and place to meet together as a school community. One of the problems with that, Chad pointed out, was that there was no space in TCA's building that could accommodate all of the students. For school-wide assemblies, teachers and students had to go across the street to a gym they rented from a local parish. "It's kind of ironic," Chad said, "that we always have to leave the building to do something that's supposed to bring us together." Michelle and Sarah had talked about converting the third floor into an auditorium, but that probably wouldn't happen anytime soon. That part of the building had been empty since it was last used in the mid-1980s—it had peeling paint, no heat, no sprinkler system, and only one ungrounded electrical outlet in each room. "That was for the filmstrip projector," Dan chimed in.

The scheduled end-time for the meeting had almost arrived, so Sarah suggested taking a vote on the ritual idea. Should TCA have a regular all-school gathering? Yes, it was unanimous. The next question, then, was how often. Toni thought twice a month would be reasonable. "I'm concerned that our plates are so full," she said. "Planning this every week would be difficult, and I just don't want us to burn out."

"But it doesn't have to be a big production," Dan pointed out. "We're such classic overachievers that everything has to be over-thought and nuanced and complex. Church is simple. And that's what we'd be creating: a secular version of church. It's a time for the community to come together and celebrate each other."

Alex, another first-year addition to the staff, agreed. "Yeah. It's about creating an environment where there's the potential for something amazing to happen spontaneously." What a great way to put it, I thought. It also was a pretty good description, it seemed to me, of the kind of climate Sarah and Michelle had helped foster among their teachers.

Sarah asked for volunteers to form a committee that would continue fleshing out the ritual idea. Eight people, including Toni, raised their hands. "The kids look at you all," Sarah told the assembled teachers, "and see a group of people who are working their behinds off, who obviously care about them, who obviously believe in them. That's why they come every day. Even if they come and don't do anything, they come. So a lot of this is already happening—this is just a way to make it more organized." She checked her watch. "OK, that's it. Smooches, everybody. Have a wonderful day."

....

JoJo walked in the room singing: "We got the chicken and the cornbread. . . ."

Book club day had arrived, and the accompanying banquet—though perhaps not as lavish as the students had originally envi-sioned—looked impressive. On four pushed-together tables in the center of Toni's room were three plates piled high with fried chicken, two large bowls of macaroni and cheese, a pan of cornbread, a homemade lemon cake, two dozen Krispy Kreme doughnuts (my contribution), a bowl of popcorn, several bags of chips, and a couple 2-liter bottles of pop. There was even a bag of Flamin' Hots that had apparently slipped through Toni's checkpoint.

"Next time we do this, I don't want to see any half-filled-in sheets," Toni told the class as she went around to see who'd completed the assignment that was supposed to be their admission ticket to the feast. "I'm going to let a couple people slide today, but next time, if you're not ready with your homework, you can't participate. The whole point of coming up with questions and passages from the reading ahead of time is so we can be ready to have a good discussion."

"I'm ready, Ms. B," said Nathaniel, eyeing the chicken. "I just didn't write everything down."

Toni wasn't having it. "What if I said I was ready for us to eat, I just didn't bring any food? We need more than food on the table to do this—we need food for thought, too. Remember that next time."

When Toni gave the go-ahead for students to begin filling their plates, they didn't need to be told twice. The chicken, the macaroni and cheese, the cake, and the doughnuts all disappeared within a matter of minutes. "JoJo hoggin'!" Felicia cried out, giggling through her outrage. "Look how many doughnuts he got!"

"That's OK," Toni said. "It looks like everybody got at least one—except for me and Mr. Michie."

Nathaniel looked down at the three doughnuts on his plate. "You can have one of mine, Ms. B."

"No, that's OK," Toni told him. After a beat, the zinger: "I just want you to wallow in the guilt for a minute." A little while later, when the class's attention was elsewhere, Nathaniel quietly slipped one doughnut each onto my plate and his teacher's.

Toni had chosen *Drive-By* to read with her class for three reasons: it was a well-crafted narrative, the vocabulary was simple enough that her students wouldn't get frustrated reading it on their own, and it addressed issues she knew concerned them. Its story centers around Tito, a 12-year-old who is pressured to join a gang when his older brother Jimmy is killed over stolen drug money. The lure of "quick dollars," according to Toni, was one of the most critical issues facing the kids she taught. "They see kids their age who aren't even in school making big money," she said. "So they're thinking, 'You're telling me to stick with this school thing, which means I have to not only finish grammar school and high school, but also possibly college if I want a career. That's a long way off. And here my seventh-grade friend is selling drugs and he has all this money in his pocket, and next year he's going to buy a car.' So when they see that, they're like—'What is all this for? My family is struggling, we can't pay the rent. I need the money now.'"

As important as Toni thought it was to make space for her students' lives and experiences in her teaching, she acknowledged that it could be a tricky balancing act. "You have this curriculum that, in your mind, you have to teach," she told me. "Even if it's not set by the administrators. You think, 'I have to get through this because I want my students to know this content.' But then the kids will come in talking about being harassed by the police or something like that, and sometimes you just have to put your lesson aside. I don't have to teach these vocabulary words today if the kids need to talk about that. But it's hard sometimes as a teacher just to say, 'Wow, this is a teachable moment—I should go with it.' I know I've missed a few."

Once the book talk started, it didn't flow as smoothly as Toni had hoped. Kids had to stop and wipe their hands every time they went from handling greasy chicken to turning pages, and many of the questions students came in with were factual—"What's a crowbar?"—rather than the interpretive variety that make for more substantive discussion. A few kids couldn't add much to the conversation because they hadn't read what they were supposed to read. Still, it was quite a scene: fifteen young people sitting around a table, enjoying each other's company, sharing homemade cake and Flamin' Hots, and talking seriously about literature. Oprah would've been impressed.

"So when the guy asked Tito 'How's Jimmy's business?' he musta been thinkin' that Jimmy was involved with the gang," Shalisa offered tentatively.

"Bam! That's it! Right there!" The words shot out of Toni's mouth. "Now you're thinking!" Shalisa smiled ear to ear. "OK, how about this passage right here," Toni continued. "On page 40. What did Tito mean when he said, 'Jimmy always said he wanted to hear life sing'?"

Students flipped to the spot and scanned the paragraph. "He sayin' he wanted to make life happy and good," JoJo said. All that was left on his plate were three naked chicken bones.

"Yeah," agreed Shontay. "He wanted to enjoy hisself, to be able to do what he dreamed about doing."

The discussion about *Drive-By*, coupled with the book club feast, struck a delicate balance that Toni tried to maintain in her teaching. On one hand, she believed in paying unblinking attention to the tough issues that affected her students' lives, and in finding ways to bridge the divide between life inside and outside of school. At the same time, she believed in making her classroom a sort of refuge, a place where happiness and goodness and even fun were plentiful, where students felt significant and valued. Toni knew there were battles for her students to fight out in the world, but also beauty to behold. Teaching them to keep their eyes open to injustices and hard realities was important. So, too, was giving them opportunities to hear life sing.

....

It was 3:35, and Toni's room was jammed with students, all waiting in line to buy candy from her three student helpers. On a table behind them, cartons of M&Ms, Skittles, lollipops, and other candy sat next to a metal money box loaded with change and a few dollar bills.

"Next—serving number 14—what you want?"

"A pack of Skittles and a sucker."

"That's 70 cents." Subtract the 40 cents those two pieces of candy had cost wholesale, and that left 30 cents profit toward the Mexico trip. Toni estimated that the excursion would cost about $1,000 per person for air fare, food, lodging, and other expenses. So far, she and the students had raised less than $2,000 through fund-raisers, but she remained optimistic. A Krispy Kreme doughnut sale was just around the corner.

As more students piled into the room, Toni was nearly swallowed up by the throng of young bodies, but she looked content to be in the eye of the storm. "What I enjoy most about teaching is the relationship I have with my students," she'd once told me. "If I was a teacher the kids didn't like, I don't know how much I could enjoy my job. In interviews, they always ask you, 'What would you do if a student didn't like you?' and you always give that answer, 'Well, it wouldn't bother me and I'd still be able to do my job.' But you can't do your job if you don't have a good relationship with the kids. I know sometimes I get on their nerves, but most of the time, they understand that I care about them and I think we have a good relationship. I can't get rid of them after school. They won't go home!"

Toni still stressed over the seemingly endless stream of paperwork she had to do, and the balance between her home and school lives remained a precarious one. But overall, she felt good about where she was—both as a teacher and as a person. "I used to complain about my job a lot," she said. "At home with my family it was complaint after complaint after complaint—especially when I was at Harrison. And even here, I used to complain: I wasn't getting enough response from the students, or they weren't doing their homework. But now that I'm seeing such success with the students, I have nothing but glorious things to say about them." She laughed. "If anybody wants to listen, I'll pull out this script and say, 'My students wrote this! And they're in seventh grade! And they wrote all of this in Spanish!'"

Part of the reason Toni's spirits were soaring, she explained, was a recent religious conversion that had helped her sort through personal issues and find some inner peace. In earlier conversations, she'd described herself as "spiritual, but not very religious." For years, she'd rebelled against what she considered the overly judgmental brand of Christianity practiced by some members of her family, and she'd felt trapped by the excessive guilt that seemed to be part of the package. "I had a lot of misconceptions about religion," Toni said. "I couldn't understand, with so many religions in the world, how anybody could be completely right. My aunt would always say, 'Well, if they're not Christians then they're not going to heaven.' But I just couldn't understand that.

No matter how much good you did in the world, you weren't going to heaven if you didn't profess Jesus Christ as your savior? It just didn't seem right."

But now she saw things both more simply and more clearly. "I've come to realize," Toni told me, "that it's all about your personal relationship with whoever you consider to be the higher being. It's not about what somebody else is doing. I've been reading the Bible, and it's all about good, you know? You shouldn't judge, according to the Bible. Jesus didn't turn his back on anybody. When nobody would talk to the lepers, he was there. If a woman was a whore, he still talked to her. And I like that. Because remember, I told you before—do good to people, and as long as you're not hurting anybody, that's pretty much what it's all about."

After about 10 minutes, the candy-buying rush died down, and the student helpers began packing away supplies and counting the day's take. "I can finish that if you need to leave," Toni told them. "You catch the bus, right?"

"Yep."

"Well, I don't want you to be here too late."

"It's all right, Ms. B. My momma know where I'm at. I can finish."

Toni looked at me. "We're going to get to Mexico this year," she said, grabbing a box the kids had filled and stashing it behind her desk. "We're definitely going to get there."

Walking to my car a few minutes later, I looked back at TCA's building and noticed, for the first time, an inscription carved in stone above the main entranceway: EDUCATE THAT YOU MAY BE FREE—A.D. 1904. Somehow, in the numerous times I'd been in and out of the school, I'd never seen it, and even then it didn't make much of an impression on me at first. But the more I thought about it on the way home, the more awed I became by the historical continuum of which Toni and the other teachers at TCA were a part.

While schools and schooling have consistently been used for shameful purposes throughout this country's past—to strip American Indians of their languages and customs; to "miseducate" and control African Americans; to erase or minimize the contributions of Chicanos; to limit the opportunities of Chinese

American and Japanese American children; and, above all, to maintain the privileges of the white, ruling class—there have always been those who resisted, who struggled for something better. Despite the persistent tendency to use schools as sites of domination and oppression, there have always been those—some whose stories are now well-known, many who will forever remain unsung—who've tried to promote and enact a different kind of education, one that opens doors, that breaks down barriers, that liberates. The thought of continuing that tradition of resistance is daunting and intimidating at times, but other times it feels possible and real. Hearing the hope in Toni's voice, and then coming out to see those 100-year-old words carved in stone, it suddenly felt both more possible and more real to me.

Photo: Nathan Mandell

6

nancy serrano

First period had just begun at Quincy Elementary, and Nancy Serrano was sitting among 17 eighth graders, a dog-eared copy of *Starting With 'I': Personal Essays by Teenagers* lying open in front of her. "Everybody, take out your responses," she told the students.

"I didn't do mine," said Fernando, the smallest kid in the room. "I only got a paragraph." His tone sounded more boastful than apologetic.

"I said a page, didn't I?" Nancy asked, but she didn't wait for an answer. "A page means a page—not a paragraph." As students rustled papers and dug inside backpacks, Nancy flipped through her book to page 129, a story called "My First Love: Too Much, Too Soon."

Though I definitely felt like a visitor in Nancy's classroom, I was a bit more at home here than in the others I'd visited, and for good reason: It used to be mine. I'd taught at Quincy for 8 years—the last 6 of them in this room—and while I'd left full-time teaching 2 years earlier, I continued to help out with the school's student video program and to do volunteer work in the community.

Nancy looked up from her book. "Yesterday we stopped reading when—when it was getting good, right?"

"Yeah! When it was getting *real* good!" Carlos said, remembering the scene they'd been reading aloud when the bell rang: a teenage girl about to have sex for the first time with a guy she thought she loved.

"So what was happening when we left off?" Nancy asked.

"The girl went to Roger's house," offered Juan, glancing down

153

at his copy of the book. "And then they went down to the basement and started fucking."

I looked up from my note-taking, unsure if I'd actually heard
what I thought I'd heard. It had been said so casually that I wondered if maybe I'd misunderstood. But the open-mouthed expres-
sions on several kids' faces told me they were thinking the same
thing I was: *Did he really say "fucking"?*

Nancy stared directly at Juan's chubby face and calmly broke
the silence. "What made you comfortable thinking you could just
say that word out loud like that?"

Juan's light skin had flushed red. "I don't know," he muttered.
"It just came out." He seemed as stunned as anybody that the
word had tumbled from his lips.

"Well, that *is* what they were doing in the story," Fernando
pointed out. "They were having sex."

"Yes, they were," agreed Nancy in measured tones. "But we
still need to be respectful and mature about how we talk about
things. Juan, I'll speak with you after class." And just like that, she
carried on with her lesson. No big commotion, no kicking the kid
out of the room, no long-winded speech about school rules or dire
consequences—none of the things I might've done my first year as
a teacher.

Then again, Nancy, at 23, was far from the naïve sort of rookie
I'd once been. Her decision to return to her community to teach
had been made not with idealistic abandon but with a clear and
sober sense of purpose. "I want to be honest with these kids," she
told me. "I want them to see a bigger picture, because when I was
growing up, my sense of the world was isolated and narrow. I
want them to question, to understand themselves in this world, to
understand why things are the way they are, and to be able to use
that to overcome whatever they need to overcome. I want to let
them know that a better future is possible."

It was with these goals in mind that Nancy took on the current
theme in three of her classes: gender roles and relationships. She'd
decided to tackle the topic after holding a series of informal conversations with groups of kids after school. "A lot of things had
been coming up," she told me. "Pregnancy and love and relationships and pressures to have sex. They had a lot of questions."

But Nancy was a language arts teacher. What about parts of

speech? What about sentence fragments? "I'm still doing that," she told me. "It's just that I'm not doing it in a traditional way. I don't use the grammar book or the literature book every day, and I don't go from one page to the next. We read interesting articles, and we analyze them, and we write about them. They're always writing. And we still do sentence fragments, too—and outlining, and paragraph structure, and synonyms and antonyms, and all that stuff—because it's important in their writing. But I don't want to just focus on that. I want to help them open their minds up to things they haven't learned about."

Nancy knew these 13-year-olds had already learned plenty about sex and relationships. A couple female students had confided to her that they were sexually active, and while Nancy's message to them—and to all her students—was one of abstinence, she believed that the sort of abstinence-only approach promoted by federal funding guidelines was both unrealistic and irresponsible. She also believed that her students' views on sex were greatly influenced by their understandings of gender roles and expectations: boys who'd come to accept machismo as the natural order of things, and girls who'd been convinced that their self-worth was measured in the amount of attention they were able to garner from guys.

"I want them to think about the ideas they grew up with," she told me. "What did their families teach them? What did their culture teach them? What did their religion teach them? What did they learn from schools, society, TV? What kinds of things have they picked up on that they've never stopped to think about? I want them to start to question all that and realize that they have control over their lives, that they can create who they are going to be. Just because your mom is the biggest *machista* doesn't mean you have to be like that. Just because your dad is homophobic doesn't mean you have to think that way."

For kids to really open up about such issues, Nancy said, relationships had to be built. Students needed to be able to trust their teacher, to feel a genuine connection. "A lot of times," she said, "kids see their teachers as being far away. But I feel like I can relate really well to my students. And it's not just because I'm Latina. It's also because I grew up poor, because I grew up in a large family, because I had a single parent, because my mom was an immigrant, because I speak Spanish, because I listen to the same music a lot of them listen to, because I lived in the neighborhood. I'm not going to say I completely, 100% understand what they're going through, because I don't. But I guess because I sat in their seats and experienced some of their experiences, I feel comfortable with them. I treat them as if they were family."

....

Nancy had eight siblings—two older sisters, three younger ones, and three older brothers—and her mother raised all nine of them on her own. "My ma's the strongest person I've ever seen in my life," she told me. "She always found ways to feed us, to keep us in an apartment, to keep us warm. In all the buildings we lived in, the landlords never gave a damn, and the apartments always sucked. In the winter it was always cold—pipes would freeze all the time—so she'd carry buckets of water over from the next door neighbor's. She was the one who put linoleum on the floor, who painted, who fixed the heater. We'd have rats—I'm not talking about mice, I mean rats—and she would always be the one figuring out how to get rid of them." Nancy said that when she was younger she hadn't had the perspective to fully appreciate her mother's contributions. "But now, I'm like, 'Wow, she did it with nine kids on her own,' you know? She's such a strong person, such a survivor."

Nancy's sisters and brothers always told her she was the one who was most like their mother, and though she didn't mind the comparison, she knew it was double-edged. Years of facing down adversities had hardened her mother, making her seem emotionally detached, and Nancy occasionally saw something similar in herself. "I'm a hard-ass," she told me. "Even with my students, I'm hard with them. They know I care about them, but I tell them, 'Look, I'm not going to sugarcoat everything. I'm not going to tell you I love you, I'm not going to hug you all the time and say "You did an excellent job." But when I'm hard on you, or I'm lecturing you, you need to see that as an example of my caring. You need to understand that what I want for you is something great, even if I don't always show it the same way as others.'"

By her own account, Nancy had grown up poor, though she said she wouldn't have described it that way at the time. "It's just the way it was," she told me. "Sometimes you don't realize you're poor until you have something to compare it to." She became accustomed to sharing most everything. Up until third grade, she and her three younger sisters slept in the same queen-sized bed with their mother. "The babies would be close to my mom, somebody would get the wall, and somebody would sleep at the feet," she said matter-of-factly. "Now that I think about it, I actually didn't mind being at the feet. Sometimes you had more space there."

When Nancy was talking about those times, her tone was neither bitter nor tragic. Though the hardships of poverty had left an impression, what seemed to linger just as vividly were memories of an apartment echoing with laughter, of *norteñas* playing on a kitchen radio, of a family forging loving bonds around tough circumstances. Someone who hadn't grown up as Nancy had—someone like me—might hear her recollections and become caught up in the "deficits" of her young life. But like poet Nikki Giovanni, who once wrote that white biographers would probably talk about her hard childhood "and never understand that all the while I was quite happy," Nancy treasured her experiences. "I feel like I'm lucky I grew up the way I did," she said. "I'm realizing now that in a lot of ways I had a beautiful childhood. Yeah, I was poor. I didn't have a dad. I didn't have a lot of things. But had I not grown up like that, I wouldn't be who I am today."

Nancy also had fond memories of her time as a student at Quincy, and of the teachers who worked hard on her behalf. But in hindsight, she saw plenty of holes in her grammar-school education. "I could count the number of Mexican teachers I had on one hand," she said. "And even then, they didn't come from a background like mine. We'd have an assembly once a year where we wore skirts and did folkloric dances, but that was as close as we ever got to embracing or celebrating our culture. I don't remember seeing myself in literature until I read *The House on Mango Street* in eighth grade, and I don't remember ever reading anything about poor people. We'd read stories about kids who had their own houses and their own rooms—and I never had that. So sometimes I'd feel like I was different, like I wasn't normal."

Nancy was accepted to Thomas Jefferson High—which, of the nonmagnet public schools available to Quincy students, had the best reputation—but she quickly learned that Jefferson's greatness was reserved for students tracked into advanced courses. Nancy's grades and test scores at Quincy had been solid but not spectacular, so she was placed in "regular" classes at Jefferson, where one of her teachers routinely spent entire class periods with his head buried in a newspaper. "As long as we didn't get too loud," she said, "he wouldn't even look up." Feeling bored and disconnected—and, maybe just as important, free from her mother's watchful eye for the first time in her life—Nancy spent much of her freshman year ditching classes. "I wasn't doing well, and the teachers made it easy for me not to do well," she said. "I'd cut class, and not much would happen." Her grades plummeted, and some of her teachers wrote her off as a troubled kid.

She hadn't written herself off, though. At the end of her sophomore year, Nancy attended a Latino leadership conference. "They had all these workshops on empowering yourself, and being proud of who you are, and moving on to your next step in life, and it just really motivated me," she said. "I saw that there really were other options after high school. I got all these brochures from different colleges and took them home to show my ma. She was like, 'What are you talking about? We can't afford college.'"

Nancy knew her mother was right about the family's financial straits: All but one of her older brothers and sisters had left high school before graduating to help pay the bills. So the next week, she went to her school counselor's office to ask about scholarships and loans. "He wasn't rude—not in a blatant, openly racist way," she remembered. "He was just like, 'Well, what's your GPA? Oh, well, it's not too high. I don't think you qualify for this.' He was all nonchalant, like he didn't care. He got out a box and gave it to me, and he's like, 'Well, look through these and see if you find anything.' Talk about a mess—it was just a bunch of papers about colleges and scholarships, not even organized or anything. And that experience made me think, 'You don't give a shit about us. If I wouldn't have come down to the office on my own you wouldn't have done anything for me!' I was really upset."

Despite the lack of support, Nancy continued to push herself, and the perseverance she'd learned from her mother paid off. Her grade-point average inched upward, and as a senior she was awarded a scholarship by the Golden Apple Foundation for students who planned to become teachers in "schools of need." She'd entertained thoughts of teaching as far back as she could remember: As a young girl, she'd collected extra worksheets at school and taken them home to "play teacher" with her three younger sisters. During her early teenage years the interest waned, but the indifference of her teachers at Jefferson had, perhaps paradoxically, revived it. "I realized that too many of my teachers weren't doing their jobs," Nancy said. "The kids in the advanced classes were getting a lot of support, but the rest of us weren't. And when you realize that, you become angry. You want to change it. When I graduated, less than a third of the seniors went on to college. Most went to community colleges. And it was mostly because we weren't getting the support we needed. So that's why I decided to become a teacher. I wanted to change things."

•••••••••••

Quincy was a four-story, red-brick, factory-style building that dwarfed the wooden two-flats and three-flats around it. Built in 1896, it had served generations of immigrant children growing up in its working-class, port-of-entry neighborhood: Irish and Germans in the late 1800s; Lithuanians, Slavs, and Poles after the turn of the century; and Mexicans following World War II. If you looked closely at the hardwood floors in Nancy's classroom, you could still see circular patterns of puttied-over nail holes every 3 feet or so—traces of the pedestal desks that were once bolted in place to make for perpetually perfect rows.

While those desks had been uprooted and tossed out decades ago, a peek inside Quincy's classrooms revealed that, for a number of teachers, perfect rows were still in vogue. But Nancy didn't have rows. She didn't even have desks. Instead, she and her students sat around the outer edges of six tables arranged to form a single rectangle—one table on each end and two lining each side. "If somebody walked in here and looked at how the room is set up and listened to some of the things we talk about, they could easily confuse it for a college classroom," she told me. "And that's the kind of atmosphere I want to create. Why is it that it isn't until you get to college that you're pushed to think and pushed to be critical and pushed to discuss issues and speak your mind and be challenged? I want my seventh and eighth graders to do those things."

Even the walls in Nancy's classroom posed questions and begged conversation. One poster depicted an Aztec man and woman in traditional dress looking at a computer screen which read, *"El futuro es nuestro"* ("The future is ours"). Another showed two older Latinas, one dark-skinned, the other light and blond, with the caption: *"Y de qué color es tu mamá?* ("And what color is your mother?"). On the door, a photo of a young black girl was juxtaposed with an excerpt from Sojourner Truth's "Ain't I a woman" speech. Filling the spaces in between were a Diego Rivera print, a map of "The Muslim World," Mohandas Gandhi's "seven deadly social sins," and dozens of vocabulary words on index cards: *internalize, perception, womanizing, acquiescence.* If the walls in Nancy's room could speak, their message, I thought, would be crystal clear: Be prepared to be challenged when you walk through this door.

Of course, not every 13-year-old is anxious to be challenged. One morning Fernando interrupted an intense discussion of sexual abuse to announce, "Hey, Ms. Serrano, you got something white on your butt." His friend Eddie responded, "Why you lookin' at her butt, dude?" Another day Fernando spontaneously launched into a schoolyard version of the *Barney* theme song: "I love you, you love me/I chased Barney down the street/with a nine-millimeter I shot him in the head/Aren't you glad that Barney's dead."

"It does get frustrating sometimes," Nancy told me. "You're having a discussion and just because the word 'sex' comes out, they're giggling and guys are looking at each other and making faces. Sometimes I have to stop and ask them, 'Are you going to be able to handle this?' Most of the time they can shake it off. But you also have to accept their immaturity and realize that they don't have experience talking about certain things in a mature way. Part of my job is to help get them to that point."

Nancy favored diving into topics with the kids in her classes— even if she wasn't certain where it would take them. Her typical procedure was to give her students a short story, newspaper article, poem, or essay, then ask them to write about it and discuss their reactions to it. "I tell them, 'This is how college is,'" she explained. "'They assign you something, you read it, you argue, you write. That's what it's all about. If you can do this, you can do college.'" Sometimes she'd have the students write first and use their written responses to get a dialogue started. Other times, they'd discuss first and write a longer reaction for homework.

Either way, most of her students were doing far more writing than they'd been accustomed to doing in school.

"You love making us write, don't you?" I'd heard a kid named Beto ask once after Nancy assigned a two-page response to three stories from Sandra Cisneros's *The House on Mango Street*.

"Yes, I do," she told him.

"You hated it when you were in eighth grade, and now you're making us do it."

"That's right, my friend."

"But why?" Beto asked, though he continued copying down the assignment.

"Because you need to be pushed."

"But we don't like to be pushed."

"Most people don't like to be pushed," Nancy said. "That doesn't mean it's not good for you."

As much as possible, Nancy told me, she let her students' concerns and questions drive her curriculum, while still keeping her own goals and objectives in sight. "You know what you want to get across, but you don't want to force it on them," she said. "You want them to bring things up themselves so that they could take ownership." Sometimes she felt compelled to be didactic, and she had no qualms about explicitly sharing her own views when she thought it was appropriate. But she worked hard to create the sort of conditions where her students could make analytical leaps on their own.

"So, could any of you relate to Sally?" Nancy asked a class of seventh graders one morning, referring to a teenage character from *Mango Street* whose father keeps her on a tight rein. Nancy had been enamored with Cisneros's collection of short stories, which centers on a Mexican American girl growing up in a Chicago neighborhood not unlike the one surrounding Quincy, when she was an eighth grader. Now she was passing the book on to another generation of kids.

"My mom doesn't let me go out," said Miriam. "She says she knows how I am but she doesn't know how other people are."

"My dad tells me I'm gonna end up like my sister," added Alicia, looking hurt.

Nancy looked toward a cluster of boys. "Guys, could you relate to that? Do your parents tell you that?" Several of the boys shook their heads.

"It's not the same for guys," said Brenda. "When I come home late, my parents start cursing me and asking where was I, but my brother comes home like an hour later and they don't say nothing to him."

"OK, who could relate to that—raise your hand," Nancy said. "I'll raise both of my hands and my feet, too, 'cause that's how my mom was. Guys, why are your parents not the same with you as they are with your sisters?"

"'Cause they think they're out there doing something bad," Daniel suggested.

"And aren't they worried that you're doing something bad, too?"

Daniel shrugged. "It's different."

"If a guy is out there having sex, people see it like he's a little Mack Daddy," explained Fatima. "But if the girl does the same thing, she's a slut."

"What if that perception was flipped around?" Nancy asked. "What if we saw the girls who had sex as cool and the boys as sluts?"

Eddie smiled. "Nah. We're pimps."

"But I'm changing the story on you, my friend," Nancy said.

"Nah, we don't want you to change it."

"Well, why are you so stuck in that mind-set? Why do we think like that?"

"I think because in some religions—maybe in all religions—girls are supposed to get married first before they have sex," offered Evelyn. "Like in the Catholic religion, we say that when you're a virgin, you're still—you know." Miriam looked around for help, but no one said anything. "You know, without nobody in your body. And when you're not a virgin anymore, you're like—you know."

"Like what?" Nancy asked.

Evelyn scribbled absentmindedly on her paper. "You're not clean. You're not pure."

Nancy scanned the room to gauge the faces. "So what do you think about that?" She paused. "It it right? Is it good? Is it fair?"

"I think we just go with tradition and we don't think about it," said Miriam. "Like in Mexico, the church controls a lot of stuff. So that's how we get these thoughts, and then they're passed on from generation to generation and we just accept it."

"All those church writings were written a long time ago," Fatima pointed out. "But they're just ideas. We could change them."

"Yeah, but a lot of it hasn't changed," said Miriam. "How come in the Catholic church men get to be archbishops, cardinals, and popes, but women can only be nuns? And in some cultures, their religion says you could have six wives at the same time, but not six husbands."

"It's not right," said Evelyn. "Supposedly we were created equal, but it seems like women are seen as inferior, like we're less."

Miriam took it one step further. "I get the feeling that, for a girl, if you lose your virginity, it's like you lose the only thing you have to give. Like that's the only thing you have of value. It seems like that's how the church sees it."

"Wow—that's deep," Nancy said. "Did everybody hear that?" The students nodded, though I wasn't sure they'd all fully grasped what Miriam was trying to say. Yet that sort of uncertainty was one of the tradeoffs of the kind of teaching Nancy had chosen to embrace. If she'd stuck to parts of speech and sentence fragments, she'd have been able to come up with a fairly accurate measure of what her students were taking away from her classes. Delving into the nuances of social issues and the complexities of the human condition, on the other hand, made assessing her students' learning—and her own success as a teacher—a much more ambiguous task.

Still, it seemed clear to me that Nancy was accomplishing at least part of what she'd set out to do. When I told Miriam after class that I'd appreciated her contributions to the discussion, she deflected the praise to her teacher. "It's because of how Ms. Serrano lets us be open about things," she told me. "This is the first class I've had where we can share our ideas and talk about issues and be comfortable. I've never experienced that in school before."

• • • • • • • • • • • •

As hard as Nancy had fought back from the brink to earn a scholarship and get to college, she'd begun to wonder almost as soon as she arrived there if it had all been a big mistake. DePaul University's Lincoln Park campus was only a 25-minute drive from her family's apartment, but it seemed a world away. "My two brothers drove me there in this old Chevy Cavalier that I'd bought for a hundred dollars," Nancy told me. "And I remember carrying in my stuff in a milk crate. I didn't have a lot—clothes, sheets, a little black-and-white TV." She didn't think much about it, she said, until she saw other students arriving in U-Hauls. "They were bringing in loads and loads—suitcases full of clothes and huge TVs and stereo systems and real storage bins. I had a milk crate! And at that moment, I realized, 'Wow, they're rich. And I guess I'm poor.' That's when it hit me. Before that, I didn't realize my experience had been so narrow. You think the world is the way it is where you grew up, and then you realize it's not."

Nancy's roommate and all of her suitemates that first year were white, and only one woman besides her had grown up in the city. "I was like, these are the white people from TV," she said. "I could just imagine the way their lives had been—the whole 'I go upstairs to my bedroom' thing." She couldn't help comparing herself to the girls on her hall, and in almost every measure she saw herself coming up short. "I felt so small, so ashamed. I felt like I stood out. And not just with material things, but with how I dressed, how I spoke. I started questioning all that. It was like I was hearing myself for the first time, and I didn't like what I heard. I was starting to hate myself, in a sense."

Things weren't much better in her classes, where Nancy was often the only Latina student. She found the assigned readings difficult, the workloads demanding, the class discussions intimidating. "I would shake and get cold and start sweating just thinking about speaking up," she said. When she got back her first paper, a two-page personal essay for a philosophy course that she'd spent days writing and revising, she got an F. "The TA who graded it wrote, 'You are in dire need of help,' and then said something about my writing capabilities. I went back to my dorm that night and cried. I was like, 'Oh, my Lord, what have I gotten myself into?' I just felt like I wasn't smart enough, like I wasn't supposed to be there."

Lonely and homesick, Nancy talked to her mother on the phone nearly every day. "We're not the kind of family that says 'I love you, I miss you,'" she said. "Our conversations are like, 'What are you doing? What'd you eat? What's going on?' That's it." Her mother would frequently leave curt messages on her answering machine, saying things such as, "*Gorda. Fea. Llámame.* Bye."

(Literally translated into English: "Fat girl. Ugly girl. Call me.")
"My roommates could never understand that," Nancy continued.
"I'd be like, oh, that just means, 'Hey Nancy, how are you? What's
new? I love you. Give me a call.'" She laughed. "I know my ma
missed me—my sisters would tell me that she wouldn't sleep
sometimes, that she'd be worrying because I was the first one to
leave home like that. But she would never say it."

Nancy's older siblings were similarly tight-lipped, but, she
added, "without them, I don't know how I would've made it.
Twenty bucks here and there, rides back and forth on the week-
ends, bringing me things I needed. Even though they hadn't been
able to go to college themselves, it was like they were living out
their dreams through me." Her boyfriend, Jaime, to whom she's
now married, was also supportive. "He's the one who first taught
me how to express my emotions, my frustrations, my fears," she
said. "I was really going through a lot then, and he'd stay up till
five o'clock in the morning listening to me."

Two other things helped Nancy survive that initial semester.
The first was that one of her instructors, an African American philosophy professor, offered to meet with her to talk through her
papers. Soaking in his advice, she continued to work to express her
ideas more clearly, and before long she noticed a marked improvement in her writing: Her F's turned into C's, then B's, and by the
end of the term, A's. "He helped me see what an essay was supposed to look like," Nancy told me. "I really didn't know. A lot of
the problem was that I'd only written one paper in high school—
Can you believe that?—and that was a phony, straight-out-of-the-
encyclopedia research paper. I don't remember ever learning how
to do it."

The other, even more significant, development came when
Nancy hooked up with a student group called DALE—the DePaul
Alliance for Latino Empowerment. She suddenly found herself
among people who not only looked like her but understood where
she'd come from, and—maybe most importantly—had a clear
sense of where they were going. "The leaders of DALE at that time
were all women, all Latinas," Nancy told me. "They were a kick-
ass group, very political, and they were the ones who opened my
eyes. I started becoming aware of things I hadn't known about—
even my own culture. I was Mexican, but I didn't really know
about Mexico's history or about what being Mexican meant. I was

ignorant like you wouldn't believe. But through them I started getting involved, going to marches, and becoming educated about
issues I never even knew existed. They inspired me to stop being
ashamed and to start being proud of who I was."

In the spring of her freshman year, she finally let the music of
Carlos y Jose—her mother's favorite *norteña* group—blare loudly
through her dorm's hallway. She'd brought the cassette with her so
she could play it whenever she missed home, but she'd always
kept the volume down if other people were around. "For a long
time, I was embarrassed of my roommate or her friends hearing
it," she said. "But by the end of that year, I wouldn't lower it down
or turn it off no matter who came in."

Thinking back on how out of place she'd felt before meeting
the women of DALE, Nancy said she could understand how some
Latino kids go off to predominantly white universities and end up
distancing themselves from their roots. "You feel like you have to
leave your world behind and join a new one, and when you try to
do that it's easy to kind of forget where you came from," she said.
"That was starting to happen to me. But you have to figure out
how to live and survive in both worlds, so you can go back and
forth and not be forced to stay in one." The experience of leaving
her neighborhood, she said, had actually opened her eyes to see it
more clearly. "Looking in was different from looking out. It made
me ask why things were the way they were."

Ultimately, it also led her back—though Nancy said she'd
never thought of returning in terms of "giving back" to her community. "To me, that seems like more of a charity thing," she
explained. "When you give back, it's like you're doing it for some
kind of gain. But I wanted to come back because when I was growing up, I don't remember anybody ever 'making it' and still living
or working in the neighborhood. I want my students to see me and
see themselves in the future. Not that I want them all to be like me,
but sometimes you need to see something tangible that says, 'Hey,
it could be done.'"

....

The day after Quincy's upper-grade talent show, Nancy wasn't
sure whether she was more upset with herself or six of her students. The night before, she'd sat in a crowded gymnasium as a
variety of student acts took to the stage. There'd been a tumbling

troupe, two fifth-grade girls doing a Tae Kwon Do demonstration, pint-sized folkloric dancers, the obligatory lip-synchers, and even a pair of daredevil bicyclists. But the act that had drawn the most attention was a group of six girls from Nancy's homeroom.

Dressed in hip-hugging jeans and tight red tops, they'd done a dance routine to the "Cha-Cha Slide." It began innocently enough, but as the song progressed the moves became more and more suggestive. While the singer intoned, "How low can you go?/Can you go down low?/All the way to the flo'?" pairs of girls faced each other and thrust their hips together to the beat as each leaned back on one hand. It wasn't anything most people hadn't seen on music videos a hundred times, but this was school, these were kids, and lots of younger siblings and parents were watching. Some students cheered the girls' every move, but other people squirmed in their seats.

Rhonda Hoskins, the school's assistant principal and one of my early teaching mentors, had been one of the squirmers. Before I arrived at Quincy the morning after the show, she'd already talked with Nancy and told her she thought the performance was inappropriate. It wasn't a scolding—Rhonda, unlike some of the other adults in the building, treated Nancy as an equal. Still, one of the questions she'd asked continued to echo in Nancy's ears: *Why did you allow it?*

"I knew they were going to do that dance," she told me later that morning. "I watched them practice it. I kept asking them, 'What kind of a message do you think that is sending?' I told them, 'Those movements are not dance movements. It looks like you're having sex. It looks really bad.' I told them I wanted them to change their act, and I guess I hoped they would eventually change it on their own. But it didn't even cross my mind that I could just say, 'You know what? You can't do that.' Why didn't I realize that I had the power to just tell them, 'You're not allowed to do that'?"

Her youthful confidence had been shaken, and the second-guessing surrounding the talent show wasn't the only reason. A few days earlier, she'd been publicly berated by a veteran teacher for using the word *crap* within earshot of students. "As soon as I said it," Nancy told me, "she said in a really loud voice, 'Excuse me! You are a teacher. You should be a better role model. You don't say those kinds of words in front of kids.' Like she was my mom.

And my students were all right there listening. I was just so shocked, I didn't know what to say. I think I must've said, 'I'm sorry,' because that whole 'Oh, my God, you're better than me' thing sometimes gets into me and I can't control it." Nancy said it wasn't the first time she'd been talked down to by a colleague, and while she chalked some of it up to first-year hazing, she thought there was more to it. "Not only am I young, but I'm a woman, I'm Mexican, I went to this school. I think some teachers subconsciously think less of me or underestimate me because of that. I don't think they necessarily mean harm, but it's there."

The flap over her students' dance routine had left Nancy questioning the impact of her teaching. During the gender unit, she'd spent a lot of time with her classes talking about the commodification of women's bodies and looking at examples of sexual exploitation in the media. "What did those girls take from all that?" Nancy wondered aloud. "Nothing? They spoke up so strongly about it in class, and then they're up there onstage looking like—" She stopped short, but I recognized her frustration.

I could think back on numerous occasions from my own teaching when I was left wondering not only if my work had made any difference but whether it had actually done more harm than good. During my last year at Quincy, one of the central themes in my reading class had been the hardships of teen pregnancy. I'd watched too many former students have babies soon after graduating eighth grade, and I'd seen the deferral of dreams that often resulted. I thought bringing the issue out in the open would be helpful, so we undertook what I'd thought was a sobering study of the realities of teen parenting. Yet within the next year and a half, four of the girls from that class had babies of their own.

"I think what it is," Nancy told me, "is that we get so sucked in to the mind-set that as women we need to look attractive and hot and sexy that we can't totally break out of it. My female students are becoming aware and conscious of it, but I guess their self-esteem is so low that they also feed off of it. They probably think that's the only way guys will pay attention to them." She said it made her both sad and angry. "In the summer, they wear those tiny shorts—I call them hoochie-mama shorts—just to get noticed," Nancy said. "That's crazy!"

Later that week she talked to the girls, but they still didn't seem to think they'd done anything wrong. "It just reminds me how complex it is," she told me. "One lesson or one unit is not going to completely change 12 years of being socialized a certain way."

When I asked what she ultimately wants for her female students, she didn't hesitate. "I don't want these girls to be housewives," she said. "Not because I think that's a bad thing—if a woman chooses it, then that's fine. But I think it's easy to lose yourself in that role. I want them to get to college, because I know they'll have their minds opened up more then. And once they get to that point, they'll be fine. I want so much for them to free their minds and become empowered and become passionate and become aware of all this shit and do something about it." She paused. "And not to dress in hoochie-mama shorts!"

············

The words POWER and PRIVILEGE, written in capital letters with a red marker, stood out on an otherwise empty dry erase board.

"OK, take out the definitions of the words we were looking at yesterday," Nancy told the class. They'd spent the first part of the period playing a grammar game.

"I lost 'em," Fernando called out. *"Se la comió mi perro."*

Nancy ignored his comment. She seemed to gather from his tone that he was joking, and besides, if she stopped every time Fernando blurted out something unsolicited, she'd be putting on the brakes every 30 seconds. "So what did we say privilege was?"

Students who'd written it down flipped through their notes. "The advantages that a certain group of people have," read Ana, stumbling over her words a bit. "And power is when a person or group has influence or control over another person or group." They were concepts I hadn't examined in any real depth until I was in my 20s. Nancy thought her eighth graders were ready.

She went to the board and wrote PARENT/CHILD. "In this relationship, who has the power?"

"The parents," several kids said.

"No, kids have power, too," said Karina. "Like the power to get in trouble."

As several students laughed, Nancy asked: "How do you know parents have the power? How can you tell?"

"'Cause they make you do stuff: Mop the floor! Clean up!"

"They make the rules."

"They could do stuff you can't," Fernando added. "Like watch pornos. I know my dad does." Again, laughter from the others.

"So they have control over you in certain ways," Nancy said. "What's another group of people that has power?"

"Cops," someone called out.

"Yeah," agreed Eddie. "Cops can do whatever they want. They take red lights like it's nothing. And they park wherever they want and don't get tickets."

"So you're saying they don't have to obey the law the same way as everyone else. Would that be considered a privilege of being a cop?"

Eddie shrugged. "I guess so. They can do it and we can't."

Nancy went back to the board and wrote TEACHER/STUDENT. "How about with this relationship?"

"The teacher's always got the power," answered Eddie.

"And do they have privileges that students don't have?" Nancy asked. I noted that she'd referred to teachers as *they* instead of *we*.

"Yous get a private bathroom," Eddie said. "We don't even got doors on the stalls."

"You get to wear whatever you want," added Ana. "We gotta wear blue and white every day."

"Yeah, and you get better chairs than us," Agustin commented, getting up and moving to where Nancy had been sitting—in a nicely padded office chair, complete with casters and armrests.

Nancy put down the marker she'd been using. "You know what? That's good that you pointed that out. I've been taking advantage of that chair because it's so comfortable. But I do think about it. I think, Man, they're all sitting in those hard chairs and I have this nice soft one."

"You're abusing your privilege!" said Agustin.

"You're right," Nancy said, walking over to him. "It is a privilege to sit there." She sat down in the blue plastic chair that had been Agustin's. "So this is what we'll do. We'll take turns. Every day, somebody new will sit in that chair." The students cheered enthusiastically. "Agustin, since you noticed it, you can be first. Tomorrow that'll be your chair." He grinned and leaned back, then spun around a full turn.

Rather than becoming frozen by Agustin's challenge, Nancy had taken a teachable moment and made the most of it. But doing so had got her off track a bit. The primary goal of her lesson had been to introduce the idea that there are substantial privileges that go along with being a white person in America—unearned benefits that someone like me accrues simply by virtue of my skin color. It's a concept that many whites find threatening because it calls into question the myth of the level playing field. While some white people are willing to acknowledge that people of color continue to be disadvantaged in a variety of social arenas, they are less inclined to concede the inverse: that they are inevitably advantaged as a result. It's been said that privilege for whites is like water for fish: It's all around them, but it's hard for them to notice it.

With time running out in the period, that lesson might have to wait for the next day. But I felt certain Nancy would come back to it. While she knew that her students learned implicit lessons about race and power in school, it troubled her that racism and its societal manifestations were rarely talked about in classrooms in explicit ways. In school books, too, race was often conspicuously absent. James Loewen (1995) analyzed 12 of the most popular U.S. history texts for his book *Lies My Teacher Told Me* and found that only five even mentioned "racism, racial prejudice, or any term beginning with *race* in their indexes" (p. 144).

"These kids have been lied to," Nancy said. "Well, not lied to, but they've only been told certain parts of the story. And I don't want to sugarcoat things. I want them to know the reality, so that they could empower themselves, so they could stand up for themselves. I want them to be more aware and more conscious—like Paulo Freire says, to learn to read the word and the world."

Race had been a subtext of my relationship with Nancy for as long as we'd known each other. When she was an eighth grader, she and four other girls had worked with me to make a homemade "book on tape" of stories from *The House on Mango Street*. Large parts of our discussions of the book involved Nancy and the other "Mango Girls" translating the immigrant experience for me, explaining references and shades of meaning that I didn't understand. The fact that I was a white man and they were all Latinas was lost on none of us, but it also wasn't something we talked

about. Though my experience growing up had clearly been different from theirs in countless ways, the bond we formed around the
reading of *Mango Street* allowed us to share stories, make connections, and build trust.

Still, I often reflected during my years in the classroom on the
relative privilege I'd enjoyed compared with the experiences of the
mostly Mexican and African American students I taught. Growing
up, I never had to worry about a teacher's having low expectations
of me as soon as I walked through the door. I never had to sit
through history or literature classes where my ancestors' contributions were given token, if any, attention. I never had to look around
my classrooms and feel as if I didn't belong: Even though I'd
attended schools integrated by court-ordered busing, system plan-
ners were always careful to maintain white majorities. And I'd
never doubted whether I could or should go to college—it was
something that seemed not only possible but natural, the obvious
and logical next step in my path.

For Nancy, of course, the thought of going to college had been
far from a given. Once she made it there, however, and worked
through her initial insecurities, she began to question the disparities and bigotry she saw all around her. I recall her going through
several stages—feeling alternately bitter, hurt, and victimized—
before finally settling into a potent, deep-seated anger. "I was
pissed off," she remembered. "I was just very, very, very angry."

That anger came to a head one morning during her sophomore
year as she and I drove together to watch one of her former Quincy
classmates graduate from junior college. "I think I'm starting to hate
white people," she told me. The comment took me aback slightly,
but considering the changes she'd gone through since going to
DePaul, I wasn't all that surprised. "The white kids in my classes—
they're so closed-minded," she continued. "Fine, they came into college unaware. So did I. But even when they're confronted with the
issues, they choose to remain ignorant! That's what pisses me off!
'Well, my family didn't do this or that, so it's not my problem.' They
don't want to shatter their perfect little world."

For the rest of the ride we went back and forth. I told stories of
undergrads I'd taught who were just as insistent about keeping
their blinders on as the ones Nancy had encountered, but I also
challenged the broad strokes I thought she'd used to paint white

students. Nancy acknowledged that she knew some whites who were socially aware and involved, but she said they were a tiny minority. Most, she insisted, were in deep denial.

Thinking back on that time, Nancy said she'd opened up to me because her anger was beginning to overwhelm her. "I was generalizing," she told me. "I'd see somebody white, and I'd think, 'You're rich, you're preppy, you must be like this.' Or I'd be on the train, and see a white woman with expensive shoes, and I'd get pissed. I'd think, 'Those shoes must've cost $200' or 'I wonder how much time she spent on her hair.' I was getting worried, because I didn't want to be like that. I didn't think I was racist. I knew I didn't really hate white people—I didn't hate you, I didn't hate my friends who were white. But I think it was just a phase of becoming aware and letting out a lot of anger and frustration that had been building up for a long time."

As a teacher, Nancy said, she still felt that anger simmering at times, and she didn't think that was a bad thing. After all, with bilingual education and affirmative action under attack, continued vast funding disparities between school districts, and so many other threats to educational and social equity, there was still plenty to be upset about. But she'd come to believe that it was important to use the anger as a catalyst for changing things—not to become swallowed or disabled by it. "You can be destructive with your anger, or you can choose to be constructive with it," she said. "I try to help the kids understand that when you first become educated about some of the injustices, there's a reaction—you're upset, you're angry. I tell them, 'So don't feel bad if you're feeling that way. But you need to move through it. You need to use it to do something good.'"

In that respect, I thought, Nancy's students couldn't have asked for a better example than their teacher.

．．．．．．．．．．．

"This is Mexican people," Karina was saying a few days later, raising one of her hands to her shoulder as if she were measuring something. She then stretched her other hand as high as it would go. "And this is white people. And Mexican people wanna go up with white people." The class was in the midst of a discussion about the psychological impact of racism on people of color.

"But we don't have to try to be like them," Ana reasoned. "We can go up another way."

"It's the media," Erika said. "We watch TV and they show women with blue eyes, blonde hair, skinny—it's brainwashing."

"That's right, sister!" Nancy exclaimed. Maybe the sexuality unit had made some inroads after all. "Just because I'm dark, thick, black hair, dark eyes—that doesn't mean I can't be beautiful!"

"So why did you dye your hair?" asked Beto. The class exploded in howls of laughter and cries of "Ooooh!" and "You feel salty!"

Nancy smiled, looking as if she knew she'd been busted. "Can I respond?" she asked, raising her arms in a sign for the students to settle down. "I did not dye my hair. They're called highlights."

Nancy told me she was glad her students felt comfortable enough to challenge her, to hold her words and actions up for scrutiny. She believed it was evidence that one of her main messages was getting through. "One thing I'm always telling them is 'Learn to question,'" she said. "'Don't accept things just because they're in a textbook.' I think a lot of the kids have the same mindset I did growing up: that whoever wrote the book is smart and educated, so whatever they tell me, it must be true. And I tell them, 'It doesn't matter who wrote it, you have to learn to analyze it and critique it and not just accept things.' So little by little, they're learning to question. They even question me—and I like that."

She may have liked it, but it also sometimes touched a nerve. When her students commented once on how many pairs of shoes she owned, Nancy had been prompted to do some soul-searching. "I do have a lot of shoes—compared to the one pair I had when I was growing up," she said. "And I hate that. I feel guilty. But in college I'd see people who had a lot of shoes, a lot of outfits, and I never had much. So in some ways I think I'm overcompensating for what I didn't have as a kid. I can see how I've become more materialistic since college." On the other hand, Nancy agreed with a Latina friend in the business world who argued that, for people of color, having an ample wardrobe is a necessary weapon—just like standard English. "So I'm aware of all that," she said, "and I'm trying to balance it."

She was even more shaken by her students' criticisms of her teaching. Earlier in the year, she'd asked her students to write evaluations of her class. Most had been favorable, but she couldn't get one boy's response out of her mind for days afterward. "He wrote, 'I think this class is a piece of good for nothing class,'" she said. "Then it said, 'I don't know why we have to do so much writing. People ain't going to look at how we write.' And then in capital letters, he wrote, 'Don't think we like to be challenged!' And *challenged* was misspelled," she recalled, laughing—though she hadn't thought it was funny at the time.

Nancy spent much of the following weekend second-guessing her motives, her methods, her apparent successes—everything. "I think my biggest concern was that they misunderstood where I was coming from," she said. "I didn't want them to think of me as a hard-ass who was just out to get them by giving them lots of work. I wanted them to see that the reason I was expecting a lot from them was that I thought highly of them, that I wanted great things for them, and that I believed they were capable of meeting that challenge."

She'd read about student resistance in critical theory courses in college, but she'd always envisioned students resisting the dreadful stuff about school, the things she was trying to change—not resisting her. "It hurt a lot," she said. "But most of all it just made me sad. Somehow this kid has been going through his education and getting by without being challenged, and he's gotten to the point where he's fine with it. So when someone comes to break that apart, he finally speaks up for himself. Why didn't he speak out before? It's just sad to see that some kids are conditioned to expect less of themselves, and they get mad when somebody asks them to expect more."

The next week she had a long talk with the boy and then with his entire class. She defended her demanding workload in principle, but agreed to ease up on the amount of writing they had to do for homework: Instead of three to four pages a night, she'd settle for two.

In large part, Nancy felt she was paying the price for the low expectations of others, for years of students' being granted what Gloria Ladson-Billings (2002) calls "permission to fail." According to Nancy, too many teachers at Quincy—and in other schools that served the urban poor—focused too narrowly on discipline as a measure of their success: If the halls were orderly and the classrooms quiet, it was assumed that all was well, that learning was taking place. But how could all be well, Nancy wondered, when so many students were coming to seventh grade lacking the most basic of skills. "A lot of the kids, at the beginning of the year, don't know how to capitalize, they can't write a paragraph," she told me. "They've never written an argument, never analyzed any-thing—in seventh grade!" Nancy believed most Quincy teachers genuinely liked their students, but liking them, she said, didn't translate into believing in them.

While I thought there was a lot of truth in what Nancy said, I'd also learned that pointing fingers of blame could be misguided. When I taught at Quincy, I'd spent many lunch periods with Bob Fabian, another upper-grade teacher, lamenting the inadequate preparation our students had apparently received in the primary grades. Then one day, Bob decided to do something proactive: He volunteered to teach a math class for second-grade low-achievers during the school's "extended day" program. Give me those kids for an hour a day for 8 weeks, Bob said, and I'll have them apply-ing the Pythagorean theorum. He confidently dubbed his under-taking "Miracle Math."

Eight weeks later, Bob came back to the third floor with his tail between his legs. He'd had a terrible time just getting the children to sit still and listen, and he never quite figured out a satisfactory way to teach his two target skills: counting money and telling time. "Miracle Math" had been a miraculous flop, and from that point on, the tone of our lunchtime conversations changed considerably.

That's not to say that Nancy's concerns over expectations were groundless. There were certainly teachers at Quincy who didn't demand enough of their students, and the more I watched Nancy at work, the more I began to wonder if I had been one of them. While I'd always thought I had high expectations in the classroom, and had tried to give my students regular opportunities to exam-ine their lives and the world around them, Nancy required as much writing in a couple weeks as I typically had in an entire 10-week marking period. Watching her in action caused me to look back at my own teaching with a more critical eye, and the most obvious lesson I'd learned was that, in so many ways, I could've pushed harder, demanded more, set the bar that much higher for my students.

Nancy knew that the world outside the neighborhood would demand a lot of these kids, and she wanted them to be ready. "I don't even see myself as a seventh- or eighth-grade teacher," she told me. "Everything I do, I do it as if they were already in high school and I was trying to prepare them for college." But finding ways to do that with students whose ability levels varied widely—some who were in a monolingual classroom for the first time—was a formidable challenge in itself.

One reason was that there simply wasn't enough time. Nancy had been trying to find a workable balance between time spent on language and writing skills and time spent on deep engagement with issues, but lately she'd begun wondering how successful she'd been. When Marlena, a soft-spoken eighth grader, turned in a paper titled "The American Dream: Is It a Reality or Is It a Nightmare?" Nancy was so proud she nearly cried. "It talked about her dad immigrating, and about the rights of undocumented immigrants, and how Mexicans come here for a better life not realizing that they're going to be exploited—and she used that word: *exploited*," Nancy said. "She talked about the history of discrimination against Mexican Americans, about the Bracero Program, and it totally seemed like she was empowered, like she was aware. When I read it, I was just overwhelmed. Sometimes you don't know if you're making an impact, but with that one, I felt I did."

On the other hand, Nancy told me, grammatical mistakes were scattered throughout the paper: run-on sentences, missing commas, jumbled verb tenses. Most of them weren't major errors, but Nancy knew that in a different context—such as on a college admissions essay—they would be viewed harshly. "I kind of looked at her paper as an evaluation of my teaching so far," she said. "I've been able to get some things across to them, and that makes me feel good. But at the same time, maybe I haven't spent enough time on other things. I want to give them the tools they're going to need to succeed and to survive—which means that they need to learn standard English. But I don't want to spend all year working out of the grammar book. It's just so hard to balance it."

Nancy was doing a better job than I ever had of finding that balance, but the curricular pendulum in her classroom still swung more often in the direction of big questions than question marks. In a time in which schools are obsessed with test preparation and standardized knowledge, such a choice seems especially daring and refreshing. But it's important to remember that it's a choice nonetheless and, as Marlena's essay showed, it doesn't come without some sacrifice.

• • • • • • • • • • • •

Not much on the streets outside Quincy announced that summer was just around the corner, but there were small signs. Blooms of pink and purple and white petunias dotted a small plot of black dirt next to an alley. A teenage girl who should've been in school somewhere ran past wearing "hoochie-mama" shorts. On down the sidewalk, two ice cream vendors nodded to one another as their pushcarts crossed paths. They were both older men—maybe in their 50s—and I wondered how many miles they pushed those carts each day, how much they took home out of each 75-cent *helado* they sold, how many mouths in their families needed feeding. I wondered if either of them had children or grandchildren at Quincy.

Inside room 305, the eighth graders in Nancy's reading class were looking over a form letter she'd just handed them outlining all the fees they'd have to pay before graduating.

"A hundred dollars! *Hijole!*"

"Damn, my ma don't got money. She just bought *ropa* for my sister."

"I know it's expensive," Nancy told them. "My ma wouldn't have been able to afford it, either. Believe me, I know how you're feeling."

Max studied the list: cap and gown photos—$16, graduation jersey—$23, eighth-grade luncheon—$20, nonrefundable graduation fee—$50. He shook his head. "My parents don't have money, man."

"I know," agreed Eduardo. "We need to grow some."

Their conversation, it turned out, was an appropriate segue to the day's lesson. The day before, they'd read an essay about growing up poor in the rural South, then written responses comparing the author's recollections to their own. But the follow-up discussion had fallen flat.

"Yesterday, when we were talking about the essay, there were a lot of you who were very quiet," Nancy said, her words seeming to still the kids once again. "And I'm not sure if it's because you were bored, or shy, or embarrassed, or uncomfortable. Why is it that we don't want to share?"

"It's depressing," a girl said in a voice I could barely hear.

"It's embarrassing," added another student.

Other kids looked down, averted their eyes. No one said anything for a few moments.

"I remember how it feels," Nancy told them, and downcast faces slowly turned toward her. "I remember not being able to pay my school fees, not having enough money for my pictures, having rats in our apartment. I woke up one time with a rat crawling on my neck." Nervous laughter bubbled up around the room. Tense bodies seemed to relax a little.

"Maybe we're poor, but at least we work," said Salvador. "At least we're not on welfare. It's one thing if people are on welfare and they really need it, but it's another thing if they're just sitting there lazy and they don't wanna work."

"Yeah," agreed Rosa. "Some of the people in the projects— they're just lazy." I was uncomfortable with the turn the conversation had taken, and I was sure Nancy was, too. I wondered how I might've responded if I were the teacher. What would I have said? What tone would I have used? How could I have pushed their thinking?

"You know what?" Nancy said to the class. "My ma was on welfare for a while." She paused, allowing the information to sink in. "It's nothing to be ashamed of. You may think people on welfare are just trying to get over, but why do you think that? Where do those ideas come from? How does the media portray the poor?"

"Dirty."

"They don't wanna work."

"That they're criminals or drug dealers."

"So don't you think that stuff gets in your head?" Nancy asked them. "It's easy to just say 'People in the projects are lazy,' but you have to think about what caused the conditions they're living in."

"Yeah," said Arturo from across the room, his beefy frame and booming voice commanding the group's attention. "I mean, there's some things people can do to clean their neighborhoods and help, but there's some stuff the government should be doing."

"Yes!" Nancy said. "Remember when it snowed so much last winter? Remember how long it took them to clean the streets around here? Why do you think that is?"

"Maybe they don't clean around here 'cause we're Mexican," answered Yessica, her face framed by huge hoop earrings.

"It's not because you're Mexican," said Marjorie, the only white student in the class. "It's because you're poor."

"They think we're not important down here," added Teresa. "'Cause the visitors to the city, they don't come here. They go straight to downtown, to the lake, to Navy Pier, so they want it to look nice around there. But not here."

"Yeah, and the landlords around here are cheap," Rosa said, anger rising in her voice. "When something is broken in my building, they take forever to fix it."

"Most of the owners don't even live around here," Marjorie said.

Nancy nodded her head. "That's a good point. It might be different if they had to live in their own buildings, right?"

"Look," Arturo said, scooting up in his chair, "we gotta open our damn eyes. Why don't we speak out against some of this stuff? One person can't change it. All of us have to get together. Let's go down to city hall and tell them bastards something!" Suddenly the room was abuzz, kids rising out of their chairs.

"This is the point of an education!" Nancy said excitedly. "For you to become aware of what's going on."

"And do something about it," added Yessica.

"Right!" Nancy said. "And do something about it. That should be the whole point of school."

The bell rang, but conversations continued as the students gathered their things.

"We're gonna protest, Ms. Serrano," Teresa said.

"Arturo for President!" two of the guys began chanting as they left. Arturo didn't even try to hide his smile.

••••••••••••

I'd like to tell you that 2 weeks later, Nancy and her students marched on the mayor's office and then on to City Hall. I'd like to tell you that Arturo gave an impassioned speech at an outdoor rally, that sanitation crews and absentee landlords had been put on notice, and that living conditions for the working poor in the neighborhood had been improving as a result. But the protest didn't happen. The kids' momentum gradually waned, the end of the year crept up, and other demands crowded onto Nancy's already overlong list of concerns. She felt guilty about not seizing the moment more fully, about not following through as she'd planned, but she reminded herself that it was her first year, and that other opportunities would come along.

Thinking about her future as a teacher was exciting for Nancy in many ways. She'd learned so much this first year, and she looked forward to building on what she'd started, to continuing to grow and evolve. "I know I have a lot to improve on," she told me. "I'm not where I want to be as a teacher. But I have my little pluses, and I'm constantly getting better. I'm not going to say I'm doing everything I want to do, because it's just so tough. But every month that I teach, I feel like I can see the bigger picture more clearly."

Part of that bigger picture involved having her work as a teacher gauged by her students' scores on standardized tests. "I feel the pressure of all that," she said. "Believe me, I'm not this carefree rebel who doesn't worry about how my kids will do on the tests. But you have to be careful that it doesn't distort your expectations or replace what you believe in. I tell myself, 'I'm not going to let this test run my curriculum.' And I'm lucky that I have a principal who gives me the freedom to make decisions about what I teach and how I teach it. But there's always that what-if. What if my kids don't perform well? What if what I'm doing doesn't give them the skills they need to survive and succeed? My main fear really is, what if what they know doesn't show up on the test? Because I know they're learning."

Another persistent challenge, Nancy said, was finding the time to do all she wants to do. "I have so many ideas, but creating your own curriculum is time-consuming, and it's hard to fit it in with all the grading and paperwork and administrative stuff teachers have to do. Sometimes I get really overwhelmed, and I'll tell my ma, 'I need to take a day off. I'm tired.' And my ma will tell me, 'What do you mean you're tired? Imagine if you had five kids and no husband and you had to go to work and then come home and cook and clean for them. Then you'd be tired.' I know what I'm doing doesn't even compare to that, so that kind of energizes me."

Most days she felt hopeful, but she worried occasionally that the enthusiasm she had for her work would be slowly drained away, that she'd somehow become jaded like the teachers who'd written her off back in high school. "Sometimes I wonder," she said, "am I doing all this just because I'm a new teacher and I have all this motivation that people talk about first-year teachers having? Or is this how I'm going to be in 5 years? I think it is. But sometimes I'm scared that I may change, that I may get frustrated. You see teachers go in with such strength and then the system and the school climate can really break them down. But I don't think that's going to happen to me. As long as people keep letting me do what I do, I think I'll be fine."

In one of the final stories in *The House on Mango Street*, the young protagonist, Esperanza, visits the home of two friends whose baby sister has just died. Their tiny house is buzzing with neighbors and relatives who've come to express their sorrow, including three elderly sisters—aunts to the dead baby—who strike up a conversation with Esperanza. They are a wise and mysterious trio, three women who seem to be able to look deep within the young girl and devine her innermost thoughts. They tell Esperanza that she's special, that she will go far. But they also leave her with a charge: "When you leave you must remember to come back for the others," one of the women says. "A circle, understand?"

Even as an eighth grader, Nancy had understood on some level what that meant—and she hadn't forgotten. Coming back to the neighborhood was about completing a circle. Teaching there was about beginning a new one.

7

teaching, stories, and troubled times

When I decided to undertake this project, I did so with the belief that one of the best ways to learn about teaching is to see it up close. I thought the stories of these five teachers—who are not only "good," in my view, but consciously fighting for the freedom and enlightenment of the students they teach—could provide examples of how other teachers might work against the grain of the grim systemic realities they sometimes face in public schools.

Of course, in many academic circles, stories and other examples of what Elliot Eisner (1995) calls "artistically crafted research" aren't seen as legitimate methods of inquiry. But I think their value is underestimated. How better to understand life in a street gang than through the stark, first-person perspective offered by Luis J. Rodriguez in his book *Always Running*? If you want to study the impact of poverty and racism on urban African American youth, you could pore over dozens of quantitative journal articles, but none, in my view, would capture the meaning of that experience in the way that *Ghetto Life 101*, a series of National Public Radio reports by Chicago teenagers LeAlan Jones and Lloyd Newman, did in the early 1990s. Similarly, you could read numerous scholarly texts on media bias without achieving the kind of understanding you get by watching and listening to the key players in *Control Room*, Jehane Noujaim's documentary about Arab and U.S. television coverage of the 2003 invasion of Iraq

None of these works attempts to make broad claims or generalizations. What they do, instead, is highlight the unique, zoom-in on individual experience in all its complexity and unpredictability, help us better understand small corners of the world in ways other forms of inquiry cannot. If I've done my job successfully, that's what the narrative portraits of the five teachers in this book do as well. They allow us to get inside classrooms and stay a while, and as we do, we're able to catch glimpses of teaching in all its moral, intellectual, emotional, pedagogical, political, and social complexity.

Such a view contrasts sharply with the compartmentalized notion of teaching often put forth in teacher preparation programs, where social contexts are typically examined in foundations courses, theoretical aspects in philosophy classes, "practical" dimensions in methods seminars, and so on. In the classrooms we've seen here—as in all real-life teaching situations—no such tidy divisions apply. Philosophy interweaves with technique, culture intersects curricular content, historical and economic realities impact purposes and goals. In a teacher such as Nancy or Toni, we're able to see the embodiment of all these elements in continuous interplay. And as we hear these teachers talk about their work, we begin to understand just how complicated good teaching really is.

But bringing the voices of teachers center stage is not just a methodological issue—it's a political one as well. In the current climate, where federally mandated accountability measures (what the editors of *Rethinking Schools* refer to as the "No Child Left Untested" policy) have left many teachers feeling disregarded and powerless, inquiry that spotlights teachers' voices and stories can stake out contested terrain in the larger conversation about public schools. Kathleen Casey (1993) calls her life histories of women teacher activists "a deliberate reversal," an attempt to move those whose voices are typically unheard in the contemporary struggle over education to the center of her analysis. I've attempted a similar turning of the tables here by directing my attention toward young teachers of color.

Still, as I discussed in Chapter 1, I'm under no illusion that these narratives are in any sense "pure" representations of the teachers' lives and work. I wondered throughout the various phases of the project about my ability as a white man to convey the experiences of women of color, and about the ways my privileged social position and subjectivity were affecting how I interpreted what I heard and saw. Taking all that into account, though, my goal was still to construct narratives that reflected how *each teacher* understood her experiences as much as how *I* understood them. It's impossible, I realize, to separate the two entirely—our interpretations are necessarily interwoven in the telling—but to me, it was a question of balance. Even though I'm having the last word now, I didn't want to have it on every page. I wanted the voices of Liz and Cynthia and Freda and Toni and Nancy to come through loud and clear.

Beyond that, I made an effort to balance my "empathetic regard" for each teacher with "critical attention" and "a discerning gaze" (Lightfoot, 1983, p. 6). One thing that gave me pause in being critical, however, was that I knew from 9 years' experience just how hard teaching is, and that trying to teach with an eye on social justice makes it that much more of an uphill climb. It's relatively easy to stand on the sidelines and critique the work of practitioners who are trying to teach against the grain, and to dismiss their efforts as watered-down or insufficient. But it's much harder to step inside a classroom and actually do something different, to enact a pedagogy that is deep and meaningful and engaging to kids—one that helps them, as Nancy puts it, "overcome whatever they need to overcome."

My assumption from the outset was that these five teachers were doing good work in their classrooms, and as Sara Lawrence-Lightfoot (1997) has noted, "The researcher who asks first 'what is good here?' is likely to absorb a very different reality than the one who is on a mission to discover the sources of failure" (p. 9). That doesn't mean I turned a blind eye to what didn't seem to be working—on the contrary. I think each portrait reveals a teacher struggling in a variety of ways. But I did feel badly for the teachers when classes or entire days seemed to unravel. I also cheered for them when lessons clicked, when students responded, when connections were made. I genuinely liked each of them as people, and I admired their dedication to their calling and to their kids. If, in the end, I was slightly more tuned in to the good things that were happening in their classrooms, I hope I can be forgiven. Teaching isn't easy. Second-guessing is.

············

When Bruce Springsteen's single "Born in the USA" was released in 1984, the song's story of a disillusioned Vietnam veteran returning home from a nightmarish tour of duty was lost on many. While Springsteen's lyrics pointed to the U.S. government's abandonment of the poor and working-class kids who'd been shipped off to fight the war, many listeners who sang along with the anthemlike chorus heard it as a patriotic declaration. I was in college at the time, and I remember seeing guys throw their fists in the air as those familiar guitar chords blared from dorm-room speakers: "Born in the USA/I was born in the USA." Advisors to then-President Ronald Reagan—who clearly hadn't listened to the song closely—even tried to use it as theme music for Reagan's reelection campaign.

Like songwriting, "artistically crafted" inquiry is an admittedly interpretive affair on many levels. Still, as the response to "Born in the USA" showed, leaving too much meaning up for grabs can be dangerous, and sometimes I worry that I've done so here, that the teachers' narratives might be read in ways that neither they nor I intended. Of course, there's no "true" reading of any story—one interpretation is as valid as any other—but having said that, let me clarify a few things I'm not trying to say in this book.

I'm not saying that success in urban classrooms comes easy to these five women simply because they are teachers of color. In fact, what stands out to me as much as anything is how hard each of them worked: Freda's two-word self-assessment—"I'm drowning"—could've been uttered by any of the other four at various points along the way. Teaching well isn't easy in any circumstance, but it requires even more determined effort of teachers working in underresourced communities or school districts, teachers who are nonetheless committed to making their classrooms places where students are educated and liberated rather than warehoused.

That might seem an obvious point to note, but I think it's important to avoid the impression that the teachers portrayed here are somehow "naturals" because they share certain cultural connections with their students. While being called a "natural" may sound like a compliment, it's really a backhanded one, as it is for black athletes who are lauded as "naturally gifted" while their white counterparts are described as "scrappy," "hard-working," or "students of the game." I consider all five of these women gifted teachers, and they certainly had cultural understandings that helped them garner respect among the kids in their classes. But I also witnessed the grinding effort that went into their daily practice, and the continual strides each teacher made to keep improving. None had the attitude that she had it all figured out. As Liz put it, "If you're really committed to being a good teacher, you commit yourself to constant study. You're always learning. You become a student of the world."

I'm also not saying that a teacher must share her students' racial background in order to be effective, or that cross-cultural teaching isn't possible or desirable. Liz, you'll remember, pointed out that she had white colleagues who do remarkable work with black kids. Similarly, Gloria Ladson-Billings (1994) has shown that both black and white teachers can teach African American children in a "culturally relevant" manner. But for a white teacher to do so—and I say this from my own experience—requires a sincere and sustained commitment to putting one's self in the role of learner. Angela Valenzuela (1999), who looks at the damaging impact of "subtractive schooling" practices on U.S.-Mexican youth at a Houston high school, suggests that teachers who are genuinely effective with students of color typically "either emanate from similar communities *or* are well versed in the literature and histories of these communities" (p. 265, italics mine). Whatever the race of the teacher, says Valenzuela, "a community's interests are best served by those who possess an unwavering respect for the cultural integrity of a people and their history." Clearly, that requires extra work on the part of "outsider" teachers, but it's far from impossible.

Finally, I'm not saying that the single (and simple) answer to the ills of our educational system lies in the hands of heroic teachers, lone crusaders seeking justice in an unjust world. One of the dangers of a book such as this is that in focusing on the particular, on the stories of individuals, it's easy to lose sight of the bigger picture, of the larger forces at work in people's lives. Because of that, some readers might conclude that if we just had more good teachers like Cynthia or Freda or Jaime Escalante, everything would be OK, and the promise of public education would be realized once and for all.

It should go without saying that the roots of the problem go far deeper, but since I'm not sure it always does go without saying, I'll say it: Yes, attracting and retaining talented and committed teachers—especially teachers of color—is a crucial component in any effort to achieve educational equity. But it's not enough. As long as we allow bilingual education programs to be dismantled, as long as a child in Illinois's wealthiest school district receives $13,000 more to fund his or her education each year than a child in the state's poorest district, as long as education reform is limited to shallow, standardized-test-driven, top-down mandates—if factors such as those remain unchanged, inequities in public schooling will persist. That doesn't mean small groups of committed teachers can't make a difference. They can—and every day, in schools across the country, they do. But if we really want what many of us say we want—equal educational opportunity for all children, along with just and fair outcomes—then we have to recognize that the challenges we face shouldn't rest only on the shoulders of caring and committed teachers but on all our shoulders—teachers, parents, citizens, everybody. None of us should be let off the hook.

••••••••••••

I didn't go into this project with a checklist of qualities that a teacher who views herself as a change agent must possess, and I didn't come out with one, either. Just as there is no single formula or blueprint for being a good teacher, I don't believe there is one best path toward teaching for change. Each of these women animates the notion in her own way, enacting a rendering that is deeply personal and inevitably shaped by her own history, values, and beliefs. Still, when we step back and look at the five portraits as a whole, it becomes clear that the teachers share certain motivations, commitments, dispositions of mind, and ways of seeing children, schools, and the world. While we can't come up with a precise definition of "teaching for change" by looking at their classrooms—and I don't know if I'd want to—we can nonetheless say something about what such an orientation might look like at ground level.

One thing that seemed important to all the teachers was valuing and building upon their students' outside-school knowledge and experiences. Sometimes this was evident in spontaneous, even silly moments that demonstrated a willingness to acknowledge or embrace youth culture—think of Freda's comparing the "adopted identities" of Hitler and Eminem, or Cynthia's allowing her girls to "do science" backed by a Christina Aguilera soundtrack. Even more substantively, though, it meant planning lessons or activities that encourage students to make connections, as with Toni's unit examining AIDS both in Latin America and in TCA's community, Liz's students' updated versions of David Walker's *Appeal*, or Nancy's use of literature that spoke to her students' lives. Curriculum, in these instances, becomes both a "window" and a "mirror" for students (McIntosh & Style, 1999), allowing them to look out on worlds previously unknown to them while also seeing their own experience with new eyes. With students whose cultural or economic backgrounds differ significantly from that of the mainstream, holding up such mirrors can be a particularly powerful practice.

The teachers' classrooms were also spaces where kids' voices were heard, where students were encouraged to make intellectual leaps, to discuss and debate important issues, to question past injustices and present wrongs. "Why would you gravitate to the religion of the people who are persecuting you?" Raymond asked during the discussion on slave rebellions in Liz's class. "How Hitler gonna try to lead Germany when he not even German?" Isaac wondered aloud in Freda's room. Agustin challenged the fairness of Nancy having a more comfortable chair than her students, and Marcellus displayed an awareness of the historical misrepresentation of people of color when he asked me, "You ain't gonna make us look bad, is you?" I heard thoughtful, incisive comments such as these on a regular basis in all five classrooms, and while they say a great deal about the intelligence and perceptiveness of the students who made them, they also say something important about each teacher's willingness to create the kind of environment where such sharing is not only allowed but actively invited.

Building strong relationships with students was a key for all these teachers as well, but as I saw it, their caring involved more than just an emotional connection. They nurtured relationships characterized by what Angela Valenzuela (1999) calls "authentic caring," which involves not only getting to know kids as three-dimensional beings but also developing a keen understanding of the social barriers they face. Think of Cynthia, who, in addition to forging genuine relationships with students such as Lynette, was animated by the fact that most of the girls she taught, because they were of color, would "have to work twice as hard as other people—maybe three times as hard—to achieve [their] dreams." Or Toni, whose childhood experiences helped her understand the brutal economic realities her students faced, which in turn strengthened her determination to give them the opportunity to travel abroad. For Nancy, authentic caring meant affirming her students' cultural identities and, at the same time, pushing them to excel—both of which, for her, were connected to an awareness that her kids were playing against a stacked deck.

As skilled as these teachers were at developing authentic relationships with the kids they taught, though, it's important to remember that all five experienced their share of resistance from students as well. While they seemed to be viewed as "cool" teachers, as adults who would listen and could be trusted, that didn't give them a free pass when it came to dealing with discipline problems or student misbehavior. It's difficult not to take such opposition personally, and sometimes these teachers did. When you believe you're doing your best to provide your students with a more humanizing and meaningful education and they still push against you, it can be tempting to throw your hands up in despair. But more often than not, I saw these women use their students' resistance as an invitation to reflect on their own practice, and I sensed, too, that each, deep down, welcomed the challenge of trying to engage her most difficult kids—even if it sometimes drove her crazy as well. Too often, teachers misread student opposition as a sign that kids simply "don't care" about their educations. Teachers working with an eye on social justice try to keep in mind that, for young people struggling against feelings of powerlessness and alienation, resistance can be a palpable sign of life.

A recurring refrain in Nancy's chapter is the high expectations she has of her students, and that theme was echoed by the other teachers time and again. "I don't want [this] to turn into an Asian support class," Freda said of her Asian studies course. "I push them—I mean *really push them*," Cynthia remarked of the girls at New Horizons. Toni wasn't satisfied with simply giving her students "an experience" with Spanish—she wanted them to have the power that came with fully acquiring a second language. In Liz's room, the atmosphere of academic rigor was unmistakable from my first visit: "It's going to be an intense quarter," she told her students that day. "So please prepare yourself for that intensity." One of the most profound realizations I had while observing these teachers was that while I thought I'd set high standards for my students during my years in the classroom, I hadn't pushed hard enough. Too often, I'd let my students' tough circumstances reduce my expectations, consciously or not, to more "realistic" ones. While I occasionally saw the teachers here do so as well, what I remember most is the resolve with which they fought such inclinations at every turn.

But having high expectations isn't enough. Equally important, from a social justice perspective, is finding ways to help kids who've continually struggled in school rise to meet them. A large body of research in education centers on identifying "what works" with "diverse" (read *poor* and *urban*) student populations, but when we look at the classrooms of these five teachers, it seems clear that—depending on the teacher, the day, the lesson, the mood—a variety of methods can be used successfully with marginalized students. I emphasize this not to suggest that identifying and describing specific teaching practices that have been shown to work well isn't helpful. But I would argue that zeroing in on methods alone without regard for the broader social contexts of one's teaching is too narrow a focus—particularly for urban educators. Indeed, what teachers of students from historically oppressed groups need, suggests Lilia Bartolomé (1996), is not "magical" methods but "political clarity" (p. 235).

For the teachers profiled in these pages, the seeds of their politicization were planted at an early age. Most looked back on their own schooling experiences with a certain degree of dissatisfaction or, in some cases, outright bitterness, and used those feelings as motivation to create a classroom environment where students felt culturally (and humanly) validated and cared for in genuine ways. Most also spoke of moments of epiphany that had sharpened their personal politics: Freda's being labeled a "twinkie" by fellow Asians, Toni's attending a Gay and Lesbian Alliance meeting in college, Nancy's carrying milk crates into her dorm while white students unpacked trailer loads of belongings. While their individual upbringings varied greatly, the life histories of these teachers show that common experiences of "exile and struggle" (hooks, 1990) do characterize the daily lives of groups in this country—people of color, women, immigrants, gays and lesbians, the poor—and the strength individual teachers draw from this can be formidable.

In her essay "A Woman of No Consequence/Una Mujer Cualquiera," Sandra Cisneros (1998) writes: "I am convinced that the power of an oppressed group is its vision, its ability to see pain where others might not see it because they have not experienced it. . . . Each of us has witnessed unique atrocities specific to our gender or race or class or sexuality; each of us, and our distinctive visions, is our gift to each other as a group and to the world at large" (p. 85). What Cisneros is acknowledging is both a shared experience among members of an oppressed group and, at the same time, differences within the group—the notion that each of us, no matter our background, has a "distinctive vision." It seems clear to me that the teachers portrayed here, in part because of their own experiences of "exile and struggle," are able to use their "distinctive visions" not only to connect with and motivate their students but to reimagine the purposes and possibilities of public education as well.

Mike Rose (1995), who criss-crossed the United States looking in on dozens of public school classrooms for his book *Possible Lives*, says he's come to believe that "a defining characteristic of good teaching is a tendency to push on the existing order of things" (p. 428). Each of these teachers, in her own way, pushes against the status quo of public education, struggles to disrupt the business-as-usual mediocrity of urban schooling. They attempt to respond to the question "What are we educating kids *for*?" with answers that go beyond empty sloganeering or taken-for-granted conclusions. They understand that arming students with the skills they'll need to become employed is crucial, but not enough. "If the purpose of schools is just to keep kids off the streets or help them get jobs, that's one thing," Liz told me. "But if we're educating kids so that they can develop critical minds and really engage in society, so that they can affect the community and demand things of their government and develop initiatives themselves, that's a completely different vision of what schools could be." It's a vision that, as much now as ever, needs to be part of the larger conversation about what's working and what isn't in public education, and why, to an unacceptable degree, schools continue to fail the kids who need them most.

•••••••••••

Three years have passed since I began spending time in the classrooms of the teachers portrayed in this book, and in many ways the educational landscape has become more bleak. Conservatives have used the terrorist attacks of 9/11 as justification for renewed assaults on multicultural curricula and ethnic studies programs. The narrow emphasis on high-stakes testing that has plagued Chicago since the mid-1990s has mutated into federal policy as George W. Bush's No Child Left Behind Act, which is on track to label nearly every public school in the country as "failing" within the next few years. Adding insult to injury, President Bush's proposed federal budget for 2005 includes the smallest increase in education funding in nearly a decade (up just 3%, to $54 billion), while requesting more than $431 billion in military spending—a total that doesn't include an anticipated supplemental request of $50 billion to bankroll the ongoing occupation of Iraq.

In troubled times such as these, the notion of teaching for change in public schools can seem little more than a defiant shout into a dark abyss. But embers of hope continue to burn. In the fall of 2002, a group of 12 teachers at Chicago's Curie High School staged a bold protest against the CASE exam, the twice-yearly assessment that had left Freda and thousands of other teachers feeling handcuffed. The "Curie 12" crafted a letter to the board of education laying out a detailed, convincing critique of the CASE, concluding with a firm declaration: They would no longer administer the test to their students. Initially the board threatened disciplinary action, but when the teachers held steadfast to their position, officials ultimately discontinued the exams—not just at Curie, but for tens of thousands of students system-wide. Umbreen Qadeer, a second-year English teacher and one of the 12 who organized the protest, told me at the time, "We're not trying to change the world. Just one really bad test." That may have been so, but what they accomplished was a small victory for teachers everywhere fighting to be heard.

What the Curie teachers refused to do—much like the five teachers we've met here—is to accept two equally disabling notions: first, that teachers don't have the power to affect change; and second, that no meaningful transformation can take place in public schools until we overhaul the entire system. Such cynicism seeps easily into copy rooms and teachers' lounges, but I agree with Lisa Kahaleole Chang Hall (1993), who writes that "radical change is the ultimate goal, but if the available options are reformist acts or political paralysis the choice seems clear. Incremental change should be valued as the means to a goal; the global begins in our backyard but obviously does not end there" (p. 166).

I'm not suggesting that every teacher who hangs up a picture of Martin Luther King in February should be lauded as a "change agent," or that we should be satisfied with token gestures toward "tolerance" and "multiculturalism," or be complacent in any way about the state of public education. A half century after the landmark *Brown v. Board of Education* decision, there is still a daunting amount of work to be done in order to move public schools closer to realizing their promise, and whether we're teachers or teacher educators, administrators or policymakers, we should all keep pushing ourselves to reach further and do more. In that regard, critique is both necessary and useful.

But I believe it's counterproductive—not to mention poisonous to the spirit—to become permanently mired in the "relentless scrutiny of failure" (Lawrence-Lightfoot, 1997) that seems so widespread in the public discourse about schools. While it's crucial that we stay wide awake to the challenges we face as educators, and to the inexcusable inequities that continue to plague schools of poor and working-class children, we must also take time to acknowledge—and learn from—the hopeful moments, the extraordinary sites where possibility is being realized, the dedicated teachers who create spaces in which kids feel respected and challenged, significant and valued. Many of these teachers understand all too well that the system is pathological, but dismantling it, at least for the moment, is beyond their reach. So they do what they can, taking small steps in the direction of more substantive change, and trying all the while to keep an eye on the bigger picture, the road ahead.

On a spray-painted wall in the heart of Harlem, a quote from poet and essayist Audre Lorde calls out: "Even the smallest victory is never to be taken for granted. Each victory must be applauded, because it is so easy not to battle at all, to just accept and call that acceptance inevitable." Teachers like Liz and Cynthia, Freda and Toni, Nancy and so many others live their classroom lives in the quest of such victories, and carry on with an abiding faith that, little by little, their collective efforts will lead to something far greater. In these ever-darkening times, their commitment and their work shine as beacons for the rest of us—illuminating our hopes, lighting our paths, guiding our way.

appendix

what i did and how
i did it: notes on method

The methodology I used in researching and writing this book draws heavily upon Sara Lawrence Lightfoot's conception of "portraiture," which she introduced in *The Good High School: Portraits of Character and Culture* (1983). Following in the qualitative tradition and echoing ethnographic aims, portraiture is an attempt to describe and depict the complexity of human experience from the perspectives of the people living that experience. It is a collaborative method, nurtured "through dialogue between the portraitist and the subject, each one negotiating the discourse and shaping the evolving image" (Lawrence-Lightfoot & Davis, 1997, p. xv). The finished portrait, like that done by a painter, does not convey a literal image of its subject but one that is nonetheless rich, multidimensional, and interpretive.

I selected the five teachers portrayed here in a straightforward, fairly informal manner. Because I was looking specifically for people of color who were 30 years old or younger and "teaching for change" in an urban public school, my pool of potential participants was naturally limited by those criteria. Other than that, I'd hoped to have some sort of balance among men and women, among people from different racial groups, and among teachers working at various grade levels, but some of those preferences didn't work out. In addition, I was looking for *good* teachers, though that term is, I realize, vague and means different things to different people.

Still, I didn't feel the need to have a precise definition of all of the components of my selection criteria. For the most part, I relied on the participant's self-identification. If a teacher defined herself as Mexican American, for example, and said she was 26 years old, that satisfied me unless I had an unusually strong reason to doubt her (which I never did). Determining if a teacher was attempting to "work for change" was a little trickier, but since that's what I was trying to explore through their perspectives, I again relied in part on each participant's self-definition. If she claimed in a screening interview that either "teaching for social justice" or "teaching for change" or "giving back to the community" was an important component of her work, she was considered for the study. Of course, if my initial observations had raised questions about the teacher's commitment to those ideas, I might have had to reconsider my selection. Fortunately, that didn't happen either.

Various personal connections and chains of events led me to each teacher. Two of them—Nancy Serrano and Freda Lin—I knew and had in mind as potential participants before I began. Nancy, as I've said, was a former eighth-grade student of mine who'd returned to her grammar school to teach. I met Freda when, for a time, we both attended meetings of a grassroots group of education activists called Teachers for Social Justice.

I selected the other three teachers in a manner resembling the "community nomination" process described by Michele Foster (1997)—except in this case, I consulted a loosely knit "progressive education community" rather than people bounded by common geography. I talked to teachers I knew, university-based site observers, principals, and other people who spent their days in schools. Toni Billingsley was recommended by an administrator friend; Cynthia Nambo's name was suggested by a teacher I knew who'd taught for several years at a community-based small school with Cynthia's husband; and Liz Kirby was recommended by a museum-based educator who'd observed in her classroom.

Several male teachers were "nominated" along the way, but for various reasons none of them worked out. One middle-school social studies teacher signed on and was eager to tell his story, but had to back out when his principal wouldn't agree to let me observe in his classroom. Regardless of the reasons, the absence of male teachers in these pages shouldn't be construed as evidence that there aren't young men of color out there doing wonderful work in the classroom. There are many, and I regret that I was unable to arrange to include any in this book.

Once I'd selected the teachers and they'd agreed to participate, I spent several days—at least ten in most cases—in each classroom. The observation days were typically spread out over a number of weeks, but I tried to visit classrooms on consecutive days when possible so I could get a sense of the flow of events from one school day to the next. In the classroom, I watched, listened, and took detailed notes on what I saw and heard. What I chose to attend to, of course, was affected by my own values, beliefs, and biases. In my role as participant–observer, I made efforts to lean more toward the observer end of the spectrum—for practical reasons more than anything else. Early on, I noticed that the more actively involved I became, the fewer notes I took, and the more I seemed to miss other things that were happening in the room. My role, then, more often approximated that of "privileged observer" rather than "active participant" (Wolcott, 1997, p. 336).

Still, it's practically impossible to spend time with a classroom of kids and not get drawn in somehow, and I did occasionally, though the extent of my participation varied from day to day and classroom to classroom. Every now and then, a teacher explicitly invited me to take part in a discussion, help with a lesson, or assist in some other way, and when asked I was glad to oblige. I also chatted with students informally as they went about their business, and many times they struck up conversations with me as well. I knew from my own experience as a teacher that having an observer in the room could change things: how the kids act, how the teacher acts, what transpires, who says what to whom. Though I was often unsure exactly what effect my being in the room was having on the classes I observed, I never doubted that my presence had an impact.

I spent most of my time in the schools in each teacher's classroom, but my observations weren't, in any of the cases, confined to that space. I sometimes went to lunch with the teachers, spent time in the faculty room, sat in on staff meetings, attended school-wide assemblies or special programs, and hung out during after-school sessions. Observing in these settings helped me get a better sense of the school as a whole and understand more clearly how each teacher's work was constrained or enhanced by institutional factors, system-wide policies, and intraschool politics.

I was able to talk with the teachers about their work and their lives in both formal and informal ways. We often had short, informal conversations between classes or, if the lesson allowed, during class, and I took notes on these exchanges. In addition to these casual talks, I also did 3 to 5 semistructured interviews with each teacher. In most cases, these were done after school, but some were squeezed in during planning periods, and in other instances we met in the evening or on a weekend at a coffee shop or restaurant. Most of the interviews, which I recorded and later transcribed, lasted between 45 minutes and 2 hours, depending on the window of time available and the topics of discussion.

Besides the observations and interviews, I used other sources of information to deepen my understanding of each teacher's work and its context. While in the classroom, I often asked for copies of handouts or readings that were being used, and I sometimes looked over the teacher's lesson plans or notes. I sketched out a floor plan of each classroom, and took careful notation on how each space was arranged. I was able to examine student essays, artwork, and projects, and in many cases to have conversations with students about the thinking behind their work. In several instances, I talked with other teachers or administrators about the history or work environment of their school, and in all cases I sought out statistical and demographic profiles of the schools on the board of education's Website.

When it came time to pore over the pages of observation notes, interview transcripts, and other documents in an attempt to find recurring themes, patterns, and narrative threads from the individual portraits, I was overwhelmed. Staring at a stack of folders on one side of my desk and a blank computer screen on the other was more than a little intimidating. Once I began writing, however, my aim was to craft rich, detailed descriptions that would convey something of the meaning these teachers give to their experiences. I wanted to create a compelling word picture of what each teacher's classroom was like, attempting to honor both what I saw and heard as well as how the teacher understood her work. Within each portrait, I sought to add depth and texture by weaving in elements of the teacher's life history, her reflections on her specific classroom issues, and her beliefs about the purposes of her teaching and the challenges of educating young people in an urban, public-school setting. To do this, I often used extended quotes from the interviews I conducted with the teachers, and while this may at times make for more cumbersome reading, it was a conscious writerly choice: I wanted to preserve each woman's words whenever possible.

I'd love to be able to say that these portraits are examples of fully collaborative, coauthored storytelling, but that would be an exaggeration. Nevertheless, I did get important input from the teachers at several points along the way. When I needed clarification on something in my notes, or needed my memory stirred about a particular event, I called and asked about it. And when I finished a draft, I sent it to the teacher to get her reaction. Typically, teachers responded by jotting things down in the margins or typing comments into an emailed document—noting factual inaccuracies, filling in holes, clarifying meaning, asking me questions. I incorporated many of the suggestions into subsequent drafts without discussion. Other times, if I disagreed with or didn't understand the proposed change, we'd talk about it further and come to some sort of compromise. The aim was to arrive at a portrait that we both felt rung true.

references

American Association of University Women. (1991). *Shortchanging girls, shortchanging America: Executive summary.* Washington, DC: Author.

Anzaldúa, G. (Ed.). (1990). *Haciendo caras/Making face, making soul: Creative and critical perspectives by feminists of color.* San Francisco: Aunt Lute Books.

Bartolomé, L. I. (1996). Beyond the methods fetish: Toward a humanizing pedagogy. In P. Leistyna, A. Woodrum, & S. A. Sherblom (Eds.), *Breaking free: The transformative power of critical pedagogy* (pp. 229–252). Cambridge, MA: Harvard Educational Review.

Behar, R. (1996). *The vulnerable observer: Anthropology that breaks your heart.* Boston: Beacon Press.

Casey, K. (1993). *I answer with my life: Life histories of women teachers working for social change.* New York: Routledge.

Cates, G. (2001). *Indian country.* New York: Grove Press.

Cisneros, S. (1984). *The house on Mango Street.* New York: Random House.

Cisneros, S. (1998). A woman of no consequence/Una mujer cualquiera. In C. Trujillo (Ed.), *Living Chicana theory* (pp. 78–86). Berkeley, CA: Third Woman Press.

Cobb, W. J. (2003). White Negro, please! *The Progressive, 67*(1). Retrieved January 12, 2003, from http://www.progressive.org/jan03/cobb0103.html

Collins, P. H. (1998). *Fighting words: Black women & the search for justice.* Minneapolis: University of Minnesota Press.

Delpit, L. D. (1986). Skills and other dilemmas of a progressive Black educator. *Harvard Educational Review, 56*(4), 379–385.

Delpit, L. D. (1988). The silenced dialogue: Power and pedagogy in educating other people's children. *Harvard Educational Review, 58*(3), 280–298.

Delpit, L. (1995). *Other people's children: Cultural conflict in the classroom.* New York: The New Press.

di Leonardo, M. (1997). White lies, black myths: Rape, race, and the black "underclass." In R. Lancaster & M. di Leonardo (Eds.), *The gender/sexuality reader* (pp. 53–68). New York: Routledge.

Eisner, E. W. (1995). What artistically crafted research can help us understand about schools. *Educational Theory, 45*(1), 1–6.

Foster, M. (1995). African American teachers and culturally relevant pedagogy. In J. A. Banks & C. A. M. Banks (Eds.), *Handbook of research on multicultural education* (pp. 570–581). New York: Macmillan.

Foster, M. (1997). *Black teachers on teaching.* New York: The New Press.

Freire, P. (1970). *Pedagogy of the oppressed.* New York: Continuum.

Giovanni, N. (1996). Nikki-Rosa. In *The selected poems of Nikki Giovanni: 1968–1995* (p. 42). New York: William Morrow.

Hale-Benson, J. (1982). *Black children: Their roots, culture, and learning styles.* Baltimore: Johns Hopkins University Press.

Hall, L. K. C. (1993). Compromising positions. In B.W. Thompson & S. Tyagi (Eds.), *Beyond a dream deferred* (pp. 162–173). Minneapolis: University of Minnesota Press.

Hall, S. (1996). New ethnicities. In D. Morley & K. Chen (Eds.), *Stuart Hall: Critical dialogues in cultural studies* (pp. 441–449). London: Routledge.

Henry, A. (1998). *Taking back control: African Canadian women teachers' lives and practices.* Albany: State University of New York Press.

hooks, b. (1990). *Yearning: Race, gender, and cultural politics.* Boston: South End Press.

hooks, b. (1994). *Teaching to transgress: Education as the practice of freedom.* New York: Routledge.

Irvine, J. J. (1989). Beyond role models: An examination of cultural influences on the pedagogical perspectives of Black teachers. *Peabody Journal of Education, 66*(4), 51–63.

Kleinfeld, J. (1975). Effective teachers of Eskimo and Indian students. *School Review, 83*(2), 301–344.

Kohl, H. (1968). *36 children.* New York: Signet.

Kozol, J. (1967). *Death at an early age.* Boston: Houghton Mifflin.

Krashen, S. D. (1985). *The input hypothesis: Issues and implications.* New York: Longman.

Kunjufu, J. (1986). *Countering the conspiracy to destroy black boys (Vol. II).* Chicago: African American Images.

Ladson-Billings, G. (1994). *The dreamkeepers: Successful teachers of African-American children.* San Francisco: Jossey-Bass.

Ladson-Billings, G. (2002). "I ain't writin' nuttin'": Permissions to fail and demands to succeed in urban classrooms. In L. Delpit & J. K. Dowdy (Eds.), *The skin that we speak: Thoughts on language and culture in the classroom* (pp. 107–120). New York: The New Press.

Ladson-Billings, G., & Henry, A. (1990). Blurring the borders: Voices of African liberatory pedagogy in the United States and Canada. *Journal of Education, 172*(2), 72–88.

Lawrence-Lightfoot, S., & Davis, J. H. (1997). *The art and science of portraiture.* San Francisco: Jossey-Bass.

Lightfoot, S. L. (1983). *The good high school: Portraits of character and culture.* New York: Basic Books.

Loewen, J. W. (1995). *Lies my teacher told me: Everything your American history textbook got wrong.* New York: Touchstone.

Malcolm X, & Haley, A. (1987). *The autobiography of Malcolm X.* Chicago: African American Images.

McIntosh, P. (2001). White privilege and male privilege: A personal account of coming to see correspondence through work in women's studies. In M. L. Anderson & P. H. Collins (Eds.), *Race, class, and gender: An anthology* (pp. 95–105). Stamford, CT: Thomson Learning.

McIntosh, P., & Style, E. (1999). Social, emotional, and political learning. In J. Cohen (Ed.), *Educating hearts and minds: Social emotional learning and the passage into adolescence* (pp. 137–157). New York: Teachers College Press.

McLaren, P., & Giroux, H. A. (1997). Writing from the margins: Geographies of identity, pedagogy, and power. In P. McLaren, *Revolutionary multiculturalism: Pedagogies of dissent for the new millennium* (pp. 16–41). Boulder, CO: Westview Press.

Meier, D. (2000). The crisis of relationships. In W. Ayers, M. Klonsky, & G. Lyon (Eds.), *A simple justice: The challenge of small schools* (pp. 33–37). New York: Teachers College Press.

Merton, T. (1978, December). Letter to a young activist (A letter to James H. Forest, February 21, 1966). *Catholic Agitator, 8,* p. 4.

Michie, G. (1999). *Holler if you hear me: The education of a teacher and his students.* New York: Teachers College Press.

Parker, P. (1990). For the white person who wants to know how to be my friend. In G. Anzaldúa (Ed.), *Haciendo caras/Making face, making soul: Creative and critical perspectives by feminists of color* (p. 297). San Francisco: Aunt Lute Books.

Perry, T. (2003). Freedom for literacy and literacy for freedom: The African-American philosophy of education. In T. Perry, C. Steele, & A. Hilliard III, *Young, gifted, and black: Promoting high achievement among African-American students.* Boston: Beacon Press.

Pillow, W. (2002). When a man does feminism should he dress in drag? *Qualitative Studies in Education, 15*(5), 545–554.

Reed, Jr., A. (2000). *Class notes: Posing as politics and other thoughts on the American scene.* New York: The New Press.

Rosaldo, R. (1993). *Culture and truth: The remaking of social analysis*. Boston: Beacon Press.

Rose, M. (1995). *Possible lives: The promise of public education in America*. New York: Penguin.

Valenzuela, A. (1999). *Subtractive schooling: U.S.-Mexican youth and the politics of caring*. Albany: State University of New York Press.

West, C. (1993). The new cultural politics of difference. In B. W. Thompson & S. Tyagi (Eds.), *Beyond a dream deferred* (pp. 18–40). Minneapolis: University of Minnesota Press.

Wolcott, H. F. (1997). Ethnographic research in education. In R. M. Jaeger (Ed.), *Contemporary methods for research in education* (2nd ed., pp. 327–353). Washington, DC: American Educational Research Association.

about the author

Gregory Michie is an assistant professor of secondary education at National-Louis University in Chicago. His previous book, *Holler If You Hear Me: The Education of a Teacher and His Students*, is a memoir of his experiences teaching in Chicago public schools. For the past 3 years he has codirected an alternative certification program for urban teachers, and he continues to work with young people in Chicago's Back of the Yards neighborhood. He lives on the city's south side.